Praise for *Modernising Money*

"Printing counterfeit banknotes is illegal, but creating private money is not. The interdependence between the state and the businesses that can do this is the source of much of the instability of our economies. It could – and should – be terminated.

...

What is to be done? ... A maximum response would be to give the state a monopoly on money creation. ... Similar ideas have come from Andrew Jackson and Ben Dyson in *Modernising Money*...The transition to a system in which money creation is separated from financial intermediation would be feasible, albeit complex. But it would bring huge advantages. It would be possible to increase the money supply without encouraging people to borrow to the hilt. It would end 'too big to fail' in banking. It wou_____ from creating money – to the public."

Martin Wolf,

their power to c

"The authors tr_____
in the context _____
policy up to the _____
the authors' sol_____

Prof. Vicky Ch

"*Modernising 1*
doesn't work w

Prof. Joseph
Martin Luther

"This 'must read, must act' book lucidly explains two things: the urgent need for a simple basic reform of the money system to make it work more efficiently and fairly for all, and an accessible way for responsible citizens to help make the reform happen."

James Robertson, _____ *...eakthrough?*

MODERNISING
MONEY

WHY OUR MONETARY SYSTEM IS BROKEN
AND HOW IT CAN BE FIXED

Andrew Jackson & Ben Dyson

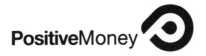

First published in the UK in 2012 by Positive Money

9 8 7 6 5 4 3

Positive Money

205 Davina House

137-149 Goswell Road

London EC1V 7ET

Tel: +44 (0) 207 253 3235

www.positivemoney.org

ISBN: 978-0-9574448-0-5

Printed in Great Britain by TJ International Ltd.

CONTENTS

ACKNOWLEDGEMENTS

We would like to thank Graham Hodgson for his numerous contributions to this book, as well as Mario Visel and Mariia Domina, for their work on historical episodes of state money creation and international finance respectively.

The discussion of the existing banking system in the first two chapters of this book is based on research and thinking by Josh Ryan-Collins, Tony Greenham, Richard Werner and Andrew Jackson for the book *Where Does Money Come From?* (published by the New Economics Foundation) and we are very grateful for their input and considerable expertise.

We are also grateful to the team at Positive Money: Mira Tekelova for holding the fort while the book was written, Henry Edmonds for his work on the design and layout, and Miriam Morris, James Murray and a number of other tireless volunteers who have helped with the editing and proofing.

We are indebted to Jamie Walton for the numerous conversations in 2010–2011 that led to the development and strengthening of these proposals, and Joseph Huber and James Robertson for providing the starting point in their book *Creating New Money*. These ideas were further developed with Josh Ryan-Collins, Tony Greenham and Richard Werner in a joint submission to the Independent Commission on Banking in late 2010.

We would also like to thank all those who have provided helpful insights, comments and suggestions on the proposals and the manuscript. We are particularly grateful for the expertise and guidance of Dr David Bholat, Dr Fran Boait, Prof. Victoria Chick, Prof. Herman Daly, Prof. Joseph Huber, Dr Michael Reiss, James Robertson, and the Positive Money Lambeth group.

Finally, we would like to express our gratitude to the James Gibb Stuart Trust and other supporters of Positive Money, without whom the book would not have been written. Of course, the contents of this book, and any mistakes, errors or omissions remain entirely the responsibility of the authors.

A NOTE FOR READERS OUTSIDE THE UK

Although this book is written with the UK banking system in mind, the analysis is equally applicable to the banking and monetary system of any modern economy. While there are minor differences in rules and regulations between countries, almost all economies today are based on a monetary system that is fundamentally the same as that of the UK.

Equally, the reforms proposed here can be applied to any country that has its own currency, or any currency bloc, with only minor tailoring to the unique situation of each country.

FOREWORD

Money ranks with fire and the wheel as an invention without which the modern world would be unimaginable. Unfortunately, out-of-control money now injures more people than both out-of-control fires and wheels. Loss of control stems from the privilege enjoyed by the private banking sector of creating money from nothing, in the form of demand deposits, and lending it at interest.

This power derives from the current design of the banking system, and can be corrected by moving to a system where new money can only be created by a public body, working in the public interest. This is simple to state, but difficult to bring about. Andrew Jackson and Ben Dyson do a fine job of explaining the malfunctioning present banking system, and showing the clear institutional reforms necessary for a sound monetary system. The main ideas go back to the leading economic thinkers of 50 to 75 years ago, including Irving Fisher, Frank Knight and Frederick Soddy.

This book revives and modernises these ideas, and shows with clarity and in detail why they must be a key part of economic reform today.

PROFESSOR HERMAN DALY

Professor Emeritus
School of Public Policy
University of Maryland

Former Senior Economist
at the World Bank

SUMMARY OF KEY POINTS

CHAPTER 1: A SHORT HISTORY OF MONEY

When early-day goldsmiths started to store metal coins on behalf of members of the public, they would issue these depositors with paper receipts. These receipts started to circulate in the economy, being used in place of metal money and becoming a form of unofficial paper money. In 1844 the government prohibited the issuance of this paper money by any institution other than the Bank of England, returning the power to create money to the state. However, the failure to include bank deposits in the 1844 Bank Charter Act allowed banks to continue to create a close substitute for money, in the form of accounting entries that could be used to make payments to others, initially via cheque. The more recent rise of electronic means of payment (debit cards and electronic fund transfers) has made these accounting entries more convenient to use as money than physical cash. As a result, today the majority of payments are made electronically.

CHAPTER 2: MONEY & BANKING TODAY

The vast majority of money today is created not by the state, as most would assume, but by the private, commercial (or high-street) banking sector. Over 97% of money exists in the form of bank deposits (the accounting liabilities of banks), which are created when banks make loans or buy assets. We explain how this process takes place and show the (simplified) accounting that enables banks to create money. We also look at the crucial role of central bank reserves (money created by the Bank of England) in the payments system, and explain why it is that banks do not need to acquire money from savers or the central bank before they can start to lend.

Chapter 3: What Determines the Money Supply?

With most money being created by banks making loans, the level of bank lending determines the money supply. What then determines how much banks can lend?

The demand for credit (lending) will always tend to be high due to: insufficient wealth, the desire to speculate (including on house prices), and various legal incentives. Meanwhile the supply of credit depends on the extent to which banks are incentivised to lend. During benign economic conditions banks are incentivised to lend as much as possible – creating money in the process – by the drive to maximise profit, and this process is exacerbated through the existence of securitisation, deposit insurance, externalities and competition. For a variety of reasons, regulations that are meant to limit the creation of money, such as capital requirements, reserve ratios and the setting of interest rates by the Monetary Policy Committee, are ineffective.

Yet despite the high demand for credit, the strong incentives for banks to create money through lending, and the limited constraints on their ability to do so, banks do not simply lend to everyone who wants to borrow. Instead, they ration their lending. For this reason, the level of bank lending, and therefore the money supply, is determined mainly by banks' willingness to lend, which in turn depends upon the confidence they have in the health of the economy.

Chapter 4: Economic Consequences of the Current System

The economic effects of money creation depend on how that money is used. If newly created money is used to increase the productive capacity of the economy, the effect is unlikely to be inflationary. However, banks currently direct the vast majority of their lending towards non-productive investment, such as mortgage lending and speculation in financial markets. This does not increase the productive capacity of the economy, and instead simply causes prices in these markets to rise, drawing in speculators, leading to more lending, higher prices, and so on in a self-reinforcing process. This results in an asset price bubble.

While the increases in asset prices may create the impression of a healthy, growing economy, this 'boom' is in fact fuelled by an increasing build-up of debt. The current monetary system therefore sows the seeds of its own destruction: households and businesses cannot take on ever-increasing levels of debt, and when either start to default on loans, it can cause a chain reaction that leads to a banking crisis, a wider financial crisis, and an economy-wide recession.

Financial crises therefore come about as a result of banks' lending activities, and the resulting creation of money. As Adair Turner, head of the UK's Financial Services Authority, puts it: "The financial crisis of 2007/08 occurred because we failed to constrain the private financial system's creation of private credit and money." (2012) The boom-bust cycle is also caused by banks' creation of excessive amounts of money.

Some measures implemented to dampen or mitigate against these effects have the perverse effect of actually making a crisis more likely. Deposit insurance, for example, is intended to make the banking system safer but in reality enables banks to take higher risks without being scrutinised by their customers. The Basel Capital Accords, again designed to make the system safer, gives banks incentives to choose mortgage lending over lending to businesses, making house price bubbles and the resulting crises more rather than less likely.

CHAPTER 5: SOCIAL AND ENVIRONMENTAL IMPACTS OF THE CURRENT SYSTEM

Much of the money created by the banking system is directed into housing, causing house prices to rise faster than the rise in salaries. As well as making housing unaffordable for those who were not on the housing ladder before prices started to rise, it also leads to a large number of people using property as an alternative to other forms of pension or retirement savings, without them realising the rising prices are artificially fuelled by the rise in mortgage lending.

The fact that our money is issued as debt means that the level of debt must be higher than it otherwise would be. The interest that must be paid on this debt results in a transfer of wealth from the bottom 90% of the population (by income) to the top 10%, exacerbating inequality. In addition, any attempt by the public to pay down its debts will result, other things being equal, in less spending. This will usually lead to a recession and make it difficult to continue reducing debt.

The state currently earns a profit, known as seigniorage, from the creation of bank notes. However, because it has left the creation of deposit money in the hands of the banking sector, it is the banks that earn interest on the vast majority (97%) of the money that exists in the economy. The loss of this seigniorage revenue for the state requires that higher taxes are levied on the population.

The instability caused by the monetary system harms the environment. The burden of servicing an inflated level of debt creates a drive for constant growth, even when that growth is harmful to the environment and has limited social benefit. When the inevitable recessions occur, regulations protecting the environment are often discarded, as is longer-term thinking with regards to the changes that need to be made. In addition, bank customers have little control over what banks invest in, meaning that they often opt for environmentally harmful projects over longer-term beneficial investments.

Finally, the current monetary system places incredible power in the hands of banks that have no responsibility or accountability to society. The amount of money created by the banking sector give it more power to shape the economy than the whole of the elected government, yet there is very little understanding of this power. This is a significant democratic deficit.

Chapter 6: Preventing Banks from Creating Money

It is possible to remove the ability of banks to create money with a few technical changes to the way they do business. This will ensure that, rather than creating new money, bank lending will simply transfer pre-existing money from savers to borrowers.

From the perspective of bank customers, little will change, except for the fact that they will have a clear choice between having their money kept safe, available on demand, but earning no interest, or having it placed at risk for a fixed or minimum period of time in order to earn interest.

The changes made to the structure of banking make it possible for banks to be allowed to fail, with no impact on the payments system or on customers who opted to keep their money safe.

CHAPTER 7: THE NEW PROCESS FOR CREATING NEW MONEY

With banks no longer creating money, an independent but accountable public body, known as the Money Creation Committee (MCC), would instead be responsible for creating money. The MCC would only be able to create money if inflation were low and stable. Newly created money would be injected into the economy through one of five methods, four of which are: a) government spending, b) cutting taxes, c) direct payments to citizens or d) paying down the national debt. Which of these methods is used to distribute new money into the economy is ultimately a political decision, to be taken by the elected government.

Ensuring that businesses are provided with adequate credit is always a concern whenever changes are made to the way that banks operate. However, rather than resulting in a damaging fall in the amount of credit provided to businesses, the reforms ensure that the Bank of England has a mechanism to provide funds to banks that can only be used for lending to productive businesses. This fifth method of injecting money into the economy could boost investment in the real economy and business sector above its current level.

CHAPTER 8: MAKING THE TRANSITION

The transition from the current monetary system to the reformed system is made in two distinct stages: 1) an overnight switchover, when the new rules and processes governing money creation and bank lending take effect, and 2) a longer transition period, of between 10 and 30 years, as the economy recovers from the 'hangover' of debt from the current monetary system. Changes are made to the balance sheets of the Bank of England and commercial banks, and additional measures are taken to ensure that banks have adequate funds to lend immediately after the switchover so that there is zero risk of a temporary credit crunch. The changes can be made without altering the quantity of money in circulation.

The longer-term transition allows for a significant reduction in personal and household debt, as new money is injected into the economy and existing loan repayments to banks are recycled back into the economy as debt-free money. The potential de-leveraging of the banking sector could be in excess of £1 trillion.

Chapter 9: Understanding the Impacts of the Reforms

In the reformed system money enters circulation in one of five ways, with each method having different economic effects. As in the current monetary system, money that increases the productive capacity of the economy will be non-inflationary, while new money that leads to an increase in spending but does not increase productive capacity will be inflationary. Because banks will no longer create new money when they make loans, lending for productive purposes will be disinflationary (slowing the rate of inflation), while lending for consumer purchases will have no economic effect. As such the Bank of England will have to closely monitor the lending activities of banks when deciding how much new money to inject into the economy.

Lending for the purchase of property or financial assets would be self-correcting, in so much as the economy is less able to support sustained asset price bubbles. As a result financial instability would be reduced, while the effect of bank failures or deflation is much milder than is currently the case, as a result of money no longer being created with a corresponding debt.

As money is created without a corresponding debt, individuals are able to pay down their debts without causing the money supply to contract. Likewise the government gains an additional source of revenue, reducing both the need for taxes and the borrowing requirement. Many of the negative environmental impacts of the current monetary system are reduced in line with the reduction of the boom-bust cycle. In particular, the pressure to remove environmental regulation in downturns is reduced as is the constant need to grow in order to service debt. Likewise, the directed nature of Investment Accounts means the investment priorities of banks will start to reflect the investment priorities of society. This also has positive effects on democracy by reducing the power of the banks to shape society in their own interests. Finally, the reformed system ensures that the creation of money is both transparent and accountable to parliament.

Chapter 10: Impacts on the Banking Sector

With money no longer issued only when banks make loans or buy assets, deleveraging of the economy becomes possible. As the level of debt falls, the banking sector's balance sheet will shrink. Because banks can now be allowed to fail, the 'too big to fail' subsidies for large banks disappear. However, at the same time it becomes much easier for banks to manage their cashflow (because all investments are made for fixed time periods or have notice periods), and regulations such as the Basel Capital Accords could be simplified when applied to the reformed banking system. An effect of the accounting changes made during the transition period is that the 'liquidity gap' that is endemic to modern banking would be significantly reduced, making banks much safer in liquidity terms.

The reforms mean that the central bank would now have direct control over the creation of new money, rather than having to indirectly control it through interest rates. As interest rates would be set by the markets, the central bank would no longer need to play this role.

From an international perspective, there are no practical implications with regards to how the reformed monetary system connects to those of other countries, and international trade and finance can continue as normal. With regards to exchange rates between pound sterling and other currencies, the common fear that the currency would be attacked and devalued is misguided; the greater risk is that the currency would appreciate. However, the design of the reformed monetary system ensures that large changes in exchange rates are self-correcting. Finally, the reforms have advantages for national security, by making the payments system more robust.

CONCLUSION

There are very real challenges facing the world over the next few decades, including likely crises in food production, climate, energy, and natural resources (including water). To focus on dealing with these extreme challenges, it is essential that we have a stable monetary system and are not distracted by crises that are caused by the design of the current monetary system. The monetary system, being man-made and little more than a collection of rules and computer systems, is easy to fix, once the political will is there and opposition from vested interests is overcome. The real challenges of how to provide for a growing global population, a changing climate, and increasingly scarce natural resources, require a monetary system that works for society and the economy as a whole. For that reason, our current monetary system is no longer fit for purpose and must be reformed.

INTRODUCTION

"Of all the many ways of organising banking, the worst is the one we have today."

Sir Mervyn King

**Governor of the Bank of England, 2003 - 2013
25th October 2010**

After the experience of the last few years, few people would disagree with Mervyn King's claim above. The 2007-08 financial crisis led to massive increases in unemployment and cuts to public services as governments around the world were forced to bail out failing banks. While the complete collapse of the financial system was averted, six years later the countries at the centre of the crisis have still not recovered. In economic terms the permanent loss to the world economy has been estimated at a staggering $60–$200 trillion, between one and three years of global production. For the UK the figures are between £1.8 and £7.4 trillion (Haldane, 2010).

Yet while the 2007/08 crisis was undoubtedly a surprise to many, it would be wrong to think that banking crises are somehow rare events. In the UK there has been a banking crisis on average once every 15 years since 1945 (Reinhart and Rogoff, 2009), whilst worldwide there have been 147 banking crises between 1970 and 2011 (Laeven and Valencia, 2012).

It seems clear that our banking system is fundamentally dysfunctional, yet for all the millions of words of analysis in the press and financial papers, very little has been written about the real reasons for this. Although there are many problems with banking, the underlying issue is that successive governments have ceded the responsibility of creating new money to the private sector corporations that we know as banks.

Today, almost all of the money used by people and businesses across the world is created not by the state or central banks (such as the Bank of England), but by the private banking sector. Banks create new money, in the form of the numbers (deposits) that appear in bank accounts, through the accounting process used when they make loans. In the words of Sir Mervyn King, Governor of the Bank of England from 2003-2013, "When banks extend loans to their customers, they create money by crediting their customers' accounts." (2012) Conversely, when people use those deposits to repay loans, the process is reversed and money effectively disappears from the economy.

Allowing money to be created in this way affects us all. The current monetary system is the reason we have such a pronounced and destructive cycle of boom and bust, and it is the reason that individuals, businesses and governments are overburdened with debt.

When banks feel confident and are willing to lend, new money is created. Banks profit from the interest they charge on loans, and therefore use bonuses, commission and other incentive schemes to encourage their staff to increase their lending, creating money in the process. The loans they make tend to be disproportionately allocated towards the financial and property markets. As a result our economy has become skewed towards property bubbles and specu-lation, while the public has become buried under a mountain of debt. When the burden of debt becomes too much for some borrowers, they default on their loans, putting the solvency of their banks at risk. Worried about the state of the economy and the ability of individuals and businesses to repay their loans, all banks reduce their lending, harming businesses across the economy.

When banks make new loans at a slower rate than the rate at which their old loans are repaid, the amount of money in the economy starts to shrink. Less new lending means less spending, and this causes the economy to slow down, leading to job losses, bankruptcies and defaults on debt, which lead to further losses for the banks. Banks then react by restricting their lending even further. This downward spiral continues until the banks eventually regain their 'confi-dence' in the economy and start creating new money again by increasing their lending.

The Bank of England maintains that it has the process of money creation under control, yet a quick glance at the growth of bank-issued money over the last 40 years (shown opposite) calls this claim into question. By ceding the power to create money to banks, the state has built instability into the economy, since the incentives facing banks guarantee that they will create too much money (and debt) until the financial system becomes unstable. This is a view recently vindicated by the chairman of the UK's Financial Services Authority, Lord

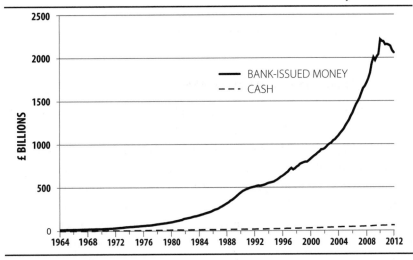

Cash vs bank-issued money, 1964-2012

Source: Bank of England Statistical Database

This chart is slightly misleading, in that it appears to show that the broad money supply continued to increase until late 2009, whereas in reality it actually started to shrink in late 2008. The appearance of an increase in the money supply between 2008 and 2009 is mainly due to changes in the way that the broad money supply statistics are reported by the Bank of England.

(Adair) Turner, who stated that: "The financial crisis of 2007/08 occurred because we failed to constrain the private financial system's creation of private credit and money" (2012).

Yet if this instability in the creation of money weren't enough of a problem, in addition newly created money is accompanied by an equivalent amount of debt. It is therefore extremely difficult to reduce the overall burden of personal and household debt when any attempts to pay down debt leads to a reduction in the creation of new money, which may in turn lead to a recession.

The years following the recent financial crisis have clearly shown that we have a dysfunctional banking system. However, the problem runs deeper than bad banking practice. It is not just the structures, governance, culture or the size of banks that are the problem; it is that banks are responsible for creating the majority of the nation's money. It is this process of creating and allocating new money that needs fundamental and urgent reform.

This book explores how the monetary system could be changed to work better for businesses, households, society and the environment, and lays out a workable, detailed and effective plan for such a reform.

OUR PROPOSED REFORMS

We have little hope of living in a stable and prosperous economy while the amount of money in circulation depends entirely on the lending activities of banks chasing short-term profits. Attempts to regulate the current monetary system are unlikely to be successful – as economist Hyman Minsky argued, stability itself is destabilising. Indeed, financial crises are a common feature of financial history, regardless of the country, government, or economic policies in place. Crises have occurred in rich and poor countries, under fixed and flexible exchange rate regimes, gold standards and pure fiat money systems, as well as a huge variety of regulatory regimes. However, a common denominator in all these systems is that the banks have been the primary creators of money. As Reinhart and Rogoff (2009) put it:

> "Throughout history, rich and poor countries alike have been lending, borrowing, crashing – and recovering – their way through an extraordinary range of financial crises. Each time, the experts have chimed, 'this time is different', claiming that the old rules of valuation no longer apply and that the new situation bears little similarity to past disasters."

Rather than attempt to regulate the current banking system, instead it is the fundamental method of create money and getting it into the economy that needs to change. These proposals are based on plans initially put forward by Frederick Soddy in the 1920s, and then subsequently by Irving Fisher and Henry Simons in the aftermath of the Great Depression. Different variations of these ideas have since been proposed by Nobel Prize winners including Milton Friedman (1960), and James Tobin (1987), as well as eminent economists John Kay (2009) and Laurence Kotlikoff (2010). Most recently, a working paper by economists at the International Monetary Fund modelled Irving Fisher's original proposal and found "strong support" for all of its claimed benefits (Benes & Kumhof, 2012).

While inspired by Irving Fisher's original work and variants on it, the proposals in this book have some significant differences. Our starting point has been the work of Joseph Huber and James Robertson in their book *Creating New Money* (2000), which updated and modified Fisher's proposals to take account of the fact that money, the payments system and banking in general is now electronic, rather than paper-based. This book develops these ideas even further, strengthening the proposal in response to feedback and criticism from a wide range of people.

There are four main objectives of the reforms outlined in this book:

1. **To have money created based on the needs of the economy.** Currently money is created by banks when they make loans, driven by the drive to maximise their profit. Under our proposals, money would be created by an independent public body, accountable to Parliament, in line with a democratically mandated target (such as in response to the level of inflation, unemployment and growth). This would protect the economy from credit bubbles and crunches, and limit monetary sources of inflation.

2. **To make possible the reduction of personal, household and government debt.** New money would be created free of any corresponding debt, and spent into the economy to replace the outstanding stock of debt-based money that has been issued by banks. Money would enter circulation via the real economy, rather than the property and financial markets. This process makes it possible for people and businesses to pay down the debts that have been built up under the current monetary system.

3. **To re-align risk and reward.** Currently the government (and therefore the UK taxpayer) promises to repay customers up to £85,000 of any deposits they hold at a bank that fails. This means that banks can make risky investments and reap the rewards if they go well, but be confident of a taxpayer-funded bailout if their investments go badly. Our proposals will ensure that those individuals who want to keep their money safe can do so, at no risk, while those that wish to make a return on their money will take both the upside and downside of any risk taking. This should encourage more responsible risk taking and reduce the 'moral hazard' intrinsic to the current system.

4. **To provide a structure of banking that allows banks to fail,** no matter their size. With the current structure of banking no large bank can be permitted to fail, as to do so would create economic chaos. Simple changes outlined in this book would ensure that banks could be liquidated while ensuring that customers would keep access to their current account

money at all times. The changes outlined actually reduce the likelihood of bank failure, providing additional protection for savers.

In order to achieve these aims, the key element of the reforms is to remove the ability of banks to create new money (in the form of bank deposits) when they issue loans. The simplest way to do this is to require banks to make a clear distinction between bank accounts where they promise to repay the customer 'on demand' or with instant access, and other accounts where the customer consciously requests their funds to be placed at risk and invested. Current accounts are then converted into state-issued electronic currency, rather than being promises to pay from a bank, and the payments system is functionally separated from the lending side of a bank's business. The act of lending would then involve transferring state-issued electronic currency from savers to borrowers. Banks would become money brokers, rather than money creators, and the amount of money in circulation would be stable regardless of whether banks are currently increasing or decreasing their lending.

Taken together, the reforms end the practice of 'fractional reserve banking', a slightly inaccurate term used to describe a banking system where banks promise to repay all customers on demand despite being unable to do so. In late 2010 Mervyn King discussed such ideas in a speech:

> "A more fundamental, example [of reform] would be to divorce the payment system from risky lending activity – that is to prevent fractional reserve banking … In essence these proposals recognise that if banks undertake risky activities then it is highly dangerous to allow such 'gambling' to take place on the same balance sheet as is used to support the payments system, and other crucial parts of the financial infrastructure. And eliminating fractional reserve banking explicitly recognises that the pretence that risk-free deposits can be supported by risky assets is alchemy. If there is a need for genuinely safe deposits the only way they can be provided, while ensuring costs and benefits are fully aligned, is to insist such deposits do not coexist with risky assets." (King, 2010)

After describing the current system as requiring a belief in 'financial alchemy', King went on to say that, "For a society to base its financial system on alchemy is a poor advertisement for its rationality." Indeed, over the next few chapters we expect readers to find themselves questioning the sanity of our existing monetary system themselves.

THE STRUCTURE OF THIS BOOK

Part 1: The Current Monetary System

Chapter 1 provides a brief history of money and banking and describes the emergence of the monetary system we have today.

Chapter 2 describes how the current monetary system works and how commercial banks are able to create the nation's money.

Chapter 3 considers the wide range of influences that affect that amount of money that the banks create.

Chapter 4 analyses the economic effects of the current monetary system.

Chapter 5 looks at the social and ecological impacts of the current monetary system.

Part 2: The Reformed Monetary System

Chapter 6 describes the changes that must be made to the operations of banks in order to remove their ability to create money.

Chapter 7 describes how new money will instead be created by a public body, and how that money will be put into the economy.

Chapter 8 outlines the transition between the current system and reformed system (with further technical details provided in Appendix III).

Chapter 9 covers the likely social, economic and environmental impacts of a monetary system where money is issued solely by the state, without a corresponding debt.

Chapter 10 considers the likely impact of these reforms on the banking and financial sector.

Part 3: Appendices

Appendix I considers historical examples of hyperinflation, and contrasts these to examples of responsible money creation by the state.

Appendix II covers issues around the national (government) debt and how it could be reduced.

Appendix III presents further detail on the accounting for money creation.

1

THE CURRENT MONETARY SYSTEM

CHAPTER 1
A SHORT HISTORY OF MONEY

In this chapter we provide a brief history of money and banking. We start by looking at the textbook history of the origins of money, before examining the alternative accounts of historians and anthropologists, which contradict the textbook history. We then discuss the development of banking in the United Kingdom and its evolution up to the present day.

1.1 THE ORIGINS OF MONEY

A textbook history

The standard theory of the origins of money, commonly found in economics textbooks, was perhaps first put forward by Aristotle (in "Politics") and restated by Adam Smith in his book "The Wealth of Nations" (1776). According to Smith's story, money emerged naturally with the division of labour, as individuals found themselves without many of the necessities they required but at the same time an excess of the products they produced themselves. Without a means of exchange individuals had to resort to barter in order to trade, which was problematic as both sides of the deal had to have something the other person wanted (the "double coincidence of wants"). To avoid this inconvenience people began to accept certain types of commodities for their goods and services. These commodities tended to have two specific characteristics. First, the majority of people had to find them valuable, so that they would accept them in exchange for their goods or services. Secondly, these goods had to be easily divisible into smaller units in order to make payments of varying amounts. It is suggested that as metal satisfied both requirements, it naturally emerged as currency. However, metal had to be weighed and checked for purity every time a transaction was made. For this reason, governments began minting coins in order to standardise quantities and ensure purity.

Adam Smith's story suggests that certain commodities come to be used as money due to their unique characteristics. In effect money was simply a token that served to oil the wheels of trade. Money can be thought of as simply a 'veil' over barter, masking the fact that people are really just exchanging one good or service for another. This would mean that doubling the supply of money would simply cause prices to double, so in real terms no one would be any better or worse off. Writing in 1848, John Stuart Mill stated the consensus view, which is still common today:

> "There cannot, in short, be intrinsically a more insignificant thing, in the economy of society, than money; except in the character of a contrivance for sparing time and labour. It is a machine for doing quickly and commodiously, what would be done, though less quickly and commodiously, without it: and like many other kinds of machinery, it only exerts a distinct and independent influence of its own when it gets out of order."

In this view, banks come on the scene much later on, initially as places where people could keep their coins safe. These banks then started to lend the coins that have been deposited with them. Yet because money is simply another physical commodity, this lending has no real effects; rather, it merely transfers resources from one person to another:

> "Often is an extension of credit talked of as equivalent to a creation of capital, or as if credit actually were capital. It seems strange that there should be any need to point out, that credit being only permission to use the capital of another person, the means of production cannot be increased by it, but only transferred. If the borrower's means of production and of employing labour are increased by the credit given him, the lender's are as much diminished. The same sum cannot be used as capital both by the owner and also by the person to whom it is lent: it cannot supply its entire value in wages, tools, and materials, to two sets of labourers at once." (Mill, 1909)

So in this orthodox view, banks are mere financial middlemen (intermediaries), passively waiting for customers to deposit money before they can start lending. This view implies that by lending, a bank transfers purchasing power from one individual to another, and thus they have no special significance for the economy.

fig. 1.1 - Common conception of banking

SAVER   BANK   BORROWER

This hypothesis has been widely perpetuated by economists and in economic models up until today. Money, banks and debt are believed to have no macroeconomic effect other than to 'oil the wheels' of trade and so can be ignored when considering the workings of the economy. This belief means that today hardly any economic models have a place for banks, money or debt. As a result, even after the 2007-2008 financial crisis, Nobel Prize[1] winning economists have been known to make statements such as "I'm all for including the banking sector in stories where it's relevant; but why is it so crucial to a story about debt and leverage?" (Krugman, 2012).

The historical reality

The problem with the idea that money emerged 'spontaneously' from barter is that, in the words of anthropologist David Graeber, "there's no evidence that it ever happened, and an enormous amount of evidence suggesting that it did not". (2011, p. 29)[2] As Graeber explains, the historical and anthropological evidence indicates that before the existence of money people did not engage in barter trades with each other. Rather, goods were freely given with

1. Technically, there is no such thing as a Nobel Prize in economics. Officially the prize is referred to as the 'Sveriges Riksbank Prize in Economic Sciences in Memory of Alfred Nobel'.

2. This is not to say that barter does not exist or has not existed in the past, merely that money did not emerge from it. In reality, barter tends to happen only between people who are strangers (i.e. they have no ongoing relationship), or is reverted to amongst people who are used to cash transactions, but for whatever reason have no currency available, such as those in prisoner of war camps. (See Radford (1945) for a fascinating example.)

the caveat that the person receiving them would have to return the favour at some point. For example, in many tribal societies the concept of having possessions and 'owning' things could disrupt group harmony, but the tribe could also promote social cohesion through a culture of gift giving. Likewise, in pre-monetary complex societies, certain conventions emerged whereby individuals would show that they desired somebody else's possession, with the owner then giving the possession as a gift, to establish a bond of obligation to be reciprocated in due course. So, rather than exchange through barter, early societies instead used a vaguely defined system of debts and credits.

The quantification of these debts and credits – the first step in the development of money as a unit of account – is thought to have come about as a consequence of the reaction of societies to disputes and feuds, specifically the attempts to prevent them from turning into matters of life and death. According to Graeber:

> "[T]he first step toward creating real money comes when we start calculating much more specific debts to society, systems of fines, fees, and penalties, or even debts we owe to specific individuals who we have wronged in some way...even the English word "to pay" is originally derived from a word for "to pacify, appease" – as in, to give someone something precious, for instance, to express just how badly you feel about having just killed his brother in a drunken brawl, and how much you would really like to avoid this becoming the basis for an ongoing blood-feud."

Ratios between various commodities were thus established to measure whether a gift or grievance had been adequately compensated, and over time, gifts and counter-gifts became quantifiable as credits and debts. In a sense this created money as a unit of account (although it didn't exist in physical form). This directly contradicts the orthodox story, which states that money emerged from barter, which itself was driven by market forces. Similar evidence is presented by economist and historian Michael Hudson, who traces the emergence of money as a unit of account to the Mesopotamian temple and palace administrations in 3500 BC:

> "It did not occur ... to Aristotle ... that specialization developed mainly within single large households of chieftains in tribally organised communities ... Such households supported non-agricultural labor with rations rather than obliging each profession to market its output in exchange for food, clothing and other basic necessities. Administrators allocated rations and raw material in keeping with what was deemed necessary for

production and for ceremonial and other institutional functions rather than resorting to private-sector markets, which had not yet come into being." (Hudson, 2004)

Money in the form of precious metals that were shaped into coins came much later, appearing in three separate places (northern China, northeast India, and around the Aegean Sea) between around 600 and 500 BC. During this period, "war and the threat of violence [was] everywhere", and as Graeber details, this was the primary reason for the shift from the convenient credit and debt relationships to the use of precious metals as money:

> "On the one hand, soldiers tend to have access to a great deal of loot, much of which consists of gold and silver, and will always seek a way to trade it for the better things in life. On the other, a heavily armed itinerant soldier is the very definition of a poor credit risk. The economists' barter scenario might be absurd when applied to transactions between neighbors in the same small rural community, but when dealing with a transaction between the resident of such a community and a passing mercenary, it suddenly begins to make a great deal of sense...

> "As a result, while credit systems tend to dominate in periods of relative social peace, or across networks of trust (whether created by states or, in most periods, transnational institutions like merchant guilds or communities of faith), in periods characterized by widespread war and plunder, they tend to be replaced by precious metal." (Graeber, 2011, p. 213)

Jewellers soon began stamping these precious metals with insignia, and in so doing created coins. However this private money was almost immediately superseded by coins manufactured by rulers who introduced the coins into circulation by paying their armies with them. They then levied a tax on the entire population payable only in those coins, thus ensuring they were accepted in general payment.

Ultimately, the evidence outlined by historians and anthropologists here suggests that:

> "Our standard account of monetary history is precisely backwards. We did not begin with barter, discover money, and then eventually develop credit systems. It happened precisely the other way around. What we now call virtual money came first. Coins came much later, and their use spread only unevenly, never completely replacing credit systems. Barter, in turn, appears to be largely a kind of accidental by-product of the use of coinage

or paper money: historically, it has mainly been what people who are used to cash transactions do when for one reason or another they have no access to currency." (Graeber, 2011, p. 40)

1.2 THE EMERGENCE OF BANKING

The first banks

The earliest prototype banks were probably associated with the temple and palace complexes of ancient Mesopotamia, where the temple administrators made interest-bearing loans to merchants and farmers.[3] By the fourth century BC in Greece, a more modern form of banking had developed (which itself had probably developed from the activities of the money changers). In addition to lending, Athenian bankers were engaged in deposit taking, the processing of payments and money changing. While Roman banking developed a few hundred years later than Athenian banking, its activities were largely confined to the financing of land purchases. However after the collapse of the Western Roman Empire in the 5th century AD the widespread use of coins and banking largely died out in Western Europe as the population reverted to peasant farming and local production, with trade conducted largely on credit. Meanwhile, the control of trade and of money passed to the Eastern Roman Empire.

Deposit banking was only able to resume in Western Europe in the 12th century following improvements in numeracy, literacy, and financial and trade innovations[4] that came about after an increase in available coinage[5] led to a resurgence in international trade (Spufford, 2002). In this environment the

---

3. However, problems emerged with this system. When the harvests failed the loans would not be repaid: everyone would start falling into debt traps (and debt slavery). The social unrest this created would be so great that the only way to stop society breaking down (or the rulers being overturned) would be to periodically forgive everyone their debts – a debt jubilee.

4. These innovations included: courier services to convey messages; carrier services for the transport of goods; double entry bookkeeping; the extension of joint enterprises for longer durations (previously these had been established for single ventures and then dissolved); the accepting of deposits by businesses for funding purposes and the payment of interest on them (rather than a share in the profits); and bills of exchange (which allowed local payments to be made without the need to transport coins or bullion).

5. Including a 24-fold increase in England between the mid 1100s and 1319.

money changers prospered, and adopted the merchant companies' practice of accepting deposits. By also holding deposits with each other, their customers were able to make cashless payments between each other (even when this took accounts into overdraft) (Spufford, 2002). Deposit banking, as it had been practised by the Athenians, was thus rediscovered.

Banking in England

In mediaeval England, there were no private money changers for banks to develop out of, since this was a royal monopoly associated with the mints (Spufford, 2002). The monopoly had however become eroded over time, as Charles I attempted to revive it in 1627, but was left to "fume in vain against the growing power of the goldsmiths who had 'left off their proper trade and turned [into] exchangers of plate and foreign coins for our English coins, though they had no right.'" (Davies, 1994) These goldsmiths offered safekeeping facilities to merchants and the public for coins, bullion and other valuables. Any coins deposited for safekeeping with goldsmiths were acknowledged with a note promising to pay out an equivalent sum. Provided that the goldsmith's name was trusted in the area where they operated, holding a goldsmith's promissory note became considered to be as good as having the actual coins in hand, as there was complete confidence that the holder of the note would be able to get the coins from the goldsmith as and when they needed. As a result, people began to accept the promissory notes as money, in place of coins, and would rarely come back to the bank to withdraw the coins themselves:

> "…the crucial innovations in English banking history seem to have been mainly the work of the goldsmith bankers in the middle decades of the seventeenth century. They accepted deposits both on current and time accounts from merchants and landowners; they made loans and discounted bills; above all they learnt to issue promissory notes and made their deposits transferable by 'drawn note' or cheque; so credit might be created either by note issue or by the creation of deposits, against which only a proportionate cash reserve was held." (Joslin, 1954, as quoted in He, Huang, & Wright, 2005)

Having noticed that their notes were now being used to trade in place of coins and that the bulk of the coins deposited in their vaults were never taken out, the goldsmiths saw a profit opportunity: they could issue and lend additional promissory notes (which would be seen by the borrower as a loan of money) and charge a rate of interest on the loan. The goldsmiths had managed to create a substitute for money issued by the state, and in the process become banks.

fig. 1.2 - Banknotes like the following (from 1889) began to be phased out following the Bank Charter Act in 1844

The corner of this note was "clipped" when the note was removed from circulation

One of the principal borrowers from the goldsmith banks was the sovereign. In 1640, Charles I had shocked the banking system by borrowing bullion (gold and silver) that merchants had deposited at the Royal Mint, in the process destroying the Mint's reputation as a safe place of custody and also damaging his own credit rating. Thirty two years later his son, Charles II, suspended almost all repayment of sovereign debts in order to finance a naval expedition against the Dutch (Kindleberger, 2007). The harm to the sovereign's credit rating of these episodes indirectly led to the founding of the Bank of England, as the state was forced to develop new ways of financing itself.

The founding of the Bank of England

In 1688 Charles II's successor, James II, was deposed in the 'Glorious Revolution' and Parliament offered the crown to his daughter Mary and her husband the Dutch Prince William of Orange. With the new King and Queen came war with France, which in 1690 led to a crushing naval defeat for Britain at the Battle of Beachy Head. In order to rebuild Britain's navy, the government needed to raise £1.2 million. To induce potential investors to fund the loan, the subscribers were to be incorporated as shareholders of a new joint stock bank, the Bank of England, which would be authorised to issue bank notes (up to the amount of the fund) and take deposits. The share issue was fully subscribed within 14 days.

Nevertheless, the government's tax revenue was still not enough to cover its debts. The government reacted by passing a Bill (in 1697) permitting the Bank to issue new shares in exchange for subscribers' own holdings of government debt (80%) and Bank of England notes (20%). As a result the Bank was further authorised to issue banknotes up to the total amount raised from the new subscribers (of £1,001,171) (Davies, 1994, p. 261), with the notes to be underwritten (guaranteed) by the government. The Bank was also granted a monopoly as a banking corporation and given limited liability for its shareholders, whilst the goldsmiths were all partnerships with unlimited liability. The Bank was thus established as a principal manager of a significant part of the government debt.

Many of the Bank's early depositors were the goldsmith banks, in spite of their hostility towards their new competitor.[6] These banks had found that the notes that they issued would often be paid across to customers of other banks, who would deposit them with their own banks. Bankers would periodically meet to exchange the notes they had received for those that they had themselves issued, and settle any differences in coin. They soon found that it was more convenient to settle using Bank of England notes, rather than carrying large amounts of coins to their settlement meetings. As a Bank of England working paper describes:

> "[S]ometime between the Bank of England's foundation (1694) and the 1770s, London bankers switched from settling in specie [coins] to settling in Bank of England notes. Such claims were a superior form of money to the notes of any other bank. The primary reason for this was the Bank's financial standing relative to other banks. This arose from the legal privilege of being the only joint stock bank allowed to issue notes, which enabled it to expand its note issue and generate widespread acceptability for its notes. Bank of England money was widely used as the settlement asset, since country banks settled inter-regional payments via correspondent

---

6.   The goldsmiths did not take to the new bank without first trying to destroy it. In 1696, England's worn, clipped and underweight silver coins had been recalled for re-minting and this led to a temporary shortage of coins needed by the new Bank of England to redeem its notes. This threatened the stability of the bank, and attempts were made by the goldsmiths to bring it down, although when they failed this only had the effect of further enhancing the Bank of England's reputation.

relationships which ultimately settled via the London clearing arrangements. And the formal provincial clearings established later in the nineteenth century settled across accounts at the local branch of the Bank of England (as for example in Manchester, the largest provincial clearing)." (Norman, Shaw, & Speight, 2011)

The Bank of England had begun to take on its role as banker to the banking system and its liabilities (banknotes) had started to be used by other banks as a means of payment between banks and a means of final settlement.

Country banking and the Bank Charter Act
The silver recoinage of 1696 (see footnote 6) was not repeated and as a result Britain's silver (and copper) coins quickly deteriorated in quality.[7] In addition, there was a constant draining of silver from the country due to both the mint price of silver being set below the market price, as well as the requirements of foreign trade. This was problematic as at the time it was silver, not gold, that was considered the monetary standard. By the 1770s, employers outside London were finding it increasingly difficult to acquire sufficient coins to pay their workers, and resorted to issuing their own tokens or credit notes. This led many into the business of banking and the creation of paper money.

After the end of the Napoleonic Wars in 1815, trade and the demand for finance increased. Likewise the opening up of South America and the Industrial Revolution sparked a wave of speculation in company start-ups, leading to increasingly reckless lending (and so banknote creation) and the inevitable wave of bank failures and crises from 1825 to 1839 (when the Bank of England was forced to replenish its gold reserves by borrowing from France). Blame for the collapse was placed at the time on over-issue of banknotes by the country banks.

In response to these crises, the Conservative government of the day enacted the 1844 Bank Charter Act, which curtailed the private sector's right to issue banknotes (and eventually phased it out altogether). The right to issue paper money became the sole prerogative of the Bank of England (although some Scottish and Irish banks were given permission to effectively 're-brand' Bank

---

7.   While gold coins were maintained to a reasonable standard they still suffered from attrition.

of England notes[8]). However, the 1844 Bank Charter Act only addressed the creation of paper banknotes. It did not refer to other substitutes for money, such as bank deposits, which were simply accounting entries on the liabilities side of the banks' balance sheets. Banks had retained, albeit imperfectly, their ability to create substitutes that could function as money.

In order to make the most of their money creation powers, banks were forced to innovate in order to find ways around the new legislation. The use of cheques became common as they made it easier for businesses and individuals to make payments to each other using bank-created money (bank liabilities, or 'deposits') in place of cash. At the same time, the development of wholesale money markets (where banks could borrow from each other) and the willingness of the Bank of England to provide funds on demand to banks in good health, further reduced the amount of Bank of England money that banks needed to hold, relative to their customer deposits:

> "[C]entral banks have facilitated settlement in central bank money by allowing low-cost transfers across their books, either of gross amounts (above all for wholesale payments, facilitating this by providing banks with cheap intraday liquidity) or of multilateral net amounts (more usually for retail payments, minimising the amount of liquidity that participating banks need to hold)." (Norman, Shaw, & Speight, 2011)

The end result of these innovations was that banks continued to create money. As Kindleberger (2007) explains, "The Bank Act of 1844 had restricted bank notes but not bills of exchange or bank deposits and these expanded in England by large amounts".

Finally, in 1866 a financial crisis brought on by the failure of the Overend, Gurney & Company Bank (to whom the Bank of England had refused an emergency loan) led to the Bank of England finally accepting the responsibility of lender of last resort. Up until that point it had often refused to intervene and provide emergency loans to struggling banks, with the result that crises were often exacerbated. By agreeing to be the lender of last resort, the Bank of England provided a further guarantee to banks that funding would be

---

8. For every banknote issued by a Scottish or Northern Irish bank, the issuing bank must hold an equivalent amount of Bank of England banknotes in their vault. These notes come in denominations of £1 million ('Giants') and £100 million ('Titans').

available should they need it, limiting the downsides to them of overextending themselves.

The Bank of England had thus taken on all the roles of a modern central bank, responsible since its inception for raising money to lend to the government (1694), assuming management of part of the government debt (1697), providing through its note issue and deposit-taking services the means for other banks to clear payments between themselves (by 1770), and standing as lender of last resort for the banking sector (1866). As the nineteenth century progressed and commerce and international trade rocketed, other major countries also developed central banks with similar functions. This system came into full use within the major economies in 1913 with the establishment of the Federal Reserve Bank ('the Fed') in the United States, a year before the outbreak of the First World War.

The gold standard

The gold standard ran from 1717 to 1931 in Britain. During this period the value of the pound was redefined only once (by the Coinage Act of 1816), at 113 grains of pure gold (about 7.3 grams). However, the gold standard was also suspended twice (from 1797-1819 and 1914-1925), in order to conserve gold to help finance the Napoleonic War and the First World War.[9] During the second suspension (in 1914), gold coins were withdrawn from circulation and convertibility of banknotes to gold was suspended. As the Bank of England was legally barred from issuing notes lower than £5 (from 1826), to replace the sovereigns and half-sovereigns withdrawn the Treasury issued its own one pound and ten shilling notes christened 'Bradburys', after the Treasury official whose signature appeared on them.[10]

In 1925, the UK returned to the gold standard at the rate set in 1816, which overpriced British exports by about 10% sparking a severe recession, a short

---

9. Although demonetisation of silver did not fully occur until the gold recoinage of 1774 eliminated silver as legal tender for sums over £25 (Kindleberger, 2007).

10. Later the Currency and Banknotes Act of 1928 transferred the outstanding Treasury notes (Bradburys) to the Bank of England and converted them to banknotes. The 1928 Act also authorised the Bank to use government debt to back the note issue rather than gold, and to use these notes rather than gold coins to redeem its higher-denomination banknotes on demand. Finally the act lifted the prohibition against the Bank of England from issuing small denomination banknotes.

general strike and a protracted miners' strike. America was however experiencing a stock market boom, created once again by excessive commercial bank lending (for the purchase of stocks and shares). In 1929 this bubble burst, collapsing the financial system and the global economy with it. As a consequence gold convertibility was suspended again and for the last time in 1933, with the pound left to find its own level against other currencies.

Towards the end of the 1930s, economies in the West began to recover through government deficit spending: civic reconstruction in the US and re-armament in the UK and Europe. Half a decade later as the Second World War drew to a close, a new arrangement was agreed such that all national central banks would hold accounts at the US Federal Reserve Bank, and the Fed would settle payments between accounts, which were redeemable, if necessary, in gold. This was the Bretton Woods agreement. Nations agreed to manage their currencies to maintain a fixed exchange rate against the dollar, and America agreed to fix the dollar against gold. The maintenance of the Bretton Woods exchange rates shifted focus onto the flow of capital into and out of countries – to prevent these flows interfering with the fixed exchange rates, the UK used a combination of capital controls (to limit the outflows due to the acquisition of foreign assets), quantitative and qualitative restrictions on bank lending, and control of interest rates (to limit the availability and demand for domestic credit which could fuel imports).

Despite the huge government deficits run up during the war, the destruction of large swathes of Europe, and a highly repressed financial system, from 1945 to 1971 growth was uniformly high and unemployment very low. For these reasons this period is commonly referred to as the golden age of capitalism.

Floating exchange rates

Between 1945 and 1971 a new dynamic developed. By international agreement, oil had always been priced in US dollars and as a consequence the oil exporting nations of the Middle East had amassed a substantial surplus of dollars, invested mainly in US Government securities (bonds). By 1965, the French President, Charles de Gaulle, was decrying the world's dependence on the US dollar and calling for a return to a national gold standard, and in 1971 Switzerland and France each demanded redemption in gold of its central bank's holdings of dollars. America, fearing a similar call from the Middle East, declared it would no longer redeem dollar holdings for gold, defaulting on its Bretton Woods obligations and leading to the collapse of the

Bretton Woods system. The final link between national currencies and gold was thereby abolished.

The oil-exporting nations of the Middle East retaliated by cutting production and quadrupling the price of oil (resulting in the 1973 oil crisis), whilst other countries struggled to maintain the fixed exchange rates they had agreed at Bretton Woods. A decade of economic chaos ensued. By the end of the 1980s the current system had emerged, whereby the major trading currencies floated freely against each other. Minor currencies were either fixed informally against one of the majors or abandoned in favour of currency union.

Meanwhile, in 1971 the Bank of England introduced 'Competition and Credit Control'. This was a package of regulatory reforms that removed the ceilings on bank lending and reduced the amount of liquid assets banks had to hold against their deposits from 28% to 12.5% (See Figure 1.3).[11] As part of the reforms, the focus switched from using direct controls to target the rate of growth of the money stock (determined by the rate of increase in bank lending) to using interest rates. Consequently:

> "This combination of regulatory and economic factors coincided with one of the most rapid periods of credit growth in the 20th century … It also contributed to an ongoing decline in banks' liquidity holdings, ultimately to below 5% of total assets by the end of the 1970s." (Davies, Richardson, Katinaite, & Manning, 2010)

Since the 1980s the focus of monetary policy has switched to the control of consumer price inflation via the use of interest rates. Meanwhile, further technological advances, such as the adoption of debit and credit cards and electronic fund transfers, have lessened the public's reliance on cash as a means of payment, with banks today needing to hold only a tiny amount of cash (around 3%) relative to the total balances of customers' accounts. Likewise, they face little restriction on their ability to create new money by making loans (for reasons explained in Chapter 3). Consequently, almost all money in circulation today takes the form of deposits created by private banks in the process of making loans.

The following chapter will describe the present day monetary system in greater detail.

---

11.   The Bank of England introduced another system to attempt to control bank lending (the corset) in 1973. However, this was abolished in 1980.

fig. 1.3 - Sterling liquid assets relative to total asset holdings
of the UK banking sector

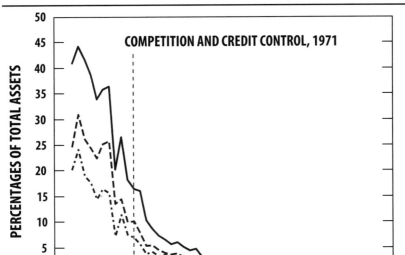

BROAD RATIO [(b)]

RESERVE RATIO [(c)]

NARROW RATIO [(d)]

Source: Davies et al. 2010

(a) Data before 1967 cover only the London clearing banks.

(b) Cash + Bank of England balances + money at call + eligible bills + UK gilts.

(c) Bank of England balances + money at call + eligible bills.

(d) Cash + Bank of England balances + eligible bills.

CHAPTER 2
THE CURRENT MONETARY SYSTEM

In this chapter we build up an understanding of the monetary system. We start by looking at the modern banking system, focussing on the role of the two key players: commercial (high street) banks, and the central bank, the Bank of England. We explain the fundamental business model of a modern bank and then look at the mechanics by which commercial banks create (and destroy) money and central banks create (and destroy) central bank reserves and cash. This chapter provides enough knowledge of the existing banking system to understand the analysis that follows in the rest of the book. However, for those who would like a much more in-depth understanding of the modern monetary system, the book *Where Does Money Come From?* published by the New Economics Foundation is very highly recommended.

2.1 COMMERCIAL (HIGH-STREET) BANKS

The banks that most of us use today are referred to as commercial banks or high-street banks. They perform a number of practical functions:

They make loans. This could be seen as the raison d'être of modern banking. It is by making loans that they expand and generate the bulk of their profits.

They allow customers to make electronic payments between each other through electronic funds transfers (accessed by internet or telephone banking) or via the use of debit cards.

They provide physical cash to customers either through bank branches or via ATM cash machines.

They accept deposits. This is the role most of us associate banks with, from our first childhood experiences of putting money 'in the bank'.

It is the first function, the making of loans, which is of crucial importance for the stability of the economy and the level of debt in society. As discussed in the sections below, banks do not make loans by taking money from a saver and transferring it to a borrower, as most of us would assume. Instead, they make loans by increasing their liabilities and assets in tandem, creating a new liability (the bank deposit i.e. the numbers that appear in the borrower's account) and a new asset (the loan contract, signed by the borrower, promising to repay the same amount). This process will be described in detail later in the chapter.

This is not however lending in the common sense of the word, as the act of lending implies that the lender gives up access to what is being lent for the duration of the loan. As economist Hyman Minsky puts it:

> "Banking is not money lending; to lend, a money lender must have money. The fundamental banking activity is accepting, that is, guaranteeing that some party is creditworthy. A bank, by accepting a debt instrument, agrees to make specified payments if the debtor will not or cannot." (1986, p. 256)

Because bank 'lending' increases the balance of the borrower's bank account without decreasing the value of anyone else's account, it increases the level of purchasing power in the economy. In effect this creates new money, just as banks did when they printed their own bank notes. Currently this 'commercial bank money' accounts for approximately 97% of the total amount of money in circulation, with cash issued by the Bank of England making up the remaining 3%. Therefore, the lending decisions of commercial banks have huge significance for the economy, for two reasons. First, because new money is created when banks make loans, the lending decisions of banks determine the total quantity of money that circulates in the economy. Second, as banks decide who they will lend to and for what purposes the loan can be used, their lending priorities determine which sectors of the economy this newly created money is allocated to. As a result banks have a huge impact on the shape and future direction of the economy. Many of the economic, social and environmental challenges that we face today are connected, in one way or another, to these two key impacts of bank lending.

We will shortly look at each of the four functions described above, showing what happens in the accounts and on the balance sheet, in order to show how the current monetary system works. But first, we need to look at the other key element of the modern banking system – the central bank.

Box 2.A - Money: What it is and what it's for

What is money for?

Textbooks tend to assign money four functions:

A store of value: Money should preserve its purchasing power – a unit of currency should be able to purchase the same amount of goods tomorrow as it does today.

A medium of exchange: Money is accepted in all circumstances in exchange for goods and services.

A unit of account: Money is the yardstick against which all other goods and services are measured.

A means of final settlement or payment: Once money has been transferred the transaction between two parties is complete. This is important as it distinguishes money from credit, which involves a future obligation or promise to pay.

What is money?

Today, there are broadly three types of money circulating in the economy:

Cash: Physical money, or cash, is created under the authority of the Bank of England, with coins manufactured by the Royal Mint, and notes printed by specialist printer De La Rue. The profits from the creation of cash (known as seigniorage) go directly to the government. Today, cash makes up less than 3% of the total amount of money in the economy.

Central bank reserves: Central bank reserves are a type of electronic money, created by the central bank and used by commercial banks to make payments between themselves. In some respects central bank reserves are like an electronic version of cash. However, members of the public and normal businesses cannot access central bank reserves; they are only available to those organisations who have accounts at the Bank of England, i.e. other banks. Central bank reserves are not usually counted as part of the money supply for the economy, due to the fact they are only used by banks to make payments between themselves.

Commercial bank money: The third type of money accounts for approximately 97% of money in circulation. However, unlike central bank reserves and cash, it is not created by the central bank or any other part of government. Instead, commercial bank money is created by private, high-street or 'commercial' banks, in the process of making loans or buying assets (as described below). While this money is electronic in form, it need not be – before computers, banks could still 'create money' by simply adding deposits to their ledger books and balance sheets, with this money being spent via the use of cheques.

2.2 THE BANK OF ENGLAND

The Bank of England is the central bank of the United Kingdom. It is crucial to any discussion of the current monetary system because it effectively provides the infrastructure and the specific type of 'base' money on which the wider system is built and operates. It is also assumed by many to be responsible for managing money creation, although as will become clear in Chapter 3, it does not currently have the tools to be able to do this successfully.

Unlike commercial banks, which deal with businesses and members of the public, the central bank typically acts as banker to commercial banks and the central government. It will also tend to hold accounts in the nation's currency for central banks of other countries. Also, while commercial banks are typically privately owned for-profit enterprises, in the UK the central bank is owned by the government.

The Bank of England performs five roles that are relevant to our discussion. These are:

1. The creation of central bank money (base money)

Although no member of the public will have an account with the Bank of England, most people will be familiar with the name for the simple reason that it is printed on most of the £5, £10, £20 or £50 notes that exist in the UK. This is the most commonly known function of a central bank: to create the cash that is used to make most smaller payments across the UK.

However, cash is not the only type of money created by the central bank. As the Bank of England describes, "Central bank money takes two forms — the banknotes used in everyday transactions, and the balances ('reserves') that are held by commercial banks and building societies ('banks') at the Bank [of England]." (2012)

These 'reserves', or 'central bank reserves', can be seen as an electronic equivalent of cash, in that they are created exclusively by the Bank of England. However, unlike cash, members of the public and normal businesses cannot access or use central bank reserves; instead they are only available to those organisations that have accounts at the Bank of England, i.e. banks and building societies. Central bank reserves are used almost exclusively by banks to settle payments amongst themselves.

Taken together, central bank reserves and cash (notes and coins) are commonly referred to in economics textbooks as 'base money', 'high powered money', or

fig. 2.1 - Hierarchy of accounts

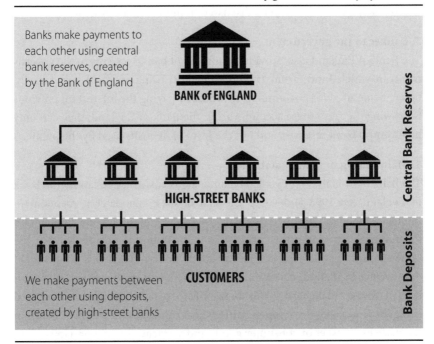

Banks make payments to each other using central bank reserves, created by the Bank of England

BANK of ENGLAND

HIGH-STREET BANKS

CUSTOMERS

We make payments between each other using deposits, created by high-street banks

Central Bank Reserves

Bank Deposits

'outside money'. The Bank of England prefers to use the term 'central bank money', but to avoid possible confusion with the similar sounding 'commercial bank money', we will use the term 'base money' throughout this book to refer to cash and central bank reserves collectively.

2. Banker to commercial banks

An important function of the Bank of England is to be the 'banker to the banks'. This involves providing commercial banks with accounts that hold the central bank reserves mentioned above. These accounts play a critical role in allowing banks to make payments to each other: in the same way that I could make a payment to you by making a transfer from my personal bank account to yours, commercial banks can make payments to each other by transferring central bank reserves between their respective accounts at the Bank of England.

In order to provide the commercial banks with the reserves they need in order to settle payments between themselves, the Bank of England also regularly lends central bank reserves to banks, on demand. The lending of reserves and the provision of accounts to banks enables the central bank to affect the interest rate at which banks lend reserves to each other, facilitating its conduct of monetary policy. This will be discussed in more detail in Chapter 3.

3. Banker to the government

The Bank of England also provides a number of bank accounts to the government, in which funds from taxation and borrowing are held, temporarily, before being used for government spending or paying the interest on previous borrowing. Because these accounts are at the Bank of England, they can only hold central bank reserves, and not the form of deposits used by the public.

4. Maintaining monetary stability

The Bank of England has two legal mandates, as enshrined in law by the Bank of England Act 1998 and 2009. The first of these mandates is to maintain monetary stability. This gives the Bank of England an obligation to maintain the purchasing power of the currency so that a pound tomorrow will buy the same amount of goods and services as does a pound today. This is equivalent to preventing inflation, commonly defined as "a sustained rise in the general level of prices" (Blanchard, 2006). In the UK these price changes are measured using the Consumer Price Index (CPI), which calculates the average change in the price of a basket of consumer goods and services over the previous year.[1] In practice, the Bank of England is currently committed to maintaining a 'low and stable' inflation rate of 2% a year.

To manage the rate of inflation in the economy the Bank of England attempts to influence the level of aggregate demand (defined as the demand for final goods and services in the economy at a particular time) by targeting the rate of interest at which commercial banks lend to each other. The target interest rate (the 'policy rate') is set by the Monetary Policy Committee (MPC) of the Bank of England, a body that is independent from the government. Section 3.4 describes the theoretical rationale behind using the interest rate to influence inflation, as well as highlighting the limitations of this approach.

5. Preserving financial stability

The Bank of England's second mandate is to protect and enhance the stability of the United Kingdom's financial system. This involves the Bank of England working to detect and reduce the threats to the financial system, which includes developing tools which allow it to monitor and to warn of impending problems, as well as ensuring the resilience of the financial system (especially the

---

1.   Although crucially the CPI basket does not include house prices.

payments system) should such a shock occur. If a threat is discovered appropriate action can be taken,[2] while in the case of unexpected shocks, such as the 2007/08 crisis, the Bank of England can intervene to protect financial stability. This may take the form of reducing interest rates, providing emergency funding for illiquid banks (the lender of last resort function), purchasing assets financed by creating base money (in order to set a floor under asset prices or reduce interest rates), and/or purchasing currency on foreign exchange markets (in order to maintain the value of the currency and therefore the price of imports/exports).

2.3 THE BUSINESS MODEL OF BANKING

Understanding balance sheets

Notes and coins today make up just three out of every hundred pounds in the economy. The other ninety-seven pounds exist as accounting entries on the books of commercial banks. For that reason, a basic understanding of accounting and balance sheets is essential in order to understand how money is created. There is no reason to be put off by the accounting terminology; if you have ever borrowed money from a friend and left a note on the fridge to remind you to repay them, then you have already done one half of the accounting necessary to understand banking.

In short, a bank's balance sheet is a record of everything it owns, is owed, or owes. The balance sheet comprises three distinct parts: assets, liabilities and shareholder equity.

Assets: On one side of the balance sheet are the assets. The assets include everything that the bank owns or is owed, from cash in its vaults, to bank branch buildings in town centres, through to government bonds and various financial products. Loans made by the bank usually account for the largest portion of a bank's assets.

---

2. This however has not always been considered possible. Before the run up to the 2007/08 crisis the consensus amongst central bankers was that asset bubbles could not be spotted in advance, that the central bank did not have the tools to prevent them, and that even if it could it would be cheaper to clean up after the bubble had burst than attempt to pop it beforehand. Naturally this view is now being questioned following the crisis.

Loans and mortgages are assets of the bank because they represent a legal obligation of the borrower to pay money to the bank. So when someone takes out £200,000 for a mortgage, this loan contract is recorded on the assets side of the balance sheet as being worth £200,000. Of course, the borrower also promises to pay interest on a yearly basis. Note however that this interest is never recorded on the balance sheet, but is recorded each year as income on a separate accounting statement, known as the income statement or 'profit and loss' statement. For example, even though the contract that the borrower signed commits them to paying £200,000 plus interest over 25 years (making a total repayable of £333,499 at 4.5% interest) only the £200,000 amount originally borrowed (the 'principal') is recorded on the balance sheet. As loan repayments are made, this principal is gradually reduced.

Liabilities: Liabilities are simply things that the bank owes to other people, organisations or other banks. Contrary to the perception of most of the public, when you (as a bank customer) deposit physical cash into a bank it becomes the property (an asset) of the bank, and you lose your legal ownership over it. What you receive in return is a promise from the bank to pay you an amount equivalent to the sum deposited. This promise is recorded on the liabilities side of the balance sheet, and is what you see when you check the balance of your bank account. Therefore the 'money' in your bank account does not represent money in the bank's safe, it simply represents the promise of the bank to repay you – either in cash or as an electronic transfer to another account – when you ask it to. The bulk of a typical bank's liabilities are made up of 'deposits' which are owed to the 'depositors'. These will generally be individuals, businesses or other organisations.

Deposits in a bank can be split into two broad groups: demand (or sight) deposits and time (or term) deposits. Demand deposits are deposits that can be withdrawn or spent immediately when the customer asks, in other words 'on demand' or 'on sight' of the customer. These accounts are commonly referred to as current accounts (in the UK) or checking accounts (in the USA), or instant access savings accounts. In contrast, time deposits have a notice period or a fixed maturity date, so that the money cannot be withdrawn on demand. These accounts are commonly referred to as savings accounts.

Equity: The final part of the balance sheet is the equity. Equity is simply the difference between assets and liabilities, and represents what would be left over for the shareholders (owners) of the bank if all the assets were sold and the proceeds used to settle the bank's liabilities (i.e. pay off the creditors).

Equity is calculated by subtracting liabilities from assets. A positive net equity indicates that a bank's assets are worth more than its liabilities. On the other hand a negative equity shows that its liabilities are worth more than its assets - in other words, that the bank is insolvent.

fig. 2.2 - Assets and liabilities

ASSETS – LIABILITIES = EQUITY

ASSETS > LIABILITIES → BANK IS SOLVENT

ASSETS < LIABILITIES → BANK IS INSOLVENT

Presenting balance sheets diagrammatically

On official annual accounts, assets are typically presented first, followed by liabilities underneath, with equity coming last, as shown below:

fig. 2.3 - Stacked balance sheet

Commercial Bank Balance Sheet
Assets
Cash, central bank reserves, bonds etc. (liquid assets)
Loans the bank has made to its customers (illiquid assets)
Liabilities
Customer deposits
Shareholder Equity
Total shareholder equity

However, it can help to present the balance sheet diagrammatically with assets on one side, and liabilities and equity on the opposite side. By definition, liabilities plus equity must be equal to assets, so the total of both the left and right sides of the balance sheet must be equal. In this book we follow the convention of American banking textbooks, with assets on the left and liabilities plus equity on the right, although in other books the columns may be reversed.

fig. 2.4 - A normal bank balance sheet

Commercial Bank Balance Sheet	
Assets *(What the bank owns +* *What is owed to the bank)*	**Liabilities** *(What the bank owes)*
Cash, central bank reserves, bonds etc. (liquid assets)	Customer deposits
Loans the bank has made to its customers (illiquid assets)	Shareholder Equity

Staying in business

For a bank, staying in business and making a profit essentially comes down to three rules: 1) stay solvent, 2) stay liquid, and 3) earn a positive margin. We'll look at each of these in detail now.

1. Staying solvent

As discussed earlier, the difference between assets and liabilities is referred to as shareholder equity. If assets are greater than liabilities then shareholder equity is positive and the bank is solvent, meaning that if it sold all its assets, it would have enough to pay all of its creditors (e.g. customers who are owed money) in full, and still have something left over to return to shareholders (the owners of the bank). However, the value of its assets is not guaranteed – borrowers may fail to repay loans, or investments such as bonds and equities (stocks or shares) may go up and down in value. If a large number of the bank's borrowers became unable to repay and then defaulted on their loans, these loans would be 'written off' and their value on the balance sheet would be reduced (possibly to zero) causing an equal reduction in equity. If a significant percentage of the assets are written off, the total value of assets may fall below the total value of liabilities, shareholder equity would become negative, and the bank would become insolvent i.e. unable to repay all of its creditors. If a bank (or any company) finds itself in this situation, with no reasonable prospect of assets recovering their value, it is required to cease trading and start liquidation proceedings.

fig. 2.5 - A bank that is fundamentally insolvent

Commercial Bank Balance Sheet	
Assets *(What the bank owns +* *What is owed to the bank)￼*	**Liabilities** *(What the bank owes)*
Cash, bonds, etc. Good loans	Customer deposits
Loans that will not be repaid	Shareholder Equity

To guard against this happening, banks try to ensure that assets are a certain level above liabilities; this difference is referred to as a capital buffer or equity buffer. For example, if the capital buffer is £10 billion, then the bank can afford to take £10 billion of losses on its assets before it becomes insolvent.

So the first rule of banking is to keep the bank's assets greater than its liabilities. Failure to do this amounts to 'game over' for a bank.

Trying to avoid insolvency depends on the bank's risk management; it needs to ensure that only a small (and predictable) percentage of loans default. Complex regulations, known as the Basel Capital Accords, attempt to give banks a standardised framework for ensuring that their capital buffer is sufficient to protect the bank from failure in the event of losses on its assets. Section 3.4 discusses these regulations and why they have been ineffective.

2. Staying liquid

Banks also run the risk of becoming insolvent through being unable to meet their liabilities as they fall due, even though their assets may be greater than their liabilities. In accounting terms, this is known as cashflow insolvency. In banking jargon it is referred to as a 'liquidity crisis'. A liquidity crisis can happen if there is a significant outflow of funds (central bank reserves) from a bank to other banks or to customers who are withdrawing cash. This process can happen very quickly, as in a bank run, or slowly if its liabilities are withdrawn slightly faster than its loan assets are repaid. If a bank becomes unable to settle its liabilities to either customers or to other banks, then it is again declared insolvent and will need to cease trading.

Avoiding a liquidity crisis relies on a process known as 'asset liability management', which involves managing and predicting inflows and outflows to ensure

Box 2.B - Confusing Reserve Ratios and Capital Reserves

It is important not to confuse reserve ratios/requirements (or liquidity ratios) with capital requirements. These two things are very different and serve completely different purposes.

Liquidity ratios or 'reserve ratios' as often discussed, requires a bank to hold base money (or other assets) against its liabilities (such as deposits). A pure reserve ratio, such as the 10% that is often given in textbook examples (which has never applied in the UK) states that for every £100 of customer deposits a bank must have £10 of base (i.e. central bank) money, in the form of either a) cash in its vaults or b) deposits (central bank reserves) at the central bank. A liquidity ratio is similar, but allows banks to hold highly-liquid assets such as government bonds in place of cash and central bank reserves, with the idea being that bonds can easily be exchanged for cash and central bank reserves if customers are making higher than usual withdrawals or payments from their accounts.

In short, liquidity ratios and reserve ratios say, "What percentage of customers could withdraw their deposits simultaneously before the bank runs out of base money?" A reserve ratio or liquidity ratio of 10% would imply that the bank could suffer a withdrawal of up to 10% of its deposits before it would become illiquid and have to seek funding (for example from other banks or the Bank of England) or close its doors.

In contrast, the capital or 'capital reserves' that are required by the Basel Capital Accords requires banks to hold capital against the assets side of its balance sheet. Capital requirements say, in essence, "What percentage of our loans can default before our liabilities exceed our assets and we become insolvent?" (Section 3.4 discusses the importance of this capital.)

that a bank is always able to make its payments as and when it needs to. In many cases, this may involve borrowing funds (central bank reserves) from other banks for periods as short as overnight in order to stay liquid and make payments to other banks.

3. Earning a positive margin

Finally, to earn a profit banks must ensure that the interest they receive across all their interest-bearing assets is greater than the interest they pay across all of their interest-bearing liabilities. The difference between the total interest paid and the total interest charged is called the 'margin' or 'spread'. The practice of asset liability management takes into account the interest rate risk of a bank's assets and liabilities (the risk that the rates determining the interest receivable from assets may deteriorate relative to the rates determining the interest payable on liabilities), to ensure that this margin remains positive (with interest rates charged being higher than interest rates paid) and sufficient to cover the costs of the bank's operations.

Banks also receive additional income from other sources. These include charging fees for services rendered and on overdrawn accounts. Universal banks, which combine high-street and investment banks, may also profit from trading securities, charging commission on securities transactions, assisting companies to issue new equity financing and by providing wealth management functions.

2.4 MONEY CREATION

With an understanding of commercial (high-street) banks, the Bank of England and balance sheets, we can now look at the mechanisms that enable banks to create money as accounting entries.

The money creation process can be difficult to understand, chiefly because we deal with money every day and so have preconceived ideas of banks and money derived from our personal experiences. As John Maynard Keynes remarked in the introduction to his General Theory (1936), "The difficulty lies, not in the new ideas, but in escaping from the old ones, which ramify ... into every corner of our minds". For example, as children we may have been given money that we put in a piggy bank to keep safe. We then carry this conception of banks and money into adulthood – when we think of money we think of cash, and banks are thought of as places to keep our money safe. Yet the vast majority of money is not cash, and banks are by their nature not places where money is kept 'safe'. As we will see, in reality the 'money' in our bank accounts merely consists of bookkeeping entries; money now is very literally just numbers on a balance sheet in a computer system. Since it is the banks that manage their own accounts, they can increase their liabilities as they wish (with some caveats which we will discuss shortly), and in doing so create and destroy the type of money that is used by the public. We will now look at how this process actually works.

In all the examples below, we ignore all balance sheet items apart from the ones in question. We also assume that balance sheet items are zero before the transaction in question takes place. This is purely to keep the examples simple and uncluttered.

Creating money by making loans to customers

How do banks create money by making loans? In this example, a self-employed builder, Jack, walks into MegaBank and asks to borrow £10,000 to buy a new van and some power tools. (Chapter 3 will show that loans to productive businesses like this make up just a small proportion of all bank lending.) Jack signs a contract with the bank confirming that he will repay £10,000 over a period of five years, plus interest. This legally enforceable contract represents an asset for the bank and when the bank comes to draw up its balance sheet it will be included as an additional asset worth £10,000. Jack, having committed to pay the bank £10,000, wants to receive the 'money' he has borrowed, so MegaBank opens up an account for him, which is a liability of the bank to Jack, and records a balance of £10,000.

There is no need, in the immediate term, for the bank to first 'find' the money from anywhere else. Once they have decided that Jack is credit-worthy and likely to repay, they can make the loan. In the words of Paul Tucker, Deputy Governor of the Bank of England: "[Banks] can lend simply by expanding the two sides of their balance sheet simultaneously, creating (broad) money." (2012) On Megabank's balance sheet this appears as so:

fig. 2.6 - Credit creation balance sheet

MegaBank	
Assets *(What the bank owns +* *What is owed to the bank)*	**Liabilities** *(What the bank owes)*
New loan to Jack £0 → £10,000	New account for Jack £0 → £10,000
All other assets £10,000	Shareholder equity £10,000

By increasing both sides of the balance sheet simultaneously, the bank has managed to issue a loan, and simultaneously create new money – in the form of deposits that appear in Jack's bank account – without affecting its other asset holdings or shareholder equity.

Notice that no money was transferred or taken from any other account; the bank simply updated a computer database. A bank cannot really be said to 'lend' money – to lend one must have money to lend in the first place.

Box 2.C - Do Banks Create 'Credit' or Money?

Some economists will argue that banks do not create money; they simply create credit. This point of view argues that bank deposits are liabilities of banks and are not declared legal tender, therefore they should not be described as money. Instead, they are promises to pay, which members of the public voluntarily accept in exchange for the convenience of being able to make payments without needing to hold large amounts of cash. When a bank fails, it becomes apparent that banks have not created money, but have simply created credit that is less safe than state-issued currency.

However, for something to be 'credit', it must have something called 'credit risk'. Credit risk is the risk that a person or company that owes you money will not repay you. If you lend £50 to an unreliable friend who still owes you money from the last time you lent to him, then there is a lot of credit risk associated to that loan.

So if the numbers that banks add to your bank account are not money, but just credit, then there must be some credit risk attached to that money. In other words, there must be a risk that the bank won't be able to repay you.

The Bank of England makes this argument in a distinction between cash and bank-created money – the 2010 Q3 Quarterly Bulletin states: "Bank of England notes are a form of 'central bank money', which the public holds without incurring credit risk. This is because the central bank is backed by the government" (p.302). They imply that cash has no credit risk because it is backed by the central bank, which is in turn backed by the government.

While this is true, it ignores the governments Financial Services Compensation Scheme (FSCS), which promises to repay the customers of failed banks up to £85,000 of their account (although if people believed a bank was about to fail the government conceivably could be forced to increase this limit even further, as it did during the financial crisis). This guarantee is supposed to be funded by contributions pooled across the banks. But if the contributions from the banks aren't sufficient – as happened during the financial crisis – then the government is required to find the rest of the money through taxation or borrowing.

As a result, the government guarantees individuals' bank accounts. Therefore, to use the Bank of England's own definition, deposits have no credit risk because they are "backed by the government", just as cash is. With no distinction between bank deposits and cash in terms of credit risk, the Bank of England's own definition of the difference between cash and bank deposits is rendered meaningless. In fact, bank deposits may incur even less risk than physical cash, as cash can be stolen or lost while bank deposits are guaranteed by the state. By providing this guarantee, the government turns risky 'bank credit' into the equivalent of state-issued money, and removes any meaningful difference between central bank money and bank deposits.

In reality a bank creates bank deposits when it advances loans. These bank deposits are liabilities of the bank, and can be used, just like physical money, to make payments in the economy (through debit cards and electronic fund transfers). No money has to be acquired from a saver before a loan can be made to a borrower. The result is that when a bank makes loans it increases both the quantity of money in the economy, as well as the quantity of debt.

Note that a bank can also create money in this way when buying financial assets, such as a government bond from a pension fund. Just as with a loan, the bond is recorded as an asset on the balance sheet and the bank credits the pension fund's account with the equivalent value.

2.5 MAKING ELECTRONIC PAYMENTS BETWEEN CUSTOMERS

Having borrowed £10,000 from his bank, Jack now wants to purchase a van. Because this is a large purchase, he prefers to make the payment electronically. We will consider two possible scenarios here: firstly that Jack and the van dealer bank at the same bank, and secondly, that they bank with different banks.

Customers at the same bank

In this example, Jack and the van dealer both bank with MegaBank (see figure 2.7). After picking out the van he likes (costing £9,500), Jack pays for it using his debit card (the end result is basically the same for both internet banking and payment by cheque). The debit card payment system (e.g. Visa or MasterCard) sends a message to Megabank, telling it that Jack wants to make a payment to the van dealer. The bank now simply updates its own internal records to reduce the balance of Jack's account and simultaneously increases the balance of the van dealer's account. No cash or central bank reserves have moved in this process; MegaBank has simply turned its liability to Jack into a liability to the van dealer, at Jack's instruction (figure 2.7).

Customers at different banks

What if the van dealer banks with Regal Bank, which is a separate entity to MegaBank? By using his debit card Jack sends a message to his bank to make a payment of £9,500 to the van dealer's account at Regal Bank (see figure 2.8). MegaBank immediately reduces the balance of Jack's account by £9,500. In order to settle this payment MegaBank will need to transfer central bank

fig. 2.7 - Exchange within same bank

MegaBank	
Assets *(What the bank owns +* *What is owed to the bank)*	**Liabilities** *(What the bank owes)*
New loan to Jack £10,000	Jack's account £10,000 → £500
	Van dealer's account £0 → £9,500
All other assets £10,000	Shareholder equity £10,000

fig. 2.8 - Exchange between banks i

MegaBank	
Assets *(What the bank owns +* *What is owed to the bank)*	**Liabilities** *(What the bank owes)*
New loan to Jack £10,000	Jack's account £10,000 → £500
All other assets (Central bank reserves) £10,000 → £500	Shareholder equity £10,000

fig. 2.9 - Exchange between banks ii

Regal Bank	
Assets *(What the bank owns +* *What is owed to the bank)*	**Liabilities** *(What the bank owes)*
Central bank reserves £0 → £9,500	Van dealer's account £0 → £9,500
All other assets £8,000	Shareholder equity £8,000

reserves from its own account at the Bank of England to Regal Bank's account at the Bank of England. It does this by sending a payment instruction to the Bank of England, to say "Please transfer £9,500 from my Bank of England account to Regal Bank's Bank of England account". Assuming that £10,000 of 'other assets' MegaBank held were in fact central bank reserves, its central bank reserves now fall to £500.

When Regal Bank receives the payment of central bank reserves into its bank account at the Bank of England, its central bank reserves increase (on the assets side - see fig 2.9). Regal Bank will also have increased the van dealer's account by the £9,500 at the point when Jack made the payment (although this would have shown as 'uncleared' until the central bank reserves arrived in Regal Bank's central bank account).

The same transaction can also be viewed from the perspective of the Bank of England's balance sheet. With both banks holding accounts at the Bank of England, transferring reserves between reserve accounts follows the same process as when two individuals at the same commercial bank make a payment between themselves; a liability to one bank (in this case MegaBank) becomes a liability to another bank (Regal Bank). While reserves appear as an asset on the balance sheet of commercial banks, they are a liability of the central bank (in the same way that bank deposits are assets of the account holders, but liabilities of commercial banks).

So, when Megabank makes a payment to Regal Bank, the transfer appears on the Bank of England's balance sheet as below (although see Box 2.D for a more complete explanation of what happens in practice):

fig. 2.10 - Central bank balance sheet during inter-bank payment

Bank of England (Central Bank)	
Assets	**Liabilities**
All assets £100,000	MegaBank's reserve account £10,000 → £500
	Regal Bank's reserve account £0 → £9,500
	All other liabilities £90,000

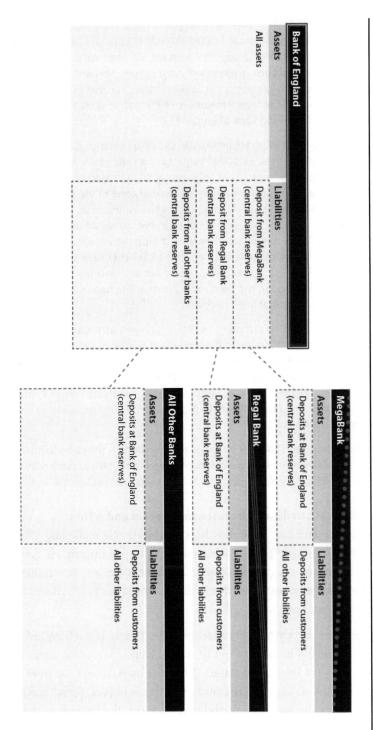

fig. 2.11 - Relation between liabilities of the central bank and assets of commercial banks

Box 2.D - A note on multilateral net settlement

We saw earlier that when a payment is made between customers of different banks, some central bank reserves will need to move between accounts at the Bank of England. However, it is certainly not the case that every pound transferred electronically between members of the public is matched by a pound being transferred at the Bank of England.

For a relatively small transaction like the £9,500 given above, MegaBank would not actually transfer the £9,500 in central bank reserves as a single payment. Instead, all the payments from its customers to customers of other banks would be queued in a computer system, namely one of the payment systems such as BACS, Faster Payments etc. Every few hours or at the end of every day (depending on the system), all the payments in would be added together to find the total flows in each direction, then payments that go in opposite directions would be cancelled out against each other to find the net amount that each bank owes to other banks. These net amounts are then settled with transfers made between the reserve accounts at the Bank of England i.e. they are settled using central bank reserves.

This process of netting out payment flows is known as 'multilateral net settlement' and significantly reduces the amount of central bank reserves that need to be held at the Bank of England. As an example of this, in 2008 a total average of £784 billion of payments was settled each day with just £32 billion of central bank reserves (Bank of England, 2009). In effect, every £1 of central bank reserves would be sufficient to support £25 of daily transactions between customers of banks.

Despite this, banks still do need to have central bank reserves on hand to make their end of day payments to other banks. How these central bank reserves are created and how banks acquire them is the subject of section 2.6.

Providing cash to depositors through branches and ATMs

Now let's assume that a few days later Jack needs the remaining £500 in his account to buy some power tools, and wants to pay in cash. He goes to the local branch, and asks to withdraw £500 from his account. The cashier hands Jack £500 and when Jack next checks his balance, it has been reduced by £500, to a new balance of £0.

The balance sheet changes are as follows. Prior to Jack receiving any money, MegaBank would have had to swap central bank reserves for cash (which it can do with the Bank of England). Then, the bank takes £500 from its own cash (which is an asset of the bank) and gives it to Jack. Simultaneously the bank reduces the value of its liability to Jack (i.e. the balance of Jack's bank account) to £0, as shown in fig 2.12.

fig. 2.12 - Withdrawing cash from an account

MegaBank	
Assets	**Liabilities**
Cash ~~£500~~ → £0	Jack's account ~~£500~~ → £0
Loan to Jack £10,000	Shareholder equity £10,000

From Jack's perspective, it appears he has taken out £500 of cash from the £10,000 that he had initially borrowed. However, in reality, Jack did not have 'cash in the bank' – he simply had a liability (a promise to pay) from the bank. Jack has swapped a promise from the bank to pay £500 (the bank's liability to him) for £500 in cash. Looked at another way, Jack has used his deposits at the bank to 'buy' an equivalent amount of physical cash that the bank already owned. We could also say that the bank has 'settled' or 'extinguished' its £500 liability to Jack by giving him the cash.

Accepting cash from depositors

Jack then takes his £500 in cash to a DIY shop and exchanges it for some tools. At the end of the day the DIY shop takes this £500 to its bank (NewBank) and deposits it there. The cash becomes the property of the bank, and so is recorded on the assets side of the balance sheet. Simultaneously, the DIY shop's account (a liability of the bank) is credited with an equal amount, and the DIY shop sees the balance of its account rise by £500:

fig. 2.13 - Depositing cash into an account

NewBank	
Assets	**Liabilities**
Cash in branch: £0 → £500 *(This is the physical cash that the DIY store deposited, which becomes the property of the bank)*	The DIY shop's account £0 → £500 *(This is simply a number in the bank's accounting system, and appears as the balance of the DIY shop's account)*
All other assets £5,000	Shareholder equity £5,000

Contrary to popular opinion, when you deposit cash into a bank, that cash does not remain your property. Instead, it becomes the property of the bank, and in return you acquire a liability of the bank – the increased balance that appears on your bank statement. This liability is a promise by the bank to either repay you in cash or make electronic payments up to the equivalent value on your behalf.

To the DIY store, it appears that the £500 has been 'put into' their account. However, it would be more accurate to say that either a) the DIY store has lent the bank £500, in return for a promise to be repaid as and when it needs the money, or b) the DIY store has exchanged £500 in cash for £500 of commercial bank money, which it can then spend electronically (or swap for cash again at a later date). Both descriptions are valid.

2.6 MONEY DESTRUCTION

As we have seen, when banks make loans, new money is created (in the form of numbers in a bank account). What happens when these loans are repaid? Exactly the opposite: whereas loans are created by *increasing* assets and liabilities simultaneously, loans are repaid by *reducing* assets and liabilities simultaneously. The reduction in liabilities reduces the amount of money in circulation; in effect, money (in the form used most often by the public) has been destroyed.

To keep the example simple, let's imagine Jack is paid £11,000 for a job he has recently completed. This payment is made electronically from a customer of another bank, so that central bank reserves are transferred from the payer's Bank to MegaBank's reserve account at the Bank of England. Jack then sees the value of his account increase by £11,000, as shown below.

fig. 2.14 - Loan repayment i

MegaBank	
Assets	**Liabilities**
Existing Loan to Jack £10,000	Jack's account £0 → £11,000
Central bank reserves £0 → £11,000	Shareholder equity £10,000

Jack decides to pay off his outstanding car loan in one go (£10,000 principal + £1,000 in interest). Upon informing the bank that he wants to pay off the loan, it reduces the balance of his account by £11,000 and simultaneously changes the amount outstanding on his loan to zero. This leaves the bank with £11,000 in central bank reserves. Consequently shareholder equity has increased by £1,000, the same amount as the interest paid on Jack's loan – this is the bank's profit on the loan, as below.

fig. 2.15 - Loan repayment ii

MegaBank	
Assets	**Liabilities**
Existing loan to Jack £10,000 → £0	Jack's account £11,000 → £0
Central bank reserves £11,000	Shareholder equity £10,000 → £11,000

The simultaneous cancellation of the asset and the liability has removed £11,000 of money, in the form of bank deposits, from the economy. However, some of it only disappears temporarily. The interest will be counted as income for the bank, and can be used to pay salaries to staff, dividends to shareholders and so on. Below MegaBank takes the £1,000 in profit and pays it out equally between its shareholders as dividends and staff as salaries:

fig. 2.16 - Bank salary payment

MegaBank	
Assets	**Liabilities**
Central bank reserves £11,000	Bank employees' accounts £0 → £500
	Shareholders' accounts £0 → £500
	Shareholder equity £11,000 → £10,000

Now that we have covered the four major functions of commercial banks, we can move on to address the functions of central banks.

2.7 LIQUIDITY AND CENTRAL BANK RESERVES

How central bank reserves are created

As we saw in the previous section, central bank reserves are a form of electronic money that banks use to make payments between themselves. In this section we show how these reserves are created by the central bank.

Initially the Bank of England's balance sheet appears as so (this is a simplified example where we've ignored everything except this particular transaction):

fig 2.17 - Creation of central bank reserves i

Bank of England	
Assets	**Liabilities**
Government bonds	MegaBank Reserve Account
£0	£0

MegaBank's shareholders have put up £10,000 of their own money, which has been invested in government bonds (known as 'gilts' in the UK). MegaBank's balance sheet is now:

fig 2.18 - Creation of central bank reserves ii

MegaBank	
Assets	**Liabilities**
Government bonds	Shareholder equity
£10,000	£10,000

If the Bank of England wishes to inject central bank reserves into the banking system (for example in response to a demand for reserves from the commercial banks), one way for it to do so is to simply purchase bonds held by the banking sector in exchange for the new reserves. This is known as an Open Market Operation. In this example Megabank sells £10,000 of bonds to the Bank of England in exchange for £10,000 of central bank reserves. The Bank of England credits MegaBank's reserve account with £10,000. This increases the Bank of England's liability (in the form of central bank reserves) to MegaBank, but at the same time it has received an asset (the gilts). As such the Bank of England's balance sheet now appears as so:

*fig 2.19 - Creation of central bank reserves **iii***

Bank of England	
Assets	**Liabilities**
Government bonds £0 → £10,000	MegaBank's Reserve Account £0 → £10,000

The Bank of England's balance sheet has 'expanded' by £10,000 and £10,000 of new central bank reserves have been created. However, from the point of view of MegaBank's balance sheet it has simply swapped £10,000 in gilts for £10,000 in reserves, without affecting its liabilities. The composition but not the size of its balance sheet has changed:

*fig. 2.20 - Creation of central bank reserves **iii***

MegaBank	
Assets	**Liabilities**
Government bonds £10,000 → £0	Shareholder equity £10,000
Reserve Account at Bank of England £0 → £10,000	

Today, open market operations are no longer used by the Bank of England as the primary method for injecting central bank reserves into the banking system. Instead, in normal times the central bank uses sale and repurchase agreements (outlined in Box 2.E) which are similar to collateralised loans (which it could also use). More recently reserves have been injected through Quantitative Easing.

How commercial banks acquire central bank reserves

Ultimately, commercial banks need to acquire central bank reserves in order to settle net transactions with other banks. These net 'settlement obligations' arise when payments by customers of one bank to another are greater than the payments coming in the opposite direction. Banks may obtain reserves in one of three ways:

a) From the central bank

The central bank retains a monopoly on the production of central bank reserves. Therefore ultimately all central bank reserves initially come from the central bank. The central bank can inject these reserves into the system through a variety of channels, including through open market operations and quantitative easing. Here we will restrict ourselves to cases where the central bank lends reserves directly to commercial banks, which it may do in one of three ways:

1. **Long term lending:** Before the financial crisis the Bank of England ran what was known as a 'reserves averaging scheme'. This allowed commercial banks to specify at the beginning of each month what quantity of reserves on average they expected to need in order to make their payments. They would then borrow this amount from the central bank using repos. However, as a result of Quantitative Easing, which flooded the banks with reserves, this mechanism is not currently required.

2. **Short term lending:** Another method of borrowing from the central bank is via what is known as the 'standing facilities'. These allow banks to borrow reserves from the central bank overnight, in case of liquidity problems (if they lack the money to pay other banks), using government bonds as collateral.

3. **Emergency lending:** Finally, the central bank, in its role as lender of last resort, stands ready to lend reserves to a commercial bank if for some reason it faces an unexpected liquidity problem (but is otherwise solvent). This is covered in more detail in section 3.4. The Bank of England may also provide reserves to the entire banking system in times of market stress through large-scale asset purchases. A recent example of this was the Quantitative Easing carried out through the Bank of England's Asset Purchase Facility.

Both the reserves averaging scheme and short term lending through the standing facilities also help the Bank of England to set the interest rate (see Box 3.A for more details). It is important to note here that the level of reserves in the banking system is usually driven by demand for reserves from commercial banks. In the words of the Governor of the Bank of England (2003-2013), Sir Mervyn King, "In the United Kingdom, money is endogenous—the Bank supplies base money [i.e. reserves] on demand at its prevailing interest rate, and broad money [i.e. bank deposits] is created by the banking system." (1994, p. 264) [Our addition in brackets]

Box 2.E - Repos (Sale and Repurchase Agreements)

The standard method by which the Bank of England creates reserves is through what is known as a sale and repurchase agreement (a 'repo'). This is similar in concept to a collateralised loan, in which the borrower must put up some collateral that they will lose if they fail to repay. It is not necessary to understand the following technical details of repos in order to understand the monetary system; the information is provided for completeness.

The process of obtaining reserves using a repo is as follows. Megabank temporarily sells an 'interest' in an asset (usually a government bond) to the central bank in exchange for central bank reserves, while agreeing to repurchase the same interest in the asset for a specific (higher) price on a specific date in the future. If the repurchase price is 10% higher than the purchase price (i.e. 10% higher than £10,000 = £11,000) then the 'repo rate' is said to be 10%. Under international accounting standards (IAS39 as adopted under the new International Financial Reporting Standard IFRS9) a repo transaction has different accounting rules from an outright sale.

Unlike in the Open Market Operation example, the Bank of England balance sheet would not actually show the gilts as the asset balancing the reserves, but the value of the interest in the gilts (valued at the £10,000 paid, not the £11,000 promised). MegaBank would retain the gilts on its balance sheet in addition to the central bank reserves but record as an additional liability its £10,000 obligation to complete its end of the repurchase agreement. The extra £1,000 does not appear on either balance sheet but, when paid, is recorded as revenue for the Bank of England and an expense for MegaBank. For simplicity, and because it is not core to understanding the monetary system, the balance sheets earlier do not show this complete accounting treatment.

Where does Megabank get the money to pay the repo rate (the interest on the repo)? The Bank of England actually pays a rate of interest on central bank reserves equal to the repo rate - so if RBS borrows £10,000 using a repo at 10% it must repay £10,000 plus £1,000 in interest. Prior to RBS's repayment the Bank of England pays interest on the reserves at 10%. This gives RBS £1,000 extra reserves which it must promptly use to repay the outstanding £11,000.

Whilst this process may seem a bit odd, there are actually two reasons for paying interest on reserves in this manner. Firstly, it means that banks are not penalised for holding reserves: having to borrow reserves at interest but not receiving interest on them (as used to be the case) meant that banks were effectively charged for holding reserves. Unsurprisingly this led to them attempting to minimise their holdings of reserves, which could pose problems for settling payments. Secondly, paying interest on reserves (and charging interest on loans) allows the central bank to control the rate of interest at which commercial banks lend to each other on the interbank market – a crucial tool of monetary policy. This is covered in more detail in Box 3.A.

Note that only the Bank of England can create central bank reserves. However, banks can also acquire pre-existing central bank reserves in other ways:

b) By attracting deposits from customers

Banks provide a deposit facility (i.e. current, checking or savings accounts) to individuals and organisations. These accounts allow individuals to deposit cash with the bank, with the money that is deposited becoming the legal property of the bank. The bank can then exchange this cash with the central bank for reserves. Likewise, banks also accept payments to their own customers from customers of other banks, either by electronic fund transfer or by cheque. These payments are ultimately settled using central bank reserves. While the bank gains legal ownership of the central bank reserves, the individual acquires a bank deposit (liability of the bank to the customer). However, while the bank may do what it wants with the central bank reserves, it also knows that the depositor may request a payment be made to a customer of another bank up to the full value of their account at any time. Banks therefore offer a higher interest rate on time deposits (such as fixed term savings accounts), to encourage depositors to 'tie up' their funds and increase the predictability of outflows for the bank. The presence of deposit insurance (a guarantee that the government will reimburse the customers of banks that collapse) on customer deposits means that depositors are less likely to attempt to withdraw when a bank faces difficulties.

c) Via wholesale funding markets

Banks may also borrow central bank reserves from other banks on the inter-bank market. This type of lending tends to be short term in nature, and is generally carried out using sale and repurchase agreements (repos – see Box 2.E). In addition, banks may also acquire reserves from other financial market participants using a variety of contracts including certificates of deposits, brokered deposits, repurchase agreements, and commercial paper. In practice, wholesale funders are typically able to withdraw their own funds from a bank before members of the public, and therefore tend to enjoy 'seniority' in terms of repayment as a result of their better access to information and the slower speed of normal depositors to withdraw their funds. As Huang and Ratnovski (2010) explain in an IMF working paper:

> "This was the main reason why in almost all recent bank failures (e.g., Continental Illinois, Northern Rock, IndyMac) short-term wholesale financiers were able to exit ahead of retail depositors without incurring significant losses. Interestingly, the well-publicized retail run on Northern

Rock took place only after the bank had nearly exhausted its liquid assets to pay off the exit of short-term wholesale funds."

2.8 MONEY CREATION ACROSS THE WHOLE BANKING SYSTEM

We have looked at the issuing of a single loan through the entry of numbers into the accounts of the bank in question. However, we should consider what happens across the banking system as a whole. There are two alternative descriptions of the process of money creation commonly discussed today. One is the 'money multiplier model' found in most mainstream macroeconomics textbooks, which is considered (by central bankers) to be an outdated and a misleading view of how the banking system operates. A more realistic description of the monetary system is 'endogenous money theory'. Both are explained below.

The money multiplier model

In 1984 Charles Goodhart, who became a member of the Monetary Policy Committee and chief advisor to the Bank of England, described the money multiplier model used in textbooks as "…such an incomplete way of describing the process of the determination of the stock of money that it amounts to mis-instruction". (Goodhart, 1984) Yet despite the fact that many economists and central bankers have long known this model to be a fallacy, it is still taught to students today as factual description of how the monetary system operates.

The model is a descriptive story of how banks' operations serve to 'multiply' the amount of money in the economy. The story begins with a man walking into a bank and depositing £1000 in cash. The bank knows that, on average, the customer won't need the whole of his £1000 returned all at once, so it keeps back a small 'reserve' of say 10% (£100), and lends out the other £900 to somebody who needs a loan. The borrower takes this £900 and spends it at a local car dealer. The car dealer takes this money and deposits it in another bank. At this point the quantity of money has increased to £1900 (the original £1000 that the first customer still has on deposit and the £900 that the car dealer has deposited). Then the car dealer's bank keeps 10% back of this new deposit as reserve (£90) and lends the remaining £810. Every time the money is re-deposited at a bank, new bank deposits (liabilities from the bank to the customer making the deposit) are recorded on the bank's balance sheet. This

fig. 2.21 - The money multiplier model

CYCLES of LENDING				TOTAL MONEY SUPPLY
1	£1,000 deposit	£100 reserved	£900 lent	£1,900
2	£900 deposit	£90 reserved	£810 lent	£2,710
3	£810 deposit	£81 reserved	£729 lent	£3,439

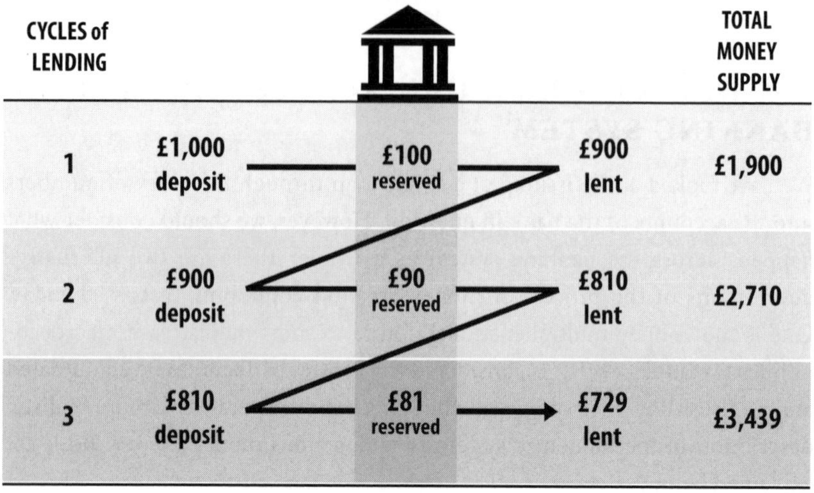

process of re-lending continues, up until the point where mere pennies are being relent, with the money supply topping out at around £10,000 despite the fact that there is only £1,000 of 'base' money (cash) in circulation.

You can imagine this model as a pyramid (fig 2.22). The cash (created by the central bank) is the base of the pyramid, and depending on the level of the reserve ratio, banks multiply up the total amount of money by re-lending it over and over again to a multiple of this original amount. More advanced treatments include central bank reserves as part of base money as well as cash, however the basic idea is the same.

The money multiplier model of banking implies three things:

1. Banks have to wait until someone puts money into a bank before they can start making loans. Essentially they are mere intermediaries and react passively to what customers do. Deposits from customers therefore precede lending.

2. The central bank has ultimate control over the total amount of money in the economy. It can control the amount of money by changing either the reserve ratio (the proportion of each new deposit that banks must keep in reserve) or the amount of 'base money' – cash (or reserves) – at the bottom of the pyramid.

3. The amount of money created by banks can never get out of control, unless the central bank deliberately or negligently allows it to.

fig. 2.22 - Relation of reserve ratio to money supply

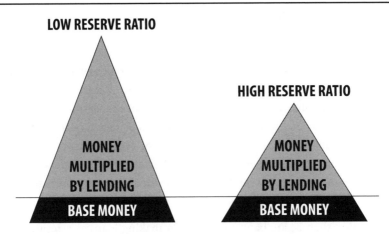

Reserve ratio determines steepness of pyramid sides

In conclusion, the money multiplier theory sees the causality in the money creation process occurring in the following way:

The central bank sets the reserve ratio, creates base money, and injects this money into the economy.

Once in the economy this money circulates before being deposited with banks. Banks then lend out a fraction of the money deposited with them and keep a fraction back 'in reserve'.

The loans are spent and the money circulates, before it is re-deposited into another bank. The bank uses this new (smaller) deposit to make a further (smaller) loan, again keeping a fraction of the deposit 'in reserve'.

The process continues until the amounts being relent are miniscule. The quantity of money in circulation is now a multiple of the base money (with the multiple being determined by the reserve ratio).

Endogenous money theory

Endogenous money theory explains that, rather than banks waiting for a depositor to come along with additional money, within certain constraints banks are able to lend as and when they want. It is by the process of lending that banks create deposits and increase the amount of money in the economy. This leads to new purchasing power in the economy, as no one has seen a reduction in the value of their account. If the bank needs central bank reserves at the Bank of England to settle any payments that arise as a result of its lending, it will be able to borrow them either from the central bank or from other banks. As Alan Holmes, then Senior Vice President of the Federal Reserve Bank of New York put it in 1969: "In the real world, banks extend credit, creating deposits in the process, and look for the reserves later." (p. 73)

The question then is, are banks restricted in making loans as a result of any potential inability to obtain reserves? In contrast to the money multiplier view of banking, in reality banks will almost always be able to obtain reserves – if not from the markets then from the central bank itself, which is required to "supply base money on demand" in order to maintain a constant interest rate. Restricting reserves would see a sharp increase in this rate (this is explained in more detail in Section 3.4).

Restricting reserves may also create a liquidity crisis, as the bank in question will not be able to settle payments on behalf of its customers due to a lack of reserves. Due to the potential for liquidity crises to turn into solvency crises, and because a solvency issue at one bank can cause a cascade of bankruptcies throughout the entire banking system, the central bank is unlikely to pursue the second option. Indeed, it goes against one of the central bank's core functions – its mandate to protect financial stability.

The validity of the endogenous money theory has been confirmed by prominent central bankers and regulators. Before he became Governor of the Bank of England, Mervyn King wrote in 1994 that:

> "In the United Kingdom, money is endogenous—the Bank supplies base money on demand at its prevailing interest rate, and broad money is created by the banking system."

In a speech at Southampton University in 2011, Adair Turner, then-chairman of the Financial Services Authority, said:

> "Banks, it is often said, take deposits from savers (for instance households) and lend it to borrowers (for instance businesses) with the quality

of this credit allocation process a key driver of allocative efficiency within the economy. But in fact they don't just allocate pre-existing savings. Collectively they create both credit and the deposit money which appears to finance that credit. Banks create credit and money."

Also in a 2011 speech, Vítor Constâncio, Vice-President of the European Central Bank, explained that:

"It is argued by some that financial institutions would be free to instantly transform their loans from the central bank into credit to the non-financial sector. This fits into the old theoretical view about the credit multiplier according to which the sequence of money creation goes from the primary liquidity created by central banks to total money supply created by banks via their credit decisions. In reality the sequence works more in the opposite direction with banks taking first their credit decisions and then looking for the necessary funding and reserves of central bank money."

Finally, in a 2010 paper, Piti Distayat of the Bank for International Settlements stated:

"This paper contends that the emphasis on policy-induced changes in deposits is misplaced. If anything, the process actually works in reverse, with loans driving deposits. In particular, it is argued that the concept of the money multiplier is flawed and uninformative in terms of analyzing the dynamics of bank lending. Under a fiat money standard and liberalized financial system, there is no exogenous constraint on the supply of credit except through regulatory capital requirements. An adequately capitalized banking system can always fulfill the demand for loans if it wishes to."

Empirical analysis has also been carried out on this topic. In a 1990 paper Finn Kydland and Ed Prescott test for whether the monetary base (i.e. reserves and cash) increases before banks make loans, as suggested by the money multiplier theory, or afterwards, as suggested by the endogenous money theory. They find that:

"There is no evidence that either the monetary base or M1 leads the [credit] cycle, although some economists still believe this monetary myth. Both the monetary base and M1 series are generally procyclical and, if anything, the monetary base lags the [credit] cycle slightly." [Our addition in brackets].

In his 1988 book *Horizontalists and Verticalists* Basil Moore also presents compelling evidence that banks lend before acquiring the necessary reserves:

> "The evidence presented strongly suggests that unidirectional causality runs from bank lending to each of the four monetary aggregates. Each monetary aggregate has been shown in turn to cause the monetary base unidirectionally."

Finally, in a survey of the empirical literature, Peter Howells finds that: "The present state of empirical knowledge appears to confirm the hypothesis that loans cause deposits". (2005)

In conclusion, the endogenous money theory sees causality in the banking system occurring in the following way:

Banks lend, creating deposits in the process.

This increases demand for reserves in order to settle payments.

The central bank provides reserves to banks on demand, thus accommodating the banking sector's lending decisions.

The fundamental implication of endogenous money theory is that it is the commercial banks, rather than the central bank, that determines the amount of central bank reserves and commercial bank money in the economy. The central bank must support the lending decisions of banks by providing sufficient reserves to ensure that all payments settle at the end of the day. For all intents and purposes it is the commercial bank tail that wags the central bank dog.

Endogenous money theory is the opposite of the money multiplier theory, which implies that the central bank determines the amount of reserves in the economy and controls the amount of money that banks create by altering the amount of reserves and setting reserve ratios. Banks then act as passive intermediaries, and simply lend the deposits that they receive.

As we will see in the following chapter, there are of course limits to money creation, although these tend to be self-imposed by the commercial banks rather than a result of oversight or control by the Bank of England.

CHAPTER 3
WHAT DETERMINES THE MONEY SUPPLY?

In the previous chapter we saw that banks create money, in the form of bank deposits, when they make loans and buy assets. In this chapter we discuss the incentives banks have for creating money in this way, as well as looking at the restrictions and regulations that prevent them from doing so.

We begin by looking at what determines the demand for bank loans, concluding that as a result of the distribution of wealth, the desire to speculate, and the effect of various laws, the demand for credit will almost always be very high. The demand for money is also discussed, as is the effect on the economy of any attempt to pay down debts in aggregate.

Second, we will look at the incentives facing banks: given the high demand for credit, why do banks not simply lend to every individual or business that applies for a loan? We will see that due to the profit motive, financial innovations and some other institutional quirks, banks will attempt to lend as much as they can as long as it is profitable for them to do so.

Third, we will look at the reaction of the regulators. Faced with a banking sector with lots of willing borrowers and an incentive to lend, is it possible to temper banks' desire to create credit and money? We conclude that none of the tools available to regulators are particularly effective, and thus banks are relatively unconstrained in their ability to lend. The main determinant of bank lending, and therefore the amount of money in circulation, will be found to be the desire and willingness of banks to lend, which in turn will rest on their confidence in the wider economy, the profitability of lending and the likelihood that loans will be repaid. In the following chapter we will see how the psychology of both borrowers and lenders changes over the economic cycle, which leads to more money creation in the latter stages of economic booms.

3.1 THE DEMAND FOR CREDIT

What determines the demand for credit? There are broadly three main reasons that people and businesses will need to borrow:

1. Due to the borrower having insufficient wealth

2. In order to speculate

3. Due to legal incentives

Borrowing due to insufficient wealth

In the UK the wealthiest 10% of the population holds 45% of the wealth, whereas the bottom 50% of the population has just 12% of the wealth (see fig 3.1). Those under the age of 44 (unsurprisingly) have the least wealth – 47% have a net wealth of less than £50,000, and almost 70% have a net wealth of less than £100,000. (HM Revenue & Customs, 2011)

Borrowing allows the purchase today something that could not be afforded otherwise. This is not to say that in a world where wealth was equally distributed there would be no borrowing, merely that if wealth were distributed more evenly, individuals would not have to borrow as much as they do now. In short, the distribution of wealth, regardless of its reasonableness/justice or lack thereof, has consequences for the demand for credit.

Lending for investment due to insufficient wealth

One group that almost always need to borrow due to insufficient wealth is entrepreneurs. Individuals between the ages of 25 and 44 are the most likely to set up or run a new business (Hart & Levie, 2011; Kauffman Foundation, 2009), yet those 45 or older hold much of society's wealth. The fact that entrepreneurs typically have a wealth of ideas but little money to implement them was noted by Schumpeter:

> "The entrepreneur – in principle and as a rule – does need credit, in the sense of a temporary transfer to him of purchasing power, in order to produce at all, to be able to carry out his new combinations, to become an entrepreneur. And this purchasing power does not flow towards him automatically, as to the producer in the circular flow, by the sale of what he produced in preceding periods. If he does not happen to possess it … he must borrow it … He can only become an entrepreneur by previously becoming a debtor… his becoming a debtor arises from the necessity of the case and is not something abnormal, an accidental event to be

fig. 3.1 – Distribution of wealth by decile, 2001 – 2003

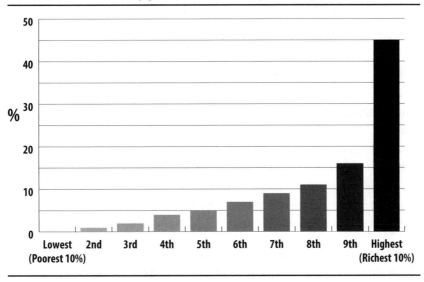

Source: HMRC Personal wealth statistics 2001 – 2003 (table 13.8)

explained by particular circumstances. What he first wants is credit. Before he requires any goods whatsoever, he requires purchasing power." (Schumpeter, 1934, p. 102)

According to Schumpeter entrepreneurs are the heroes of capitalism – creating jobs and prosperity for all. Yet, as the above quote attests, when wealth is not equally distributed they are they are highly dependent on creditors to facilitate their entrepreneurial activities. And for small entrepreneurs, unless they are able to raise money from friends/family, banks are often the only available source of credit.

Larger established businesses also need to borrow, for two main reasons:

To expand: A firm that wants to buy new machinery or open new stores must pay for the goods and equipment before it can actually sell anything. For that reason it needs to borrow upfront and repay the loan once the new store or equipment is generating income.

To manage the cashflow gap between payments coming in and out of the business. This is common when a firm receives a large order: it must pay for the materials it uses to produce the order before it actually gets paid for the finished goods, so it needs to borrow for a short period of time with the loan (or overdraft) being repaid as after the finished goods are sold and paid for.

Lending for property purchase due to insufficient wealth

Individuals also need to borrow to purchase property. Houses are the most expensive purchases that most individuals will ever make, with only a small minority wealthy enough to afford to buy a house outright. Most people will need to take out a mortgage, typically to be repaid over a period of 25 years.

The level of demand for mortgage lending is partly a function of house prices (in addition, as we will see in chapter 4, house prices are also influenced by the amount of mortgage lending). When house prices are on average £165,000, as they were in mid-2012, the amount people need to borrow will be higher than when average house prices were £58,000, as they were in 1997 (Nationwide, 2012). Expectations also matter: rising house prices will increase the demand for mortgage lending, as people will either want to 'get in early' to avoid being priced out of the market or in order to profit from rising prices.

Lending for consumption spending due to insufficient wealth

Individuals may also borrow in order to spread their payments over a period of time. Historically people made purchases on consumer credit for durable goods, such as washing machines or cookers, which allowed them to spread the cost of an expensive item over a period of years. Economists term this 'consumption smoothing'. More recently, there has been an increase in the supply of and access to consumer credit, (through credit cards for example), as well as changes in the cultural acceptability of debt. Taken together, these factors have resulted in an increase in the number and type of goods that are commonly purchased on credit. According to a government report, in the UK "the longer term trend, would, on balance, tend to suggest that debt is becoming a problem for an increasing number of households". (BERR, 2007)

Borrowing for speculative reasons

The second reason people might wish to borrow is in order to speculate – by borrowing to speculate an individual can increase their returns over that which they could achieve if they used only their own money. This can involve borrowing to buy an asset (financial or real) whose price is rising, and then selling the asset again when it has reached a higher price. Most people may associate this type of behaviour with traders in the City or on Wall Street, but it is also the business model of every buy-to-let investor who bought a second or third house in order to benefit from rising house prices. The demand for credit in order to speculate is naturally highest in a time of rising asset prices.

As we will see in later chapters, speculation can become a self-fulfilling prophecy. In certain markets rising prices can lead to an increase in demand, as people borrow to purchase the asset in expectation of even further price rises. The extra purchases push up prices, which leads to further borrowing, increases in demand, and price rises in a self-reinforcing mechanism.

Markets in which supply does not change much in response to demand, such as financial and property markets, are particularly vulnerable to this type of asset price speculation. It can be particularly damaging when the asset in question is a necessity (e.g. housing). The dynamics of this situation and its impact on the economy will be covered in more detail in Chapter 4.

Borrowing due to legal incentives

The third reason that borrowing may be higher than it otherwise would be is due to legislation. Specific laws may change the incentives for borrowing. For example, limited liability laws that apply to companies alter the demand for credit through the incentives they place on corporate management:

> "As Stiglitz and Weiss (1981) have pointed out, the legal construct of corporate entities with limited liability of directors creates an asymmetric incentive structure, where directors who borrow money to build up their business may gain much if they succeed, but their downside will be limited if they don't. ... If they succeed they may be the next Bill Gates. If they fail, they will lose their paid-in equity capital, but not more. The actual demand for credit is therefore always relatively large (even if from crank entrepreneurs with high risk ideas)." (Werner, 2005, p. 195)

Tax laws also alter the demand for credit. For example, in 1965 corporation tax was introduced in the UK. One of its features was that loan financing was to be treated differently from financing raised through equity – debt financing was tax deductible whereas equity financing is not. This is despite the fact there is no good economic reason for this to be the case. The result is that UK companies are incentivised to take on more debt than they would otherwise.

3.2 THE DEMAND FOR MONEY

Imagine an unlikely scenario in which nobody in the nation wanted to borrow: everyone would be living within their means, people would save up before making large purchases, and banks would have nobody to lend to, as no-one would be willing to take on debt. But even in this situation, there would still be a need for money as a means of payment so that people could trade with each other. There is a certain level of 'demand' for money, independent of the desire of some people to borrow.

'Demand' is a specific concept in economics: it refers to "the willingness and ability to pay a sum of money for some amount of a particular good." (Bannock, 1978) The demand for money refers not, therefore, to how much money people would like (presumably most people would like to have millions), but to how much they are willing and able to retain in their wallets and bank accounts at any one time instead of spending it on goods, services, holidays or exchanging it for other financial assets such as bonds or shares. What determines the level of this demand for money?

Most obviously, people choose to hold (i.e. 'demand') money because it is useful whenever they need to buy something. While cash is useful for smaller purchases, for larger purchases and shopping online, electronic means of payment are essential. So there is a need for electronic money in the economy simply to allow trade to take place. People will typically hold at least enough money to cover their planned spending from one pay-cheque to the next.

Others may also want to hold a certain additional amount of money aside in case of unexpected developments, such as urgent car repairs or to cover an unexpected loss of income. Therefore in addition to the demand for money in order to make transactions, people also hold money because the future is inherently uncertain. Even individuals who make significant investments in other financial assets (such as shares) may keep some 'money in the bank' to limit their losses in case their other investments fall in value. In this sense, holding money is a safety measure. Traders may even hold money in order to speculate – if they believe a financial asset they hold is going to fall in value they could sell it for money and wait for the value to fall before buying it back at the new, cheaper price.

In conclusion, there is a clear demand for money as:

1. A means of payment.

2. A contingency measure due to the uncertainty of future expenditure and income.

3. A contingency due to uncertainty over the value of other assets.

How then do people obtain this money? Currently the banking sector is the only issuer of bank deposits. As we have seen, banks create deposits in the process of making loans. So, in the current system, unless somebody is first willing to go into debt to a bank, no one will be able to hold a bank deposit.

The other form of money that individuals are able to hold is of course cash. However, as well as a cash-only economy being highly inconvenient (not to mention risky for those holding large amounts of cash), it is also now an impossibility. Under the current monetary system the central bank sells notes and coins to the banks in exchange for central bank reserves, meaning that the only way for this cash to enter the economy is for individuals to withdraw it from the bank, in exchange for a reduction in their bank deposits. Without somebody first holding bank deposits – i.e. unless someone has first borrowed from a bank – there is no way for cash to come into circulation.

This problem points to one of the quirks (or flaws) in the existing monetary system. Economists distinguish between the need for credit (for investment, consumption smoothing or speculation) and the need for money (as a means of payment or a hedge against uncertainty). Yet in the current monetary system there is only one source of money, and that money is always credit created through bank lending. The demand of one person to hold money in the form of bank deposits therefore creates a requirement for someone else to be in debt to a bank. Thus, in order for there to be money so that the economy can function and people and businesses can trade, someone must first have borrowed from a bank.

Conclusion: the demand for money & credit

We have seen that credit is demanded in order to make investments in businesses, smooth consumption over a period of time (such as housing or consumer finance), or to speculate. The legal construct of corporations and tax incentives can increase the level of demand for credit from businesses. As such there will always be substantial demand for borrowing from banks.

However, because the banking sector (i.e. licenced deposit taking institutions) is the only source of both cash and bank deposits, there is also a structural demand for borrowing from the economy itself, determined by the demand for money (although this will not directly result in an increase in the demand for credit). Individuals operating within an economy require money, but because bank deposits are created when banks make loans, for an individual to obtain money – whether to make transactions or to store against future contingencies – someone else must have previously gone into debt. This means that, in the current monetary system, for there to be money, there must also be debt.

What's more, if people *en masse* try to repay their debts money creation by banks will fall. As described in section 4.2, the lower spending this leads to can cause a debt deflation,[1] bankruptcies, increased unemployment and lower growth. Under such conditions it is reasonable to expect that both individuals and firms will be forced to borrow in order to make ends meet, increasing the debt that they were initially trying to pay down. This leads to the paradoxical result that an attempt to pay down debts in aggregate may invoke economic conditions that actually lead to an increase in the demand for credit/debt.

In conclusion, in addition to the demand for credit that occurs as a result of people wanting to borrow, there is also a need for credit to ensure the economy has the money it needs to function. Any significant attempt to pay down debts is paradoxically likely to lead to an increase in demand for credit/debt. The demand for credit will therefore always be very high – at least within the current monetary system.

3.3 FACTORS AFFECTING BANKS' LENDING DECISIONS

The previous section looked at the factors that influence the demand for credit, concluding that the demand for borrowing from banks will always be very high. The following section looks at the incentives banks have to lend. Will they try to meet the level of demand for credit by making loans to everyone who is willing to go into debt (in the same way that Apple would supply an iPhone to everyone who is willing to pay the asking price)? Or will they turn away potential borrowers who are willing to sign on the dotted line?

The drive to maximise profit

The business of banking is in general a private for-profit enterprise. Banks profit by extending loans, with the profit being the interest charged on the loan, minus any costs (such as the interest paid on their liabilities, the wages of staff, losses on loans that aren't repaid, etc.). During relatively benign or stable periods banks are understandably keen to lend: the more (successful) loans they make, the higher their profits. This profit incentive is exacerbated by three additional factors: the ability of banks to securitise their assets, the

---

1. See Chapter 4 for more details, or Irving Fisher's paper, 'The Debt Deflation Theory of Great Depressions' (1933).

provision of deposit insurance, and the ability to externalise some of their costs (i.e. because the costs of excessive money creation are borne not by the banks but by society as a whole).

Securitisation

Traditionally for a bank to make profits it was important that its loans were repaid. When a borrower defaults (refuses to repay) on a loan, the assets side of the bank's balance sheet shrinks, yet the liabilities side remains the same. Defaults eat into shareholder equity, decreasing the net worth of the bank. With enough defaults shareholder equity can be completely wiped out, turning the bank insolvent. Therefore, as described by Davidson (2008), because "loans were illiquid assets and had to be carried on the books till the person either paid off the mortgage or defaulted", banks made their profits gradually as loans were serviced and eventually repaid. Therefore, "Before making a loan, the banker checked the classical three C's: collateral, credit history and character of the borrower."

However, more recently banks have switched from a model of banking in which they make profits over the lifetime of a loan to one in which profits on loans can be booked within weeks of it being made. This is the "originate and distribute" model of banking made possible by securitisation. Securitisation is the practice of pooling multiple loans (which may include mortgages) together, and then selling these consolidated loans to investors as Collateralised Debt Obligations (CDOs). The bank receives an up-front payment, and the investors receive a stream of income over the life of the financial instrument. The bank's profit comes from a fee for arranging the loans, instead of collecting the interest as the loan is repaid. Accordingly, banks no longer needed to worry about the three C's: "When you securitize mortgage you don't care about the risk, because you're going to pass it off". (Davidson, 2008) The ability to securitise loans means banks can make profits not by the quality of the loans they make, but by their quantity. The willingness of banks to lend to the US subprime market was partially (and possibly predominantly) attributable to securitisation.

Government guarantees, deposit insurance & 'too big to fail'

"Bank runs are a common feature of the extreme crises that have played a prominent role in monetary history. During a bank run, depositors rush to withdraw their deposits because they expect the bank to fail. In fact, the sudden withdrawals can force the bank to liquidate many of its assets at a loss and to fail. During a panic with many bank failures, there is a disruption of the monetary system and a reduction in production." (Diamond & Dybvig, 1983)

When a company becomes insolvent, creditors to that company will usually lose a proportion of their money. In the case of a bank, this would involve depositors only receiving a percentage of the full value of their account. However, in the UK (and in most other countries) the government guarantees that if a bank fails, the customers of that bank will be able to claim a certain percentage or a capped amount of their deposit back from the government. This guarantee on the money in a bank account is known as 'deposit insurance'. In a country with deposit insurance, in the event of insolvency the insolvent bank will have its assets sold off. Any funds raised in this way are used to reimbursed depositors, with any shortfall being made up by taxpayers and deposit insurance schemes banks have previously paid into.

The first system of deposit insurance was established in America in response to the Great Depression. Its purpose was to prevent the bank runs that contributed to the depression from ever happening again. Deposit insurance is based on the idea that depositors will not attempt to withdraw their deposits *en masse*, even if they find out the bank is insolvent, as long as they know that the government will reimburse their deposits in the result of a bank failure. This is intended to prevent runs on banks that are rumoured to be insolvent or experiencing financial difficulty. In addition those banks that are insolvent will not have to undertake a fire sale of their assets in order to quickly raise money. Fire sales are undesirable because they can lead to a crash in asset prices, which can also lead to the insolvency of others (including banks) that hold similar assets. Left unchecked, a debt deflation may result (as outlined in section 4.2).

In the UK today the government provides deposit insurance (via the Financial Services Compensation Scheme, FSCS) to most bank accounts up to a limit of £85,000. In theory the FSCS is funded by levies on banks whose customers are covered by the guarantee, but in practice the major contributors to the cost of the scheme have been taxpayers. Due to the failure of certain banks in 2008-09, just £171 million of the £19.86 billion (less than 1%) was funded through levies, while the rest was provided by government (Financial Services Compensation Scheme, 2009).

There are two main problems with deposit insurance. The first is that by being insured, customers will take little or no interest in the way that the bank lends and takes risks. This is known as 'moral hazard'.[2]

In a system without deposit insurance, depositors would have a strong incentive to monitor their bank's behaviour to ensure the bank does not act in a manner that may endanger its own solvency. For example, a depositor would be concerned with the types of loans their bank was making and the amount of capital their bank had (capital acts as a buffer, protecting depositors from losses when loans go bad). Other things being equal a bank with a higher capital ratio would be considered safer and in consequence could be expected to attract more customers than a bank with a smaller capital base. However, in a system with deposit insurance there is no incentive for customers to monitor their bank's behaviour, as depositors are guaranteed to receive their money back regardless of the level of risk taken by the bank. This lack of scrutiny from customers (or the financial press) means that banks are not restricted to taking the level of risk that their depositors would be comfortable with. Instead, they are free to lend as much as they like to whomever they like, in the process lowering their capital ratio (increasing their leverage).[3] Thus the presence of deposit insurance removes one potential constraint on the banks' desire to lend and therefore removes a potential constraint on their ability to create money. It also increases the riskiness of their lending.

The second problem with deposit insurance regards the insolvency procedure and its costs in the case of a bank failure. In a country with a deposit guarantee scheme, bank insolvency normally means either a) a government bailout of the bank in question, or b) the closing of the bank, the sale of its assets and compensation for deposit holders up to the designated amount. How likely

---

2. Moral hazard is when the provision of insurance changes the behaviour of those who receive the insurance, usually in an undesirable way. For example, if you have contents insurance on your house you may be less careful about securing it against burglary than you might otherwise be.

3. Furthermore, instead of caring about their bank's solvency, depositors are incentivised by the interest rate on different bank accounts. In order to attract funds, banks will have to offer higher rates of interest on their accounts than their competitors. Thus, in order to maintain their profit margins they will have to charge borrowers higher rates of interest. Other things being equal those willing to borrow at higher interest rates will be those taking the greatest risks, which increases the risk of default.

are governments to take the second option? The case of RBS (Royal Bank of Scotland) is useful here.

When RBS ran into trouble during the financial crisis, the government had the option to close the bank and let it fail (as would happen to any non-bank business that became insolvent). However, because of its obligation to reimburse the (insured) depositors of RBS, the government would have been obliged to find approximately £800bn – greater than the entire national debt at that time, and similar in size to the UK government's annual tax take. Of course, in an ideal world much of this could potentially have been raised by the sale of RBS's remaining (good) assets. However, the government was constrained in its actions – it had to resolve RBS quickly, otherwise millions of account holders would lose access to the payments system. Any delay could cause the panic to spread to other banks, amplifying the original problem. Finding buyers for £800 billion of assets is hard at the best of times, especially when those assets are from a failed bank. In the middle of a financial crisis it is close to impossible. As a result the government would have most likely had to accept a price for the assets far below their market value, and would need to make up the shortfall from taxpayer's funds or borrowing. In addition, the majority of RBS's assets were loans. These are difficult to value quickly (due diligence takes time), and in consequence the government would once again have had to accept a price below market value. Invoking bankruptcy procedures against RBS would have therefore been highly costly to the government.

A further problem with allowing a large bank to fail in the current system is that it could lead to problems at other banks. First, because banks often owe each other large amounts of money a failure could lead to insolvencies at other banks due to the non-repayment of loans. This can lead to a cascade of bankruptcies throughout the entire system. Second, insolvency at one bank can lead to runs on solvent banks as depositors panic about their own bank's position. The belief a bank is insolvent can become a self fulfilling prophecy, as a fire sale of assets reduces their value. Third, the payment system itself may be affected by bank insolvency: many smaller banks do not have direct access to the high value payment systems, instead accessing them indirectly through a larger bank known as a settlement bank. If the settlement bank became insolvent this could create problems in the payment system, as the 'customer bank' would not be able to make or receive payments. In addition, insolvency at either the customer or the settlement bank could lead to insolvency at the other bank. For example, if a settlement bank makes payments with their own liquidity on behalf of their customer banks, they are in effect lending to their customer bank until the accounts are settled at the end of the day. Likewise, if a settlement bank receives more payments to their customer bank than the customer bank makes during the day then in effect the customer bank is lending to the settlement bank (again until the accounts are settled at the end of the day). Depending on who owes who, bankruptcy (and therefore default on borrowings) of either bank during the day may create problems for the other bank. These are not simply theoretical risks: "During the great depression 247 US banks were closed between January 1929 and March 1933 due to the failure of a correspondent [bank]". (Salmon, 2011) Similar issues almost materialised in the 2007/08 financial crisis:

> "In one of the UK payment systems, a UK bank that got into difficulty made its payments through a much smaller bank, in terms of balance sheet size. These exposures could well have put the smaller bank in significant financial difficulty had the authorities not intervened in the failing bank."

These risks may also spill over into the rest of the payment system if banks start delaying their payments due to uncertainty as to the status of one or more banks.

Fourth, the failure of a bank may negatively affect the flow of credit (i.e. lending) to the economy, particularly if the bank services a large proportion of the lending market. For example, RBS accounts for a significant proportion of all lending to UK businesses, meaning that its failure would have been devastating for small and medium sized businesses (which employ around half of all workers in the UK).

For all of these reasons, banks can be deemed 'too big', or 'too systemically important' to fail.[4] As a result of these costs and potential risks, a cheaper and safer option for the government was to effectively give RBS £45.5 billion in exchange for newly issued shares. This became an asset of RBS, making its net worth positive again.

Large banks fully understand that deposit insurance means that if they become insolvent, the choice facing government is between repaying all their customers due to deposit insurance, or rescuing the bank through an 'injection of capital' (a bailout). In practice, it will always be many times cheaper

---

4.   The idea of something being too big to fail runs contrary to the very principle of capitalism – under a capitalist system a business that does badly is meant to fail!

and safer to rescue a bank than to let it fail. This knowledge will lead the bank to take higher risks, knowing full well that the government will be unable to afford not to rescue it if it should fail. The larger the bank, the greater the cost to government of allowing it to fail, and the more confident the bank will be that it has a guaranteed safety net even if the risks it takes backfire and it becomes insolvent. Banks will therefore lend greater amounts and lend to riskier borrowers than they otherwise would do. This in turn leads to a expansion in the amount of money in circulation.

Externalities and competition[5]

Banks may also make more loans than is socially optimal because they don't face the full costs of their lending (i.e. they externalise costs onto other members of society). For example, when banks make loans they increase the amount of purchasing power in the economy and this can result in inflation in consumer and asset prices (discussed in detail in Chapter 4). Both asset and consumer price inflation impose costs on society as a whole, with asset price inflation particularly problematic due to its potential to cause financial crises. This is the classic economic externality problem: if the costs of inflation and financial crises were borne solely by the banks, they would have no incentive to create too much credit, or allocate credit into asset price bubbles.

The problem of excess money creation is amplified by competition between banks. To gain market share and increase profits, banks must make more (successful) loans than their competitors. This in itself creates a tendency for banks to make too many loans. In a recent paper, Hart and Zingales (2011) create a simple framework to analyse the effect of bank lending on inflation in the economy, asking the question:

> "Does a competitive banking sector generate the socially optimal amount of the means of payment [i.e. money]? In this paper we show that the answer is no, even if we abstract from any moral hazard and asymmetry of information. In particular, we analyse the general equilibrium effects that the availability of money has on prices and identify two pecuniary externalities: more money increases the equilibrium price of the goods that those with the money buy; but it also increases the wealth of the

---

5.　An externality can be defined as a cost or benefit that is not transmitted through prices, or alternatively a cost or benefit that is incurred by a party who was not involved in the transaction. A common example of a negative externality is pollution.

agents supplying these goods and so the prices of the goods they buy. A competitive bank, which ignores the externality imposed on other buyers, will generate too much money ... As a result, we show that the private provision of inside money [bank deposits] is generally inefficient." (p. 2) [Our addition in square brackets]

In short, the impossibility of internalising these inflationary externalities means that the private banking sector will never be able to create the socially optimal amount of money and will normally create more money than the economy needs.

3.4 FACTORS LIMITING THE CREATION OF MONEY

Because of the negative impact excessive bank lending can have on the economy, historically the authorities have implemented various regulations in an attempt to control the quantity and direction of their lending activities. The following section will look at the effectiveness of some of these regulations. In particular, it will look at the effectiveness of controlling bank lending through capital requirements, reserve requirements, and interest rates.

Capital requirements (the Basel Accords)

As outlined in section 2.3, shareholder capital (or equity), is thought to be important for two reasons. First, it provides a buffer for depositors and other bank creditors when a bank's assets fall in value. In this situation, rather than depositors losing money (or the state losing money in countries where deposit insurance exists), shareholders take the first hit. This is intended to give depositors and other creditors confidence in the bank and hopefully the banking sector as a whole.

Second, it is thought that the ratio of capital to assets can be used as a regulatory tool to control a bank's lending. This is a key aspect of the Basel Capital Accords, which stipulate that the ratio of a bank's capital to its (risk-weighted) assets must not fall below some pre-determined amount. For Basel I and II, this was 8%. For Basel III the ratio will rise to 10.5%.[6] In theory under Basel

---

6. However, banks classified as 'Systemically Important Financial Institutions' (SIFIs) will be required to hold up to 3.5% in additional capital, and, depending on the level of credit in an economy all banks may be required to hold an additional

II if the ratio of a bank's capital to its risk-weighted assets falls below 8% the bank would be unable to increase its lending any further.

However, capital requirements do not fully constrain bank lending for several reasons. First, banks profit through charging interest on loans. Any profits that are retained increase shareholder equity, and therefore capital. This higher capital allows a bank to further increase its lending, which, providing the loans are repaid, will lead to further increases in profits and shareholder capital. As long as a bank's lending is profitable (such as in a boom) this cycle will be able to continue.

Second, banks are able to raise additional capital through new share issues. During boom periods, banks' profits tend to be high, and this leads to higher dividends and an increase in the price of banks' shares. Consequently banks will face little difficulty increasing their capital through this avenue during booms.

Third, as discussed earlier, banks can also engage in a process known as 'securitisation'. This allows banks to package assets (loans) on their balance sheet and sell them on to 'special purpose vehicles', receiving a payment in exchange. This has the effect of freeing up the capital which was being held to cover potential losses on the loans. As a result more (new) loans can then be made and the pace of lending (and money creation) can increase.

Fourth, the Basel Accords allow banks to calculate their capital requirements using what is known as the 'Internal Ratings Based Approach'. A bank that uses this approach can, given the consent of its local regulator, develop its own empirical models to calculate the amount of capital it is required to hold against its assets. Any bank using this approach could therefore theoretically hold less capital than it would otherwise be required to. As such this could be considered de-regulation. Of course, whether Basel II increased or decreased regulation depends on the approach taken by the regulator. In the UK, the Financial Services Authority (FSA) regulation was based on the philosophy that:

> "Markets are in general self correcting, with market discipline a more effective tool than regulation or supervisory oversight through which to ensure that firms' strategies are sound and risks contained.....

2.5% in capital as a countercyclical buffer. As a result the total level of capital some banks will be required to hold under Basel III may be as high as 16.5%.

"The primary responsibility for managing risks lies with the senior management and boards of the individual firms, who are better placed to assess business model risk than bank regulators, and who can be relied on to make appropriate decisions about the balance between risk and return, provided appropriate systems, procedures and skilled people are in place." (Financial Services Authority, 2009)

Before the financial crisis the FSA's regulatory stance borne out by this philosophy was commonly referred to as 'light touch'. Although there has been a change of direction since then, as a result of the other issues highlighted in this section, capital remains an ineffective tool for controlling money creation, by banks, even taking into account the countercyclical buffer proposed by Basel III.

Reserve ratios & limiting the supply of central bank reserves

Recall that central bank reserves are used by commercial banks in order to make payments between each other, and the central bank has the monopoly on their creation. In theory, by forcing banks to hold a certain percentage of central bank reserves relative to their deposits, the central bank can restrict the quantity of deposits to a multiple of the quantity of central bank reserves.

The belief that the central bank can manage the money creation process through the creation of central bank reserves is prevalent in mainstream economics textbooks. This is largely due to their belief in the money multiplier model (outlined in section 2.7), in which the central bank first creates base money, and banks then use this base money to lend, with the total amount of lending limited by the quantity of reserves and the reserve ratio. However, as explained earlier, "In the real world, banks extend credit, creating deposits in the process, and look for the reserves later." (Holmes, 1969, p. 73)

If banks make loans first then go looking for the reserves later, is it possible for the central bank to restrict lending by limiting the supply of reserves? Currently there is no compulsory or even advisory reserve ratio in place in the UK. But if such a reserve ratio was in place, then in theory, if a bank had an insufficient quantity of reserves (that it needed to make inter-bank payments arising from its customers making payments to customers of other banks) then the bank in question would need to restrain its loan making. This would decrease the number of payments its customers made to customers of other banks, reducing the outflows of reserves from the bank in the process.

However, in reality the Bank of England cannot manage private banks money creation by restricting the supply of reserves unless it is willing to create either a liquidity (and possibly a solvency) crisis, or see interest rates rise above the level at which it has committed to maintain them. As Charles Goodhart (1994) explains:

> "Virtually every monetary economist believes that the central bank can control the monetary base [i.e. the stock of cash and central bank reserves]...Almost all those who have worked in a central bank believe that this view is totally mistaken." [Our addition in brackets.]

To see why this is the case, imagine that the central bank tried to control bank lending by limiting the quantity of reserves in accounts at the Bank of England. As outlined previously, reserves are used to make payments, and by limiting the supply of reserves to banks, the ability of those banks to make payments between each other is also reduced. If a bank, either deliberately or through miscalculation, made too many loans and this resulted in an outflow of reserves in excess of its holdings, would the central bank be forced to provide more?

If the central bank refused to create excess reserves, then the bank in question would be unable to make payments to other banks. Under such circumstances the bank may attempt to raise reserves by selling some of its assets. While liquid assets may be sold quickly for their full value, quick sales of illiquid assets often mean accepting a price below fair value. Liquidity problems can therefore soon become solvency problems, with a solvency issue at one bank causing a cascade of bankruptcies throughout the entire banking system. Accordingly, the central bank is unlikely to refuse any request for additional reserves, indeed doing so would go against one of the central bank's core functions – its mandate to protect financial stability. As the Bank of England describes it:

> "If there is a shortage of liquidity, then the central bank will (almost) always supply the need...As regards a shortage of commercial bank reserves held at the central bank, the risk is that a shortage would mean payments could not be cleared at the end of the day. It is to avoid this risk that central banks have in place credit standing facilities (SFs) — though they will normally aim to supply liquidity via open market operations (OMO) — to avoid spikes in market interest rates." (Gary, 2008)

As the above quote attests, there is another reason why the central bank may wish to supply reserves to the banking system on demand: any excess demand for reserves above their supply will push up the price of reserves (i.e. the interest rate they are lent at). At this point the central bank, which is committed to maintaining the interest rate on interbank lending, will be able to bring the interest rate back down only by injecting reserves into the system. By doing so, it will have failed to constrain bank lending by implementing reserve ratios. As Victoria Chick (1992) explains:

> "If a policy of stable interest rates is in place ... reserves virtually disappear as a constraint on bank behaviour. Banks are now able to meet any reasonable rise in the demand for loans. Deposits will rise as a result and the shortfall of reserves is met by the system. This mechanism has been used often enough in Britain for the Bank of England to be referred to as 'lender of *first* resort.'"

There are also other reasons why reserves may not constrain lending or payments. First, to the extent that payments are made between customers of the same bank, no reserves will be required. The more a banking system is dominated by a few large banks (such as in the UK) the greater the number of payments that can be made across the banks' own books, and the less banks will need central bank reserves to make payments.

Second, when a bank lends money it will usually result in an outflow of reserves from the bank (when the customer spends their loan). However, every flow must go somewhere, so that one bank's outflow of reserves is matched with another bank's inflow. Therefore, if all banks increase their lending in step with each other, the payments between customers of different banks will tend to cancel each other out and therefore a fixed quantity of reserves will be able to support an increasing quantity of payments (and lending). This point was made quite explicitly by Keynes (1930) in his Treatise on Money:

> "The rate at which the bank can, with safety, *actively* create deposits by lending and investing has to be in a proper relation to the rate at which it is *passively* creating them against the receipt of liquid resources from its depositors. For the latter increase the bank's reserves even if only a part of them is ultimately retained by the bank, whereas the former diminish the reserves even if only a part of them is paid away to customers of other banks; indeed we might express our conclusion more strongly than this, since the borrowing customers generally borrow with the intention of

paying away at once the deposits thus created in their favour, whereas the depositing customers often have no such intention.

[...]

It is evident that there is no limit to the amount of bank money which the banks can safely create *provided they move forward in step*. The words italicised are the clue to the behaviour of the system. Every movement forward by an individual bank weakens it, but every such movement by one of its neighbour banks strengthens it; so that if all move forward together, no one is weakened on balance. Thus the behaviour of each bank, though it cannot afford to move more than a step in advance of the others, will be governed by the average behaviour of the banks as a whole – to which average, however, it is able to contribute its quota small or large. Each Bank Chairman sitting in his parlour may regard himself as the passive instrument of outside forces over which he has no control; yet the 'outside forces' may be nothing but himself and his fellow-chairmen, and certainly not his depositors."

The argument that the central banks cannot restrict bank lending through reserves is therefore not new or obscure – the above statement was made over 80 years ago by arguably the most influential economist of all time. Furthermore, during the monetarist experiment of the 1980s, the theory that central banks could control bank lending by limiting the monetary base was put to the test and failed.[7] Yet despite this, many economists still believe the central bank can control bank lending and money creation by restricting the level of cash and reserves in circulation.

In the next section we will consider a related argument – that the central bank can control bank lending, money creation and spending (and thus the level of aggregate demand and inflation) by manipulating interest rates.

Controlling money creation through interest rates

Currently, one of the Bank of England's two core purposes is to maintain price stability, which in practice means keeping inflation at a target level of 2% a year. It attempts to achieve this by manipulating the short term interest rates at which banks lend reserves to each other on the interbank market. In this

---

7. Although technically they attempted to do this through interest rates rather than by limiting reserves, as to limit reserves could have in the extreme caused banks to become insolvent.

Box 3.A - Setting the interest rate

The central bank's ability to set interest rates comes from its position as the monopoly issuer of central bank reserves. By changing this rate the central bank attempts to influence borrowing by businesses and households, affecting the rate of money creation and therefore affecting aggregate demand in the economy. This should affect the level of inflation. In the last ten years the Bank of England has used three different methods to set the interest rate:

Pre-2006: In order to set interest rates the Bank of England artificially limited the quantity of reserves in circulation, so the banking sector would always find itself short, in aggregate, of the amount it needed to settle payments. This forced the banks to approach the Bank of England to borrow the reserves they required. By choosing the interest rate on the reserves that it lent, the Bank of England could influence the interest rate on reserves in the system as a whole. This approach was management-intensive, involving the injection of reserves twice and sometimes three times every day.

2006 – 2008: In 2006 the Bank of England moved to what is known as a 'reserves averaging' scheme. Under this scheme, at the beginning of every month the commercial banks informed the central bank as to how many reserves they would need on average over the course of the month. The central bank then supplied this quantity of reserves to the commercial banks (using repos) and the commercial banks were required to hold this quantity of reserves on average across the month. If any bank found itself with excess reserves then it could either lend these reserves to another bank, or, if there were no borrowers, deposit these reserves in the 'deposit facility' at the Bank of England. Likewise, if a bank found itself short, it could borrow reserves from other banks or, if there were no willing lenders, from the Bank of England's 'lending facility'. The central bank incentivised banks to hit their reserve target by paying interest on reserves at the policy rate when they were within a narrow range of their target.

By standing ready to lend reserves to banks at a higher rate of interest (than the policy rate), and pay interest on reserves deposited with it at a lower rate of interest (than the policy rate), the central bank controlled the interest rate at which private banks lent reserves to each other on the interbank market (known as the London Interbank Offered Rate, or LIBOR for short). This is because a bank looking to borrow reserves from another bank on the interbank market would not pay more than the interest rate at which it could borrow from the Bank of England. Similarly, a bank lending reserves would not accept a lower interest rate than that which it could receive by leaving its reserves in its own account at the Bank of England. These two interest rates created a 'corridor' around the interest rate at which the Bank of England wanted banks to lend to each other (the policy rate).

Post 2008: Since 2008 the central bank has operated what is known as a 'floor system' of setting interest rates. In 2008 the central bank flooded the commercial banks with excess reserves through its Quantitative Easing program. This led to the reserves targeting scheme being dropped, with all reserves then remunerated at the policy rate. Because banks now had more reserves than they required, the need to borrow reserves on the interbank market was greatly diminished. Consequently, the overnight interbank lending rate now closely mirrors the policy rate.

section we discuss how the central bank attempts to control inflation through interest rates, the transmission mechanisms from interest rates to inflation, and the effectiveness of the interest rate as a tool to limit the growth in money creation by banks. We begin with a short outline of what inflation is and its links to money creation.

Inflation, bank lending and money creation

Inflation is defined as "a sustained rise in the general level of prices." (Blanchard, 2006) In the UK inflation is measured using the Consumer Price Index (CPI), which calculates the average change in the price of a basket of consumer goods and services over the previous year.

Economists disagree on what causes inflation. Some believe inflation is entirely due to the creation of new money, as the holders of the newly created money push up the price of goods and services. This was a view held by Milton Friedman, who famously asserted that "inflation is always and everywhere a monetary phenomenon" (1970). Others believe that "inflation usually does not have monetary origins" (Tymoigne, 2009, p. 40), and instead focus on non-monetary explanations such as wage increases.[8] In his textbook Olivier Blanchard tries to forge some common ground between these disparate groups by showing that while in the short run inflation might be caused by non-monetary phenomena, in the long run "unless they lead to higher nominal money growth, factors like the monopoly power of firms, strong unions,

---

8. In the short run the price level can change for a variety of reasons. For example, sudden increases in demand for goods and services may push up their prices (demand-pull inflation). Or increases in the cost of production may force producers to increase the price they charge in order to maintain margins (cost-push inflation). Or workers may bid up their wages, either individually or collectively, in order to maintain their real wage (the wage-price spiral). Other theories link the change in the rate of inflation to deviations from a 'natural' rate of growth/unemployment (the non-accelerating inflation rate of unemployment).

strikes, fiscal deficits, the price of oil, and so on have no effect on inflation." (2006, p. 191) One explanation for the lack of consensus between economists might be that:

> "Inflation is a complex social process, and it seems unlikely that there is any one explanation of the phenomenon valid for all times and all places. For any theory which asserts, for example, that higher growth is always associated with higher inflation, it is always possible to point to empirical instances of the opposite, either stagflation (low growth with high inflation) or, more benignly, non-inflationary growth." (Smithin, 2003, p. 190)

However, despite the fact that in the short run inflation can be caused by other factors, there seems to be little doubt that monetary factors are important in the long run. Indeed, the Bank of England is quite explicit:

> "In the long run, there is a positive relationship between each monetary aggregate and the general level of prices. Sustained increases in prices cannot occur without accompanying increases in the monetary aggregates. It is in this sense that money is the nominal anchor of the system." (Bank of England, 1999)[9]

In the current monetary system bank lending increases spending in the economy (and the amount of money in circulation). If spending grows in excess of the productive capacity of the economy it will create inflation:

> "In the long run, monetary and credit aggregates must be willingly held by agents in the economy. Monetary growth persistently in excess of that warranted by growth in the real economy will inevitably be the reflection of an interest rate policy that is inconsistent with stable inflation. So control of inflation always ultimately implies control of the monetary growth rate." (Bank of England, 1999)

Because high and variable rates of inflation impose costs on society, central banks are charged with keeping the inflation rate low and stable. How the central bank sets the interest rate, its effectiveness in controlling the growth in lending, and the subsequent effects on inflation are discussed below.

The interest rate and inflation

Currently, the Monetary Policy Committee is the group within the Bank of England charged with keeping inflation at a target rate of 2%. Its main tool

---

9.   Sustained increases in prices could also occur with a constant monetary aggregates and a continual fall in productive capacity, although this is unlikely.

for doing so is the 'policy rate' of interest. The Bank of England designs its operations in such a way so that short term interest rates (in particular the rate at which banks lend reserves to each other on the interbank market) closely follow the policy rate.

> "Policymakers attempt to achieve a certain inflation goal by using their control over interest rates to restrain the total demand for goods and services in the economy." (IMF, 2010, p. 9)

However, this was not always the case; the interest rate was in fact first used by the Bank of England in order to defend the exchange rate and therefore the country's gold reserves (note these are not the same as central bank reserves). Crucially, the way in which monetary policy was conducted was designed:

> "with a view towards making the central bank's chosen key short-term rate effective in determining the set of other shorter-term market rates, and not in order to achieve any predetermined level of monetary base." (Goodhart, 2001)

Although the target of monetary policy has changed, the central bank still attempts to achieve its objectives by influencing short term interest rates, which in this case is the rate at which banks lend reserves to each other on the interbank market. The theory is that higher rates of interest lower the level of economic activity, which leads to a reduction in aggregate demand, hence lessening the upward pressure on prices. Conversely, lower rates of interest are thought to increase the level of economic activity, which leads to an increase in aggregate demand and an increase in the upward pressure on prices.

The transmission mechanism of monetary policy (interest rates)

Suppose that due to an expected increase in inflation, the Bank of England raises the policy (base) rate. If a bank wants to make loans, but does not have sufficient reserves to make the additional payments that the loans will (likely) entail when the loans are spent, it will now cost it more to acquire reserves. In order to maintain its profit margin the bank must increase the interest rate it charges on its new loans to businesses and individuals. In theory this is likely to decrease the demand for loans, with banks then lending less than they otherwise would. As such there will be less borrowing by individuals and firms, a lower rate of growth of money creation, and this will lead to lower spending. Lower spending on both assets and on goods and services reduces the demand for them, and in so doing reduces their prices. This is the 'direct' effect of monetary policy on aggregate demand and inflation.

fig. 3.2 - Transmission mechanisms of monetary policy

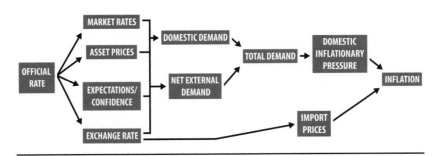

For simplicity, this figure does not show all interactions between variables.
(Bank of England, 1999)

There are also several 'indirect' routes through which changes in interest rates may affect inflation. First, changes in interest rates alter the expectations and confidence of individuals and organisations as to the future path of the economy, as well as to the future path of interest rate movements (and therefore the viability of certain business models). Other things being equal, falling interest rates reduce the proportion of income needed to service debt and increase the perceived value of expected future profits relative to the immediate costs of new investment. This should in turn engineer positive views of the future which are likely to lead to higher levels of spending and borrowing. As a result inflation should increase (or at least, deflationary pressures should decrease).

Second, a change in the interest rate has an effect on the exchange rate. In general, a reduction in interest rates will tend to lead to depreciation of the currency, as investors sell their domestic currency for foreign currency, whereas an increase in interest rates is likely to lead to a currency appreciation, as investment in the country increases demand for the currency. Changes in the value of the domestic currency vis-à-vis foreign currencies then leads to changes in the price of imported goods and services.

Third, a change in the interest rate alters the wealth of individuals and firms. In particular, a reduction in the interest rate make savers worse off (as they receive lower returns on their savings) while making borrowers better off (as they pay lower levels of interest). These effects then feed through into people's spending and borrowing behaviour.

Finally, changes in wealth also affect the ability of individuals and businesses to borrow. Lower interest rates increase the price of financial assets, increasing the wealth of those holding them. Other things being equal, an increase in asset prices will increase the asset owner's ability to borrow (as they can use the assets as collateral). With more collateral available, banks will be more willing to lend. If this lending materialises, then money creation, spending, and inflation will all increase.

Problems with using interest rates to control inflation

The above section outlined the orthodox interpretation of how interest rates affect inflation. However, there are several problems with this analysis. It is the view of the central bank that monetary policy has "little direct effect on the trend path of supply capacity", instead working "largely via its influence on aggregate demand in the economy." (Bank of England, 1999, p. 3) Yet this is not necessarily true. If bank lending funds investment by businesses in the real (non-financial) economy, it may increase the productive capacity of the economy (even at 'full' employment). This would mean that more could be produced using the same quantity of resources, and consequently prices would fall. For example, if there is a decrease in the policy rate, and this disproportionately increases borrowing by firms to finance investment (over borrowing for other reasons), then the higher borrowing will increase the amount of goods and services available to purchase in the economy. As as result, a lower interest rate could potentially lower inflation, in contrast to the orthodox position. The empirical observation of this effect is termed Gibson's Paradox.

Second, "it is a long and uncertain chain of events from an adjustment in the interest rate controlled by the central bank to a desired change in the rate of inflation." (Arestis & Sawyer, 2003, p. 17) This is likely to pose difficulties for those on the Monetary Policy Committee when setting rates. Figure 3.2 outlines this 'long and uncertain' chain of events. Yet this diagram is actually a simplification - many of these factors interact with each other in unpredictable ways. As a result it would only take a small miscalculation for the effect of an interest rate change to be quite different from that which was predicted.[10]

---

10. An increase in the interest rate might make speculation on assets unattractive, but have little effect on borrowing for investment. Or the same increase might make borrowing for investment unattractive but leave asset speculation unchanged. While the change in the interest rate is the same, the effect on demand and inflation is likely to be very different. For example, take the situation whereby a rise in the interest rate primarily lowers the demand for borrowing to purchase assets. Under these conditions fewer assets will be purchased and this should

Third, the impact of monetary policy on the exchange rate places constraints on its use as an instrument to reduce inflation. As Arestis & Sawyer explain:

> "In light of the relationship between the exchange rate and the interest rate posited by economic theory, there are constraints on the degree to which the domestic interest rate can be set to address the levels of aggregate demand and inflation without destabilizing the currency." (2003, p. 17)

The central bank is also likely to be limited to the extent that it cares about the competitiveness of exporters and the balance of trade. If increases in the interest rate lead to large inflows of foreign currency, the price of the domestic currency will be pushed up, making domestic goods more expensive to foreign purchasers and leading to a loss of competitiveness of the export sector.

Changes in the interest rate may also affect prices and demand through the exchange rate in other ways. For example, Marcel Sanchez of the European Central Bank has found that the link between changes in interest rates and changes in exchange rates depends on whether the increase in prices of foreign goods following an exchange rate depreciation leads to reduced economic activity (contraction - because raw material costs have increased) or increased output (expansion - because consumers switch to cheaper home-produced goods). With expansion, falling interest rates are associated with exchange rate depreciation and therefore increased import prices, whereas with contraction, falling interest rates are associated with exchange rate appreciation and therefore decreased import prices. (Sanchez, 2005)

Fourth, the use of interest rates to stem inflation is inherently flawed. Interest payments are a cost to businesses, and higher interest rates will either eat into the profit margins of businesses (making it more difficult for them to invest from retained earnings) or will drive firms to pass on costs to customers by raising prices, which is by definition inflationary. Interest rates also change the wealth of individuals and businesses in the economy – increasing interest rates makes savers richer and borrowers poorer, and this affects their decisions to spend and their ability to borrow. The effect of an increase in interest rates on

---

lower asset prices. Asset owners will find that their wealth has decreased, and so will be less likely to spend and less able to borrow (less collateral). Yet savers will now receive a higher interest rate on their savings, increasing their wealth and so improving their ability to spend and borrow. What effect dominates will be hard to say - all that can be said with certainty is the wealth and imperfect information channels of monetary policy (as outlined above) are difficult to predict.

inflation will depend to an extent on whether the effect of increasing savers' wealth cancels out the decrease in debtors' wealth, or whether one dominates the other. Moreover, if savers and borrowers have different consumption patterns then the effect of increasing rates will be to increase the demand for the goods that interest earners buy, pushing up their prices. (Tymoigne, 2009)

Fifth, the control of inflation by interest rates can place the two core central bank functions – price stability and financial stability – into conflict with each other. For example, if asset price inflation is high, then it will take a large increase in the interest rate (above the rate of asset price inflation) in order to stem the rise in credit creation for asset purchase and burst the bubble. This is likely to create strong disruptive effects on the productive economy (possibly bankrupting firms). If this asset inflation is not spotted early, the likelihood will be that a large number of economic agents will be drawn into speculative positions (buying a house as an 'investment' is one example of how ubiquitous speculative behaviour has become). Any decrease in asset prices can impair the ability of speculative investors to repay their loans, increasing the risk of defaults, and potentially leading to bank bankruptcies and financial crisis (damaging financial stability). This can spill over into the real economy, leading to rising unemployment, recession (or even depression) and possible debt deflation.

In conclusion, the theoretical arguments that the interest rate can be used to control the creation of money by the banking sector, and therefore inflation are at best weak. In addition, there is some empirical evidence to suggest that rather than increases in interest rates limiting aggregate demand (and therefore inflation) instead interest rates "tend to be positively correlated with economic activity and there is at least as much evidence that … causality runs from economic growth to interest rates" (Werner, 2011). Taken together, the empirical and theoretical work suggests that interest rates are an ineffective tool for limiting demand and therefore inflation.

Unused regulations

It is not impossible to control the amount (or direction) of credit created by banks in the current monetary system. Credit/window guidance can and has been used to control both the amount of credit banks create, as well as to which sectors of the economy it is allocated. Werner (2010) describes the process used in Japan:

"[T]he central bank (or the finance ministry) imposes quantitative and qualitative quotas on the entire banking sector, allocated according to a principle that is accepted by the banks, while maintaining competitive behaviour between them (proportionally to existing size). Furthermore, strict limits or even bans are imposed on the creation of credit by banks for particular transactions that may otherwise create more harm than good, especially financial and asset market transactions (i.e. transactions not directly contributing to GDP) and to some extent also consumer loans."

Almost every major industrialised nation (with the exception of the USA) has used some form of credit guidance since the Second World War. However, it has since fallen out of fashion, with the result being that banks face little restriction on the amount of credit they create and what they create this credit for.

3.5 SO WHAT DETERMINES THE MONEY SUPPLY?

The aim of this chapter was to make several things clear. First, there will always be a substantial demand for credit (and money). Wealth disparities ensure that individuals will need to borrow more than they otherwise would to buy houses and to smooth consumption, while businesses will need to borrow to invest. Borrowing also allows people to increase the returns to speculation and investment, and limited liability and tax laws lead businesses to favour debt over equity financing.

Second, banks are overwhelmingly incentivised to make as many loans as possible during benign economic periods. Traditionally the major source of profit for the banking sector was lending – more loans mean greater profits, provided that the loans are repaid. However, the ability to collateralise and securitise loans has meant even this constraint is no longer binding – banks can even make profits from loans that aren't repaid (as it is the buyer of collateralised debt obligations that takes the loss). As a result bank lending became quantity rather than quality driven. Likewise the existence of deposit insurance and the 'too big to fail' safety net, the externalisation of the social and economic costs of excess money creation, and competitive pressures all combined to push banks to increase their lending.

Third, the high demand for money and credit and the willingness of banks to provide it would not matter if the various regulations that are meant to limit bank credit creation actually worked. However, they do not. Capital requirements are flawed and do not significantly limit money creation. This is because the extra profits that come from increased lending boost capital and increase the lending capacity of the bank in a pro-cyclical fashion. Nor can central banks restrict the quantity of central bank reserves made available to banks, because to do so would risk either a liquidity crisis and possibly a solvency crisis, or cause the base rate of interest to move away from the Bank of England's target rate. Finally, the Bank of England cannot reliably limit money creation by changing the price of central bank reserves – the base or policy rate of interest – for the wide variety of reasons discussed above.

Credit rationing

What then determines the level of bank lending, and therefore the quantity of money in circulation? Faced with a huge demand for credit, and little limit on how much they are able to supply, banks could simply supply as much lending as is demanded, by granting a loan to everyone who applied for one. With such high demand, however, the market-clearing rate of interest would be very high. As Stiglitz and Weiss (1988) point out this will create two problems. First:

> "among those who are most likely to bid high interest rates are risk lovers (who are willing to undertake very risky projects, with a small probability of success, but high returns if successful); optimists (who overestimate the probability of projects succeeding and the return if successful); and crooks (who, because they do not plan to pay back the money anyway, are virtually indifferent to the interest rate which they promise).

> "As a consequence, as the bank raises the rate of interest, there is an adverse selection effect; the mix of loan applicants changes adversely, so much so that the expected return from those receiving loans may actually decrease as the interest rate charged increased."

The problem of adverse selection has long been known: Adam Smith noted in the Wealth of Nations that when interest rates are high the only people wishing to borrow would be "prodigals and projectors":

> "Sober people, who will give for the use of money no more than a part of what they are likely to make by the use of it, would not venture into the competition. A great part of the capital of the country would thus be kept out of the hands which were most likely to make a profitable and advantageous use of it, and thrown into those which were most likely to waste and destroy it. Where the legal rate of interest, on the contrary, is fixed

fig. 3.3 – Relationship between interest rate charged on loans and profits

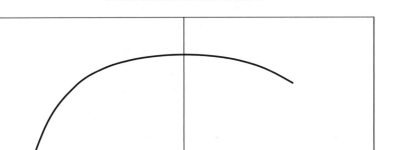

BANK PROFITS vs INTEREST CHARGED

but a very little above the lowest market rate, sober people are universally preferred, as borrowers, to prodigals and projectors." (Smith, 1776)

The second problem is that in order to compensate for the higher loan cost, "there may be an adverse incentive effect; borrowers take riskier actions, which increases the probability of default." (Stiglitz & Weiss, 1988) Therefore, if banks charge interest rates at the market clearing level they will drive the less risky borrowers out of the market, leaving only the high-risk borrowers. Higher risk implies a higher number of defaults on loans, which will adversely affect bank profits. The relationship between bank profits and the interest rate charged on loans is shown in figure 3.3.

In response to these theoretical issues and anecdotal and empirical evidence on the number of rejected loan applications, Stiglitz and Weiss (1981) developed a theory of credit rationing. Credit rationing implies that banks respond to a situation whereby they have imperfect information (i.e. they cannot perfectly tell good borrowers from bad) by setting interest rates below the market clearing rate (to a level which maximises their profits – i* on figure 3.3) and ration credit instead.[11] In conclusion, the credit rationing theory sees causality in the banking system occurring in the following way (see overleaf).

---

11.   In addition, in their model banks cannot overcome the problem of imperfect information by increasing their collateral requirements on borrowers, due to adverse selection issues.

Faced with a large demand for credit, banks set interest rates below the market clearing rate and ration credit instead (by rejecting some loan applications).

When banks lend, deposits are created.

This increases demand for reserves in order to settle payments.

The central bank provides reserves to banks on demand, thus accommodating a bank's lending decisions.

We can conclude that the primary determinant of bank lending is how profitable banks believe that lending will be. For banks, profitability depends on the proceeds of a loan (the interest charged) exceeding the costs of making a loan (the interest paid to acquire the funds needed to settle net payments to other banks, plus other costs – e.g. salaries). As long as the costs of making a loan are below the profits expected from the loan at the rate of interest that maximizes bank profitability (due to imperfect information/credit rationing) then a bank will make the loan. If the bank is planning to keep the loan on its books then the loan's profitability will depend upon it being repaid. Positive economic conditions, such as high growth and low unemployment, increase the probability of a loan being repaid, as businesses are more likely to succeed and individuals are less likely to lose their jobs. The opposite is true of negative economic conditions. This point has been made quite clearly by Adair Turner:

> "[B]anks can create credit and private money, and unless controlled, will tend to create sub-optimally large or sub-optimally unstable quantities of both credit and private money." (2012)

However, if a bank plans to securitise the loans it makes then it doesn't have to worry about repayment – it can make the loan safe in the knowledge that it can sell it off to someone else. Likewise, when a loan is collateralised with an asset that is not expected to fall in value (such as a house), the bank can make the loan safe in the knowledge that if a default does occur it may take control of the asset, sell it, and so still make a profit.[12] Freed from the downside of

---

12. The NINJA mortgages made in the run up to the financial crisis are an example of such lending in action (so called because they were made to individuals with No Income, No Job or Assets, who were unlikely to be able to repay).

default, the profit motive causes banks to maximise their lending, increasing the quantity of money and debt in the process.

So how much money has been created by banks?

The chart of "Cash vs Bank-Issued Money" from the Introduction shows the effect on the quantity of money in circulation of a high demand for credit combined with a lack of regulation. Between 1970 and 2012 banks increased the total amount of money in the economy from £25 billion to £2,050 billion – an 82 fold increase. In the same time period prices only have increased 13 fold.

What have banks been lending for? Figure 3.4, overleaf, shows the total sterling amounts of loans outstanding in the UK since 1997. By far the greatest proportion of bank lending is to the property market: In March 2010, 46.3% of the value of total loans outstanding in the UK was to individuals (and secured on property), with an additional 13.2% to commercial real estate companies.[13] A further 22.8% of lending was for financial intermediation,[14] 6.3% was unsecured personal debt, 1% went to insurance companies and pension funds and 2.8% was to 'public and other services'. Meanwhile, the value of loans outstanding to the productive part of the economy (i.e. those sectors which contribute to GDP) accounted for just 7.6% of total lending.

13.   'Business services' account for a tiny proportion of this figure.

14.   This includes lending to financial leasing corporations, securities dealers, investment and unit trusts and other financial intermediaries.

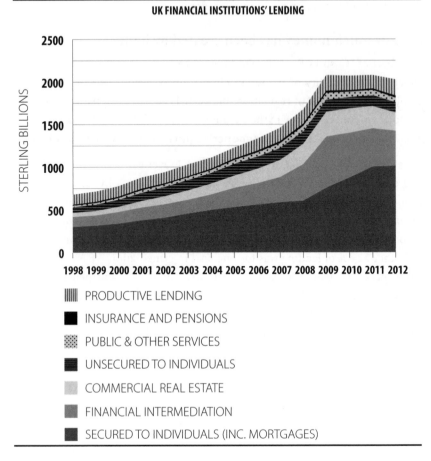

fig. 3.4 - UK resident monetary financial institutions' lending

UK FINANCIAL INSTITUTIONS' LENDING

PRODUCTIVE LENDING

INSURANCE AND PENSIONS

PUBLIC & OTHER SERVICES

UNSECURED TO INDIVIDUALS

COMMERCIAL REAL ESTATE

FINANCIAL INTERMEDIATION

SECURED TO INDIVIDUALS (INC. MORTGAGES)

Source: Bank of England Statistical Database

This chart is slightly misleading, in that it appears to show that the broad money supply continued to increase until late 2009, whereas in reality tit actually started to shrink in late 2008. The appearance of an increase in the money supply between 2008 and 2009 is mainly due to changes in the way that the broad money supply statistics are reported by the Bank of England.

CHAPTER 4

ECONOMIC CONSEQUENCES OF THE CURRENT SYSTEM

Chapter 2 discussed the mechanics of bank lending, showing that when a bank makes a loan it creates new money, increasing both the amount of money and the level of debt in the economy. Chapter 3 showed that banks profit from making loans, that the demand for credit tends to be very high, and that banks face little constraint on their ability to lend. Consequently, in the current monetary system it is the commercial banks, rather than the central bank, which determine both the quantity of money and debt in the economy, as well as the first use of newly created money.

In this chapter we analyse the economic effects of such a monetary system. For non-economists this chapter may be the most challenging, although we have attempted to convey the theories as simply and with as little jargon as possible. Some readers may wish to skip to Chapter 5 and return to this chapter after reading the rest of the book.

We begin by looking at the short-run impact of bank lending, distinguishing between lending to the 'productive' and 'non-productive' sectors of the economy. Particular attention is paid to the effect of money created (via bank lending) to fund purchases of financial assets, in contrast to the effect of money created to invest in businesses that contribute to GDP. We also consider the links between asset and consumer price inflation.

The longer-run dynamic effects of bank lending on the economy are then discussed with reference to Hyman Minsky's 'Financial Instability Hypothesis'. Minsky's theory explores the role of the financial sector in driving the boom-bust cycle, financial crises and debt deflation, showing that in the long term stability is itself destabilising. Evidence for the effect of bank lending on financial stability and business cycles will then be examined.

Finally, we consider the economic distortions that occur when the government intervenes to stabilise the banking system. Ironically, deposit insurance is shown to incentivise risky behaviour by banks, increasing the likelihood that the insurance will be required to be paid out whilst at the same time providing a large subsidy to the banking sector. The effects of the Basel Capital Accords on banks' lending decisions are also shown to have the potential to make crises more rather than less likely.

4.1 ECONOMIC EFFECTS OF CREDIT CREATION

Non-economists might expect that the economics profession takes money, banks and debt seriously; after all, these institutions are at the centre of almost all economic activity on the planet. Yet the reality is that the economics profession tends to ignore them:

> "In the monetarist view of Friedman and Schwartz ... but also in the recently dominant Neo-Keynesian synthesis ... macroeconomic outcomes are largely independent of the performance of the financial system." (Schularick & Taylor, 2009)

Some of the reasons economic theories ignore finance were briefly alluded to in Chapter 1: if money emerges naturally out of barter (as a token that serves to oil the wheels of trade), money can be thought of as simply a 'veil' over barter, masking the fact that people are still just exchanging one good or service for another. Consequently, money can be thought of as neutral - doubling the supply of money simply doubles prices, so in real terms no one is any better or worse off. While some economists might concede that changes in the stock of money have short run effects (for example, due to prices reacting slowly), once they have adjusted (in the long run) money can again be safely ignored. Similarly, if lending is a transfer of purchasing power from one person to another, then the amount of debt in the economy has no effect unless debtors and creditors behave differently (in terms of spending). Likewise, in Chapter 3 we saw that the central bank believes monetary policy has "little direct effect on the trend path of supply capacity", instead working "largely via its influence on aggregate demand" (Bank of England, 1999, p. 3).

The problem is that none of this is true – money is not a commodity or a token – today the vast majority of money is created by banks when they make loans. As a result the amount of lending determines the amount of purchasing power in the economy – for this reason (and others) the quantity of debt does matter. Similarly, the amount of lending determines the productive capacity of the economy – as Schumpeter (1936) points out, entrepreneurs in general can only become entrepreneurs by previously becoming debtors. In short, finance matters:

> "we cannot understand how our economy works by first solving alloca-
> tion problems and then adding financing relations; in a capitalist economy
> resource allocation and price determination are integrated with the financ-
> ing of outputs, positions in capital assets, and the validating of liabilities.
> This means that nominal values (money prices) matter: money is not
> neutral". (Minsky, 1986)

In the following section we will attempt to unravel the effects banks have on the economy, firstly by discussing Richard Werner's 'Quantity Theory of Credit', followed by Hyman Minsky's 'Financial Instability Hypothesis'.[1]

Werner's Quantity Theory of Credit

In his 2005 book, 'New Paradigm in Macroeconomics', Werner sets out a simple framework which describes the effects of bank lending upon output and prices (see Werner (1992, 1997), and The Economist (1992) for earlier presentations.) This framework is useful for the following discussion, where we see that the impact of money creation on the economy depends on two factors: First, how much money is created, and second, what that money is used for.

Werner starts with the quantity equation of money, which sets out the rela-tionship between money, prices and the number of transactions in the econ-omy, shown below.

(1)
$$MV = PT$$
Money x Velocity of that money = average Price x number of Transactions

In the equation above, M stands for the quantity of money in circulation, V for the velocity of money (the number of times money is used for a transaction in

---

1.   It is important to note that the following section outlines various economic models. These models are not intended to describe how the economy functions as a whole; rather they are devices to aid the reader's understanding of the effect of different types of money creation on output and prices.

a given time period), T for the number of transactions in that period, and P for the average price level of the transactions. The left hand side (MV) of this equation represents the total spending for a given time period, whereas the right hand side (PT) shows the total value in monetary terms of the number of transactions for the same time period. The quantity equation is not only an equation but an equality – it is true by definition. The quantity equation simply states that the total revenue from all the goods and services sold in a given time period must equal the amount of money spent on goods and services during the same time period.

The quantity equation can theoretically be used to analyse how a change in the stock of money (M), can lead to a change in prices (P). However, the traditional version of this equation has several problems.

First, there is no reliable data on the number of transactions (T), so in order to estimate the equation economists had to find a suitable proxy. There is data available on the quantity of national income/output measured (real GDP, represented by the symbol Y) in volume terms, so economists decided to use this in place of transactions. The new quantity equation then became MV = PY. The right hand side of the equation (PY) is then real gross domestic product (Y) multiplied by prices (P) which together make up nominal GDP. However, as Werner (2005) points out, replacing T with Y is rational only if PT = PY, that is if all transactions (T) are accounted for in real GDP (Y). Unfortunately this is not the case – T measures all transactions in an economy, including those for pre-existing assets (such as financial assets and pre-existing property). Because these are not included in measures of GDP (which only measures the quantity of new goods and services), PT does not equal PY, so Y cannot be used in place of T.

Second, the formula does not identify what is meant by money (M). Should just money created by the state be included? Or should money created by private banks be included as well? And what about things that have money-like properties, such as bonds?

In response to the first difficultly, Werner (2005) separates out the quantity equation into the two separate equations. One equation comprises the money, prices, transactions and velocity in the part of the economy that produces goods and services that are included in GDP, which we will refer to as 'real economy'. The other comprises the same variables but for transactions that do not contribute to GDP (generally financial transactions on assets).[2] This 'disaggregated quantity theory of credit' is show below:

(2)

$$M_R V_R = P_R Y$$

Equation for transactions which contribute to GDP (subscript R stands for real).

Money in the real economy x Velocity of that money = Prices for goods and services x Total output

(3)

$$M_F V_F = P_F T_F$$

Equation for transactions which do not contribute to GDP (subscript F stands for financial).

Money used for financial transactions x Velocity of that money = Prices of financial assets x Total trade in those financial assets

In these models, any increase in money (given a constant velocity, V_R) used for transactions in the real economy (M_R) will lead to a rise in nominal GDP (either through its effect on prices, output, or both).[3] Likewise any increase in money spent in the financial sector will, given a stable velocity, lead to an increase in the price of financial assets.

In response to the second difficulty – the unclear definition of money – Werner uses data on bank loans (that is credit/money creation) as a proxy for M. This has two benefits. First, because people borrow to spend, this measure of money is a record of money being used. Conversely, traditional measures of the money supply (such as M4), are simply measures of money that is sitting in bank accounts – there is no way of knowing how much of these deposits are active (i.e. being used for purchases) and how many are simply lying dormant.

---

2.   Werner uses the symbols C in place of M, to stand for credit, and Q in place of T to stand for the quantity of transactions. However, apart from these presentational differences the equations are the same.

3.   In recent years, velocity (V) has declined. This is often thought to be due to technological innovation. However, Werner (2005) shows that V has actually remained constant, with the decline due to an increasing number of transactions not included in GDP. For a discussion see Werner (2005), chapters 13 & 14.

Box 4.A - Output (GDP), potential output, and growth

The term 'Output' simply refers to the total amount of goods and services produced in an economy within some given time period. An economy's output may rise or fall depending on economic conditions. On the other hand potential output is the output the economy could achieve if it was utilising all its resources fully.

In the long run potential output is dependent on two factors. The first is the 'quantity of factor inputs' (QFI). These inputs include land and labour (which are considered the 'fundamental' factors) as well as capital (such as machines).

For example, for a bakery the quantity of factor inputs would include ingredients, equipment (capital), the land the kitchen is built on as well as the people (labour) doing the baking. The second factor which contributes to potential output is 'total factor productivity' (TFP). TFP is the output in an economy over and above that which is accounted for by the quantity of inputs. Some think of it as the skill of those within the economy in combining inputs, or alternatively the level of technology in the economy. If we return to our example of the baker, then total factor productivity could measure the skill of the person doing the baking. It may also represent an improvement in the technology used by the baker. Putting the two together, Potential Output (Y*) is dependent on the 'quantity of factor inputs' and 'total factor productivity' so that:

(5)
$$Y^* = f\,(QFI\,;TFP)$$

Potential Output is a function of the quantity of inputs and total factor productivity

Potential output therefore measures the maximum level of output that an economy could achieve if everyone who wanted to work was working as efficiently as they could and every machine was running at full capacity. However, in reality what the economy actually produces will be determined by how much demand there is in the economy for these goods and services.

Each year the value of all the final goods and services produced within a country are added together giving the economy's output. This is known as the Gross Domestic Product of an economy and is represented in the quantity equations as the price of goods multiplied by the quantity of goods sold ($P_R\,Y$).

Gross Domestic Product can be split into further sub categories: those purchases which are for consumption (C), those which are for investment (I), those which are due to government spending (G), and net exports, which is made up of Exports (X) minus imports (M), so that the equation for output is:

$$Y = C + I + G + (X\text{-}M)$$

The Output (Y) of an economy consists of Consumption (C), Investment (I) and Government (G) spending plus net exports. For simplicity, we'll ignore net exports in the analysis below. Because the government does not typically borrow from banks to fund its spending (though it could), government spending does not lead to money creation, so we will not concern ourselves with its effects either and instead focus only on consumption and investment. Returning to Werner's Quantity theory of credit, GDP is determined by purchases of investment and consumption goods.

(6)
$$M_{IR} V_{IR} + M_{CR} V_{CR} = P_R Y$$

Subscript I stands for investment,
Subscript C for consumption, R for real economy.

(Money for investment x Velocity of that money) + (Money for consumption x Velocity of that money) = Average prices x Total output

This equation says that GDP (the right hand side of the equation) depends upon money spent in the real (non-financial) economy on investment ($M_{IR} V_{IR}$) and money spent on consumption ($M_{CR} V_{CR}$).

We now have a framework in place to analyse the effects of money creation (via bank lending) when that lending is for either consumer spending or investment purposes.

Second, bank lending includes information on the intended use of the loan, which allows the quantity equation to be disaggregated, so that a loan to a sector which contributes to GDP shows up as an increase in money in the real economy (M_R), whereas a loan for a mortgage or to buy shares shows up as an increase in the amount of money in the financial economy (M_F).[4]

With an updated quantity equation of money that accounts for the true nature of money as well as financial transactions, Werner's model reveals that bank

---

4. Steve Keen (2011) presents a similar model to Werner's which distinguishes between pre-existing money and new bank credit creation:

(i)   Income + change in debt = (price level x output) + net asset sales

(ii)   Net asset sales = asset price level x quantity of assets x fraction of assets sold

lending will have different effects on the economy depending on how that money is used. This point was also made by Keynes, who spoke of two circulations of money – industrial circulation, i.e. money used to undertake normal business operations; and financial circulation – money used to buy and sell financial assets. The following sections detail the effects of different types of lending, such as for consumption (consumer spending), investment and financial transactions.

Money creation for consumer spending at full employment

Assume (and suspend disbelief for a moment) that the economy is operating at its full capacity, so that actual output is equal to potential output (see Box 4.A) and all resources are fully employed, including labour. Under these conditions if a bank extends a loan for consumption purposes (C) then this credit creation increases the purchasing power in the economy (the M_C component of M_R), with no corresponding increase in output (Y). With increased demand but no increase in output, the only effect (with a stable velocity of money, V) would be to push up prices. Thus, we should expect credit creation for consumption at full employment to be purely inflationary, so that:

(4)
$$(\uparrow M_R)\, V_R = (\uparrow P_R)\, Y$$

$\uparrow$ stands for 'increase in'

Money creation for productive purposes at full employment

What about money creation (via bank lending) for investment in productive capacity i.e. for a business investing to increase its output? As with money creation for consumer spending, this increases the purchasing power in the economy (the $M_{I\,R}$ portion of M_R), but also increases the quantity of goods produced – the productive capacity of the economy. For example, investment includes money spent on research and development, which can lead to the discovery of new technology, inventions, and production techniques that increase the potential output of the economy beyond its current level (i.e. they increase 'total factor productivity'). Credit creation for investment also allows firms to put in place new technologies or production techniques (i.e. increase the quantity of factor inputs).

In a situation where the economy is operating below potential output (less than full employment, however it is defined) credit creation for productive purposes will increase the quantity of goods and services produced in the

Box 4.B - 'Full employment'

In neoclassical economics the term 'full employment'[i] has a very specific meaning. It is not the level of employment where there is no unemployment, as one might expect, or even the level of employment which allows for a small amount of temporary unemployment as people shift between jobs. Instead the term full employment refers to the level of employment at which any increase in employment leads to an acceleration in the rate of inflation. In economics this is known as the Non Accelerating Inflation Rate of Unemployment (NAIRU).

Despite its name, the NAIRU theory is actually remarkably simple. The theory supposes that in the long run the level of unemployment depends on structural, or 'supply side' factors in the economy, such as tax rates and regulation. With the unemployment rate in the long run determined solely by these 'supply side' factors, the government is not thought to be able to alter the long-term level of unemployment through spending.[ii] Any attempt by the government to decrease unemployment below its NAIRU level in the short run will lead to upward pressure on wages, which will increase costs to firms and lead them to increase their prices (so leading to an acceleration in inflation). Higher prices lowers demand and this feeds through into an increase in unemployment back to its pre-intervention (NAIRU) level. Essentially therefore the NAIRU is the idea that the economy has a maximum capacity – any increase in demand beyond this level will only lead to inflation.

There are however numerous theoretical and empirical issues with the NAIRU, a good summary of which is given by Galbraith (1997). Most of these have long been known – indeed, a central theme of Keynes' 'General Theory' (1936) is that markets, left to their own devices, will not necessarily deliver full employment. Nevertheless, despite these problems it will be useful to consider the effects of bank lending in a scenario where the economy is at its 'full capacity'. The rationale for doing so is to examine whether bank lending – i.e. increasing demand through the creation of new purchasing power – can actually be non-inflationary, despite the economy being at full capacity.[iii]

i. Full employment is a controversial term amongst economists. Some (such as Tobin) argue the term should be taken literally, that is full employment refers to a 0% unemployment rate. Similarly, some use the term to refer to the level of employment that would exist if there were no 'structural' (i.e. long term) unemployment, so that 'frictional' unemployment (i.e. those between jobs) would not be counted as unemployed. Conversely, full employment is used by mainstream economists to refer to a level of employment that does not lead to an acceleration in inflation (the NAIRU).

ii. Under the more extreme 'rational expectations' hypothesis the government cannot even increase output in the short run. Such theories are however clearly contradicted by both common sense and empirical reality, and so will not be pursued here.

iii. This idea was previously mentioned in section 3.4, which questioned the prevailing wisdom that monetary policy worked largely through changes in demand rather than changes in supply.

economy, without bidding up the price of any inputs (as they are currently idle). As a result it should increase output without increasing inflation (Werner, 2005, p. 212).

(7) $$(\uparrow M_R)\, V_R = P_R\, (\uparrow Y)$$

However, if the economy is already running at full capacity and a firm borrows to invest in new machinery, the borrowing would in theory bid up the price of inputs by virtue of the economy running at full capacity. This would increase prices without increasing output (and so cause inflation). However, even in this full employment scenario, credit creation may not necessarily be inflationary. For example, even in the so-called 'boom' years, when unemployment was relatively low, many people (at least in the UK) were employed in sectors that did not contribute directly to GDP. In this environment it is possible for credit creation for investment purposes to be non-inflationary, even if unemployment is low.

For example, a loan may allow a company to hire more workers. In a world where everyone was working in a productive company (i.e. a company whose output contributes to GDP) then this would involve bidding up the price of labour in order to attract workers from one company to another. With no change in the total amount of hours worked output would be the same and therefore the only effect would be to increase inflation. However, in today's economy workers may move from the non-productive sector to a productive sector, and in so doing increase output and GDP. Even within companies there may be scope for increasing output. In the words of Hyman Minsky:

> "Only a portion, and in many cases only a small portion, of the cost of doing business reflects labor and purchased inputs that are technologically necessary. The labor employed in executive offices, advertising, marketing, sales, lobbying, research, product development, corporate lawyers, and so forth is not required by the technology embodied in capital assets. The services supplied by this labor may be vital to the functioning and survival of the organization in a given business environment, but in no sense are these costs technologically determined." (Minsky, 1986, p. 173-174)

In today's economy increases in lending for investment may also be non-inflationary at full employment so long as it attracts labour and capital that was previously not used to produce goods and services – that is, it must lead to an increase in the amount of goods produced in an economy.

In an economy operating below full capacity

It is unlikely that many people would argue that today's economy is at 'full employment', even allowing for 'natural' or 'frictional' unemployment. In a situation where the economy is operating below potential output (less than full employment, however defined) many resources are lying idle. Credit creation for productive investment purposes should therefore increase output.

(8)
$$(\uparrow M_R) \, V_R = P_R \, (\uparrow Y)$$

Likewise, an increase in credit creation for consumption purposes at below full employment would not increase prices. Although the loan would increase the level of demand in the economy, it would also increase output, as firms would start to use some of their unused capacity.

Money creation for house purchases and financial assets

As well as creating credit for investment and consumer purchases, banks may also lend money for the purchase of pre-existing assets, such as housing or shares. Unlike when credit is created for investment, credit creation for asset purchases does not increase the quantity of goods produced in an economy.

Consider Werner's quantity equation for financial transactions ($M_F \, V_F = P_F \, T_F$). An increase in bank loans for house or asset purchases (M_F) will lead to an increase in the price of the asset purchased (P_F), as long as the number of transactions (T_F) remains relatively constant.

(9)
$$(\uparrow M_F) \, V_F = (\uparrow P_F) \, T$$

This is not surprising – mortgage lending creates new money and allocates it into the property market, increasing the demand for houses. With no change in the quantity of houses available to purchase, the most likely effect will be to increase house prices. As Steve Keen (2011) puts it:

> "Population dynamics – even immigration dynamics – have nothing to do with house prices. What determines house prices is not the number of babies being born, or immigrants – illegal or otherwise – arriving, but the number of people who have taken out a mortgage, and the dollar value of those mortgages ... For changes in house prices, what matters is the acceleration of mortgage debt."

In response to the suggestion that mortgage lending increases house prices it could be argued that an increase in the price of an asset acts as a signal (in the housing market) to developers to build more houses: increasing house prices lead to an increase in the number of houses being built, increasing their supply and so leading to a fall in their price. However, this argument falls down on two fronts. First, an increase in house prices tends to increase the price of land. As a result although developers see their revenues rise they also see their costs rise and so rising prices do not turn into increased profit margins. Second, rising prices attract speculators:

> "Though debt acceleration can enable increased construction or turnover, the far greater flexibility of prices, and the treatment of housing as a vehicle for speculation rather than accommodation, means that the brunt of the acceleration drives house price appreciation. The same effect applies in the far more volatile share market: accelerating debt leads to rising asset prices, which encourages more debt acceleration." (Keen, 2012, p. 25)

That asset price rises are inherently pro-cyclical is a point that has also been made by Adair Turner, chairman of the Financial Services Authority. In addition to increasing the demand for credit, he notes that asset price rises may also increase a bank's ability to supply credit:

> "We need also to recognise the role that credit can play in driving asset price cycles which in turn drive credit supply in a self-reinforcing and potentially destabilising process. Thus … increased credit extended to commercial real estate developers can drive up the price of buildings whose supply is inelastic, or of land whose supply is wholly fixed. Increased asset prices in turn drive expectations of further price increases which drive demand for credit: but they also improve bank profits, bank capital bases, and lending officer confidence, generating favourable assessments of credit risk and an increased supply of credit to meet the extra demand." (Turner, 2010, p. 37-38)

That asset price inflation and credit creation by banks interact with each other in potentially destabilising ways will be looked at in more detail in section 4.2. The next section will discuss the possibility that asset price inflation may feed into consumer price inflation.

How asset price inflation can fuel consumer price inflation

The previous section showed how the banking system, through its ability to create credit and channel it to non-productive purposes, can create both asset price and consumer price inflation. In particular, the creation of credit for purchase of pre-existing assets, such as property, was shown to push up its price. However, it is also possible for some of this inflation in asset prices to eventually 'spill over' into consumer prices. This section outlines the channels through which this might occur.

For example, take the case where the price of housing has been pushed up due to an increase in credit creation for house purchases. Any increase in house prices that are considered to be permanent will also increase the perceived life-time wealth of homeowners. The empirical literature suggests a major determinant of consumption spending is wealth, therefore any increase in wealth will likely lead to an increase in consumption.[5] This consumption, however, must be financed in some way. One method is out of savings – for example, an individual may consider their wealth to be the sum of the value of their financial assets (including their house) and the money they have in their bank account. If the value of their house increases, then they can spend some of the money in their bank account whilst leaving total wealth unchanged. This can affect consumer prices, as money which was being treated as savings (and was essentially out of circulation) is now being spent. To the extent that this money is spent on consumer goods, prices will increase. However, increases in consumption through this channel are limited to the extent of an individual's savings.

Rather than spend their savings an individual could choose to borrow against the value of their house. One method of doing so would be to simply borrow more from banks through pre-existing arrangements, such as credit cards and overdrafts, i.e. to increase the uptake of already available credit. However, increases in wealth may also increase the total amount of credit available to individuals (this is known as the financial accelerator; see Box 4.D for more details). To briefly sum up, because of asymmetric information between

---

5. Of course, if only a small percentage of people own their home then any increase in housing wealth will not increase consumption in the population as a whole. And if increases in housing wealth lead to either increases in rent or expected rents then the effect on consumption will depend on the percentage of people renting. In 2002 69% percent of UK households owned property.

borrowers and lenders, financial markets suffer from moral hazard and adverse selection problems. As such lending to households is largely determined by the amount of collateral they can offer – increases in the price of housing (which can be used as collateral) increase the quantity of credit available and decrease its price (the interest rate; Goodhart & Hofmann, 2007).[6] Furthermore, to the extent that a bank's loans are secured on property, increases in house prices may lower the amount of capital banks feel it is prudential to hold against these types of loans, and so increase their lending capacity. In short, rising house prices increase wealth, and this increases both the willingness of homeowners to borrow and banks to lend. More lending increases the amount of money spent on goods and services. With no corresponding increase in production (at full employment), an increase in consumer prices will result.

An additional method through which rising house prices may lead to an increase in consumer price inflation is through the effect on workers' wages. For example, rising property prices will tend to lead to an increase in rents as landlords seek to maintain the rate of return on their investments. Both the increase in rents and house prices are likely to lead to workers who do not own a home demanding higher wages in order to maintain their standard of living. The success of any such demand is likely to rest on multiple factors, some individual to the employee and others determined by the economy (e.g. the unemployment rate). If successful, these demands will increase firm's costs, which may be passed on to the consumer in the form of higher prices.

4.2 FINANCIAL INSTABILITY AND 'BOOM & BUST'

The previous section looked at how, by lending to different sectors of the economy, banks affect economic growth and inflation in consumer and asset prices. In particular the economic effects of bank lending were shown to vary depending on what the newly created money was used for. However, certain elements, although implicit, were missing from the analysis. Chiefly, the long-run dynamic implications of credit creation were ignored, such as the self-reinforcing nature of asset price bubbles, the long run implications of increasing debt, the speculative behaviour of individuals and businesses, and

---

6. To borrow against rising house prices will also depend, to an extent, on the availability of housing equity withdrawal products.

the potential for recessions, depressions, financial crises and debt deflations. This section explicitly outlines these effects using Hyman Minsky's Financial Instability Hypothesis.

Minsky's Financial Instability Hypothesis

Hyman Minsky developed the 'financial instability hypothesis' as an explanation of how financial crises are endogenously created by a modern capitalist economy. Minsky's fundamental insight was that periods of stability led to greater risk taking and debt – that is, stability is itself destabilising. Furthermore this instability tended to be upwards – capitalism tended towards unsustainable booms. Over time booms, their subsequent busts and the response of the authorities to them lead to changes in the vulnerability of the economy to financial crises, which, if they occur, can lead to depressions and debt deflations.

Minsky's analysis begins in a growing economy that has just emerged from a prolonged recession. As a result of recession induced bankruptcies, write-offs and deleveraging, firms and individuals tend to have low levels of debt relative to their equity. In addition, due to the recent recession firms are conservative in their borrowing decisions and banks are conservative in their lending decisions (i.e. only small, low risk investments are undertaken). Borrowing in this stage is broadly of the hedge type (see Box 4.C), so that the revenue expected from the new investments would be sufficient to cover both the interest and principal repayments on the investment loan.

Conservative investments combined with a growing economy results in the majority of loans being repaid and the projects that the loans funded succeeding, with those firms that borrow the most making the highest returns. This apparent success vindicates firms' decisions to borrow and banks' decisions to lend, and it becomes apparent that margins of safety can be revised downwards – i.e. more debt can be taken on and cash flow projections can be revised upwards. Greater investment, financed by an increase in lending from the banking sector, increases profits, lowers unemployment and increases economic growth. Increasing confidence in the future state of the economy leads to asset prices being revised upwards, and this, combined with the revision of acceptable debt structures, increases firms' 'borrowing power'.

The increase in investment, employment, asset prices and growth, financed by an acceleration of debt provided by the banking sector, leads to the beginning

Box 4.C - Minsky's Hedge, Speculative and Ponzi Units

To facilitate his analysis Minsky classified firms and individuals by the way in which they finance their activities, with these classifications being hedge, speculative and ponzi.

Hedge units expect to be able to fulfil their financial obligations (including debt obligations) through their income alone. Hedge units are the most robust type of unit as they are only vulnerable to changes in demand for their goods or the costs of their inputs.

Speculative units are not able to fulfil their debt obligations through their income alone. In the short term their income is only expected to be enough to cover the interest on their loans, not the principal – their debts must be rolled over as they mature. Thus, in order to carry out their day-to-day business, speculative financing units require access to financial markets, making them vulnerable to changes in the interest rate and the availability of finance.

Ponzi[i] units do not earn sufficient income to pay either the interest or the principle on their debts. To pay their debts they must either continually borrow more or sell their assets. These ponzi units make money either through turning into a hedge or speculative units after some time (the unit may have been engaging in a long term investment, for example), or by selling their assets at a higher price than they purchased them for. In addition to having the same vulnerabilities as hedge and speculative units, ponzi units' balance sheets also deteriorate over time as more debt is taken on.

The weight of each type of financing in the economy determines the fragility of the economy to financial crisis. Economies which have a higher weight of firms which fund their operations through ponzi and speculative financing arrangements are more vulnerable than those with a large proportion of hedge firms, which can rely on the income from their investments to service both the interest and principal repayments on their debt.

---

i. The term 'ponzi' is in no way meant to entail that the firm is engaged in any illegal or unsavoury behaviour. It is a normal state of business that some firms will become ponzi financing.

of what Minsky called 'the euphoric economy'. Minsky defined euphoria as when:

> "gross profits in the present-value calculations that had reflected expected recessions are replaced by those that reflect continuing expansion. Simultaneously there is less uncertainty about the future behaviour of the economy." (Minsky, 1966, p. 8)

Growing confidence means firms are happy to take on more debt, debt-to-equity ratios are further reduced, and this makes firms more susceptible to a rise in interest rates.

With rising asset prices and low interest rates (due to the recent recession) economic agents can profit by speculating on the price of assets, and banks can make profits by introducing speculative financing methods. Lending for speculation on assets pushes up the price of assets (as described by Werner's disaggregated quantity equations), and increases feelings of wealth. From the bank's perspective, rising asset prices mean loans are almost always repaid. Collateralised loans can be made to those who cannot afford them (for example, sub-prime/NINJA mortgages), safe in the knowledge that even if the borrower defaults, the loan collateral (the house) can be repossessed and sold for a profit. Secondly, the increased demand for lending increases profits as long as banks are able to meet the increased demand for loans. This puts pressure on banks to innovate in order to increase their lending as much as possible (e.g. through 'regulatory arbitrage').[7]

The ability to profit from speculating on asset prices leads to the emergence of the 'ponzi unit' (which borrows to invest in rising asset prices). Because the cash flows generated by the assets the ponzi unit purchases with borrowed money are not enough to cover either the interest or principle repayments on the loan, the loan can only be repaid if the assets can be sold for more than the value of the loan. The longer the euphoric stage of the economy lasts and the longer assets prices continue to rise, the more units will shift to ponzi positions, relying on rising asset prices in order to be able to service debts (and make profits). The more economic units that shift into ponzi positions the more fragile the economy becomes to any kind of shock that stops speculation on the asset - without increases in the price of the asset ponzi units loans cannot be repaid, potentially leading to bank insolvency and financial crisis. Meanwhile, the interest rates on liquid assets increases, as people sell them in order to purchase those (less liquid) assets whose prices are rising.

Under euphoric conditions the economy becomes increasingly indebted. As these debts are used to finance non-productive asset price speculation, the debt of the economy increases without a corresponding increase in the capacity

---

7. A prominent example of such innovation in the run up to the most recent crisis was the creation of collateralised debt obligations, which allowed banks to move assets off their balance sheets, freeing up capital for more lending.

Box 4.D - Irrational exuberance

"Historians will marvel at the stability of our era."

Gerard Baker
The Times, January 2007

Prior to the most recent financial crisis, optimistic expectations within financial markets, the economics profession, and the general public were not hard to find. Belief in a 'great moderation' – that improvements in understanding the economy led to greater control of the business cycle through monetary policy – were endorsed by a wide range of economists including Ben Bernanke, Governor of the Federal Reserve (Bernanke, 2004). This behaviour is not surprising – psychologists have shown that success boosts confidence (Shiller, 1999). Thus extended periods of stability lead economic agents to revise what they believe to be 'safe' debt-equity ratios, spurred on by the proclamations of 'experts' (who believe themselves to have tamed the business cycle).

One cause of over-optimism as to the future state of the economy is 'disaster myopia'. Guttentag and Herring (1984) describe disaster myopia as the systemic underestimation by decision makers of the likely occurrence of low frequency events, such as asset price collapses. The lower the frequency of an event and the greater length of time since the last event occurred the less accurate decision makers' predictions will be. When applied to economics and banking, disaster myopia explains the psychological reasons why bankers are unable to incorporate the risk of asset prices falling into their lending decisions.

An example of disaster myopia can be seen in Herring and Wachter's (2002) model, in which real estate markets are prone to bubbles because the supply of real estate is fixed (in the short term) and difficult to short sell. As a result house prices rarely fall, and this leads to disaster myopia amongst bankers, who therefore lend more money than they otherwise would into the property market, pushing up prices in the process.

Disaster myopia also occurs during a crash. The occurrence of a low frequency shock (such as a bubble bursting in the housing market) in the recent past leads decision makers to overestimate the probability of a similar shock occurring soon after. Banks react by cutting lending by more than the true probability of a crash reoccurring suggests they should. Regulators, who also suffer from disaster myopia, will likewise overestimate the probability of the event reoccurring, and increase regulation more than they otherwise would which may lead to further contractions in lending (Herring & Wachter, 2002).

of the economy to pay back its debt. Furthermore, due to profit opportunities brought about by the economy's apparent stability, the proportion of economic units engaged in 'speculative' and 'ponzi' financing increases. While the economy may be booming, the increased debt burden and over reliance on borrowing from financial markets have made the economy more vulnerable to financial crisis.

As interest rates continue to rise, either because of market forces or because of the central bank trying to prevent the economy from overheating, some projects that were 'hedge' (self-financing) at the lower rates of interest become 'speculative' (dependent on further borrowing), and some that were 'speculative' become 'ponzi' (dependent on capital gains). Because ponzi units have to sell their assets in order to service their borrowings, the increasing number of ponzi units results in more assets being brought to market. Meanwhile, the increase in the interest rate reduces the level of new borrowing for asset purchases. The sudden increase in the supply of assets along with the decrease in demand for them leads to a reduction in their price (or a slowing down in the rate of price increase). Consequently, ponzi units find that neither the sale of their assets nor the cash flow which the asset generates is enough to cover the debt incurred in the purchase of the asset, and are therefore unable to repay their loans.

The bursting of the bubble

The increase in nonperforming loans and the drop in the price of assets leads banks and businesses to revise their expectations of the future downwards. Banks respond by reducing lending, as well as by increasing the price of loans (the interest rate), which pushes even more borrowers into speculative and ponzi positions. Decreased optimism about the future also lowers the demand for funding from businesses, as does the rising price. As a result bank balance sheets, which expanded during the boom, begin to contract. In the absence of government intervention the reduction in lending, spending and the stock of money creates deflationary pressures in the economy, increasing the real value of debt and making it even harder for indebted firms to repay their loans. As defaults occur on debts, bank assets shrink, which can result in a financial crisis as banks become insolvent or see their capital fall below levels mandated by the Basel Capital Accords (see section 3.4), leading to further contractions in lending. The unwillingness of banks to lend due to increased pessimism about the future of the economy, a general increase in debt to equity ratios due to capital attrition through debt defaults, and the desire to rebuild balance sheets makes it hard for businesses to acquire funding, including those which were not directly affected by the crisis. Even those businesses that can acquire funding may find interest rates too high. The focus on paying down debts,

Box 4.E - Supplementary reasons for asset bubbles

The Financial Accelerator: Bernanke and Gertler (1989) present a model as to how asset price rises can fuel further asset price rises. Imperfect information between borrowers and lenders (i.e. the borrower knows more than the lender as to their likelihood to repay) creates 'agency costs' for banks. Borrowing is accordingly more expensive than it would otherwise be. Because of their ability to post collateral, higher net worth borrowers have lower agency costs. This reduces asymmetric information and moral hazard problems, making the bank more willing to lend. When asset prices rise during a boom, agency costs fall for those that hold the assets. This is the 'financial accelerator' mechanism: higher net worth during booms (due to higher asset prices) leads to lower agency costs and therefore increased borrowing. This borrowing tends to increase demand for assets, raising their prices. This increases net worth further, which reduces agency costs and so allows further borrowing.

Leverage targets: The leverage ratio for a bank is given, broadly, by dividing the bank's shareholder equity (including retained earnings) by its aggregate tangible assets.[i] Its leverage, or level of leverage, is the inverse of this ratio. Adrian and Shin (2008) find evidence that financial institutions target a specific level of leverage. As a bank holds capital assets, during a boom an increase in asset prices strengthens the bank's balance sheet. This leads to a fall in the bank's leverage.

As banks target a specific level of leverage, in order to restore the desired ratio they borrow more, and use the proceeds to buy more of the assets that they already hold. Increased asset purchases pushes up asset prices, which leads to a fall in the level of leverage, which in turn leads to further purchases – a positive feedback loop. Conversely, during asset price downturns the exact opposite occurs – falling prices lead to higher leverage ratios, and as the bank is targeting a specific level of leverage they start selling off assets. If this leads to a fall in the price of the asset then leverage will increase, requiring further asset sales – a positive feedback loop. Adrian and Shin conclude that the pro cyclical behaviour of banks in response to changes in leverage is likely to exacerbate fluctuations in asset markets.

i. Technically, it is defined as Tier 1 capital/(Total assets – intangible assets) – see D'Hulster (2009).

combined with lower investment, leads to lower output, lower employment and downward pressure on wages. This lowers demand for goods and services, with the end result that otherwise healthy businesses that were not directly involved in the bubble can go bust.

This decrease in demand is likely to be particularly painful for smaller firms – without access to capital markets small firms are likely to find it difficult to roll over their debts, increasing their likelihood of bankruptcy. For example, after 10 years of recession in Japan "193,000, mainly small and medium-sized companies" had gone bankrupt (Werner, 2005, p. 303). Large firms, on the other hand, are likely to have access to capital markets and the ability to pledge collateral for bank loans.

When the bubble bursts the fundamental problem facing the economy is that the debts incurred in purchasing assets cannot be repaid with the earnings the assets generate. As a result, Minsky argued that the bursting of an asset price bubble could result in a variety of outcomes, depending on the level of inflation and extent of government intervention. These are detailed below.

No government intervention, high inflation:
If the rate of inflation is high when the bubble bursts, the cash flows from assets will soon increase to a level where they cover the costs of debt repayment (which do not rise with inflation), despite the fact that investment and growth have decreased. Because of this bankruptcies are limited, although liquidity is decreased. While a depression is avoided, little else is changed, and this, combined with the absence of a 'real' crisis sets the stage for a repeat performance.

No government intervention, low inflation:
If after the bubble bursts the rate of inflation is low, the cash flows from investments will not increase quickly enough to a level which allows investors to repay their debts. In this situation the bursting of the bubble can lead to a mass selling off of assets, resulting in a debt deflation process of the type described by Irving Fisher. In Fisher's (1933) formulation, the process is as follows:

"(1) Debt liquidation leads to distress selling and to (2) Contraction of deposit currency, as bank loans are paid off, and to a slowing down of velocity of circulation ... cause[ing] (3) A fall in the level of prices ... [as a result] there must be (4) A still greater fall in the net worths of business, precipitating bankruptcies and (5) A like fall in profits, which in a "capitalistic," that is, a private-profit society, leads the concerns which are running at a loss to make (6) A reduction in output, in trade and in employment of labor ... lead[ing] to (7) Pessimism and loss of confidence, which in turn lead to (8) Hoarding and slowing down still more the velocity of circulation. The above eight changes cause (9) Complicated disturbances in the rates of interest." (p. 342)

Thus the actions of market participants serve to exacerbate the initial fall in asset prices, and the economy enters a downward spiral from which it is difficult to escape.

Debt deflations are likely to be particularly painful for smaller firms. Minsky (1986), shows that in the event of a modest decline in demand (e.g. in a recession), firms that are price takers will be forced to lower prices. With costs fixed in the short run, lower prices may affect firms' ability to repay any outstanding debts. Conversely, those firms which are price setters (i.e. those that have market power) will be able to resist the downward pressure on prices. Because of this, Minsky concludes that: "Market power, which allows a firm to constrain price movements when demand falls, may be a prerequisite for the use of expensive and highly specialized capital assets and large-scale debt financing" (1986, p. 181). Essentially, banks will favour lending to firms with market power, as their ability to constrain downward price movements during recessions and depressions decreases the risk of them defaulting on a loan.

Due to the negative effect of debt deflations on small firms and banks preferring to lend to firms with market power, once the economy recovers prices are likely to increase, as the remaining large forms exercise their market power in order to increase prices.

With government intervention:
Alternatively, the government may choose to intervene and attempt to increase cash flows to prevent the debt deflation and associated depression. The most visible interventions in 2007-08 crisis were the bank bailouts, which were mainly designed to ensure the continual functioning of the financial markets and prevent the spread of panic. In addition, the government may increase spending – so called countercyclical spending. In a country with a social safety net a proportion of this spending will occur automatically, as an increase in unemployment results in an increase in transfer payments to individuals (e.g. benefits). Both autonomous and non-autonomous spending will at least partly offset the fall in demand by increasing cash flows to businesses and the newly unemployed.

The government may also intervene (through the central bank) in order to attempt to prevent bank lending from contracting. This commonly takes the form of a reduction in interest rates. However, as shown in section 3.5, confidence, not the interest rate, is the primary determinant of bank lending. As a result during the current financial crisis the central bank also engaged in direct purchase of government bonds from non-banks (Quantitative Easing), which effectively increased both broad and base money in equal amounts, as well as the price of gilts and other assets. It was thought that the increase in asset prices (and reduction in yields) would lead to an increase in spending via 'wealth effects'. Monetary policy interventions have therefore attempted to maintain asset prices and spending, and prevent the stock of money from shrinking.

The government may also attempt to engineer higher levels of consumer inflation, in an attempt to make debts easier to repay (as above). As Minsky describes, "Inflation, which increases nominal cash flows, can become a policy instrument to validate debt" (1986, p. 190).

Problems with intervening – unintended consequences of fiscal policy

Government intervention can create problems for the economy in the long run. Taking the case of fiscal interventions first, the suggestion that the government should act counter-cyclically is relatively uncontroversial and has been standard economic practice since Keynes. However, financial crises and their accompanying recessions/depressions require government interventions of a different order of magnitude than the standard boom-bust cycle. In particular, the most recent set of bank bailouts have pushed UK government debt to a record post-war level.[8] While a country that has the power to print money cannot default on its debts denominated in its own currency (as it could in extreme cases simply print money to pay its debts), there are economic and political reasons to want to keep the government debt burden within a particular range.

First, an increase in national (government) debt necessitates large interest payments to bond holders which may lead to political pressure to cut government spending on public services. To the extent that some of these services are crucial for the private sector to prosper, lowering spending on them may slow the long-term potential growth rate of the economy. Furthermore, high levels of government debt may limit (politically or economically) the government's ability to engage in countercyclical spending that may help the

---

8.   This is mainly as a result of the growth of the British banking industry relative to the size of the economy – currently in the UK the ratio of domestic banking assets to GDP is the highest it has been at any comparable time in history (from 50% of GDP in the 1950s to 550% of GDP in 2010).

economy emerge from recession. This result has been found empirically by Taylor (2012):

> "Exposure to a credit boom can make recessions painful, but when combined with an adverse fiscal position at the onset of the crash, economies are perhaps even more vulnerable. Such empirical evidence would suggest that even if the stakes are lower in normal recessions, countries with more "fiscal space" are better able to withstand a financial crisis, perhaps by having room to offer stabilizing support to their economy (or at least dodge austerity)."

Second, rather than cut spending the government may attempt to increase taxes in order to pay back its debt. An increase in taxes may harm any recovery, by lowering disposable income and therefore demand for goods and services. Third, although not a problem in the middle of a recession, public debt may crowd out private sector investment when the economy picks up again.

Problems with intervening – unintended consequences of monetary policy
Monetary policy interventions may also create unintended consequences. When the central bank lowers the interest rate in response to recessionary conditions it benefits borrowers at the expense of savers. Pension funds in particular may suffer: lower interest rates increase the net present value of future liabilities, increasing the need for higher current fund contributions. Financial crises may also lead to unorthodox monetary policy (such as Quantitative Easing). Because quantitative easing pushes up the price of bonds it also lowers their yield, again increasing required contributions to pension funds.

Furthermore by decreasing the yield on bonds, QE increases the desirability of other assets, pushing up their prices. This can have long run effects. By purchasing assets the central bank may prevent prices from falling, and so 'set a floor' under their price, implicitly guaranteeing prices and legitimising prior investment decisions.[9] Rightly or wrongly the investor is led to believe that asset prices will not be allowed to fall below a certain level. With the investor

---

9. A recent example of such behaviour was the 'Greenspan put', which was the name given by financial markets participants to the belief that when financial markets unravel the chairman of the Federal Reserve (Alan Greenspan), would come to the rescue. Nobel Laureate in Economics Joseph Stiglitz cited the 'Greenspan put' as one of the causes of the speculative bubble which led to the financial crisis (Stiglitz, 2010).

gaining from the upside but not suffering from the downside of his or her decisions, further risk taking and speculative behaviour is encouraged, which may lead to further asset price inflation and financial crisis. In effect profits are privatised and losses are socialised.

Consequently, while the government may offset the worst of a financial crisis, its actions may have unintended consequences, namely increasing inflation and making a future crisis more likely:

> "the economic relations that make a debt deflation and a long-lasting deep depression like that of the 1930s unlikely in a Big Government economy can lead to chronic and, at times, accelerating inflation. In effect, inflation may be the price we pay for depression proofing our economy." (Minsky, 1986, p. 165)

The Financial Instability Hypothesis

To sum up, the essence of the Financial Instability Hypothesis is that booms and busts, asset price bubbles, financial crises, depressions, and even debt deflations all occur in the normal functioning of a capitalist economy. What is more, periods of relative stability increase the likelihood of instability and crisis by increasing returns and thus the desirability of leverage. The banking sector, with its ability to create credit, facilitates this desire for leverage, which sets in train a series of events that culminate in recession and in some cases a financial crisis and depression. In short, Minsky considered the capitalist system to be inherently unstable. The next section will examine some recent evidence for the role of credit creation by banks in causing booms, busts, and financial crises.

4.3 EVIDENCE

The central contention of the previous section was that bank lending has real macroeconomic effects. In particular, it was argued that bank loans – i.e. money creation– for the purchase of pre-existing assets, such as property, leads to an increase in its price. Over time price increases lead to a self-reinforcing and destabilising process whereby price increases lead to more lending and so ever increasing debt, until eventually the debt burden becomes too large and the asset bubble bursts. Often this will lead to a recession, and in the most extreme cases it may also lead to a financial crisis as defaults on loans set in train a chain of events that result in bank runs, bankruptcies and potential debt deflation.

The following section will briefly look at the evidence for this theory, by examining the role of private debt – predominantly bank loans – in financial crises, including the Great Depression of the 1930s and the Financial Crisis of 2007/08. It will also examine evidence for whether recessions that are not associated with financial crises are also the result of excessive bank lending.

Financial crises

Figure 4.1 shows data on private and public debt in the US since 1920. Prior to both the 1930s and 2007 private debt – bank lending – increased dramatically relative to GDP, with debt levels plunging thereafter.

This data is unsurprising considering what we know about financial crises. In the 1930s banks were primarily lending for the purchase of securities on the stock market. The increase in the demand for securities led to an increase in their price (the 1920's stock market boom). Eventually bank lending slowed, lowering demand, and this fed through into lower (or decelerating) securities prices. The bursting of the bubble triggered a wave of defaults, bank runs and insolvencies, a debt deflation and a depression.

Likewise, as shown by figure 4.1 for the US and 4.2 for the UK, the run up to the 2007/08 financial crisis was characterised by banks rapidly increasing lending and therefore their creation of money. Much of this new money went into the financial and property markets, pushing up the price of property in the process (outlined in detail in Box 4.E). As Adair Turner (2012) put it: "The financial crisis of 2007/08 occurred because we failed to constrain the private financial system's creation of private credit and money". When the debt burden became too large, speculators began selling property, leading to a large drop in its price and a wave of defaults as 'ponzi' investors could no longer afford to make loan repayments. This bursting of the property bubble precipitated the financial crisis as financial products backed by these mortgages (mortgage backed securities) fell in value, which led to a crisis in the shadow and normal banking systems as the institutions holding these products saw the asset sides of their balance sheets shrink.

Increased lending by banks in the run up to a financial crisis is in fact a common feature of all financial crises. Looking at a dataset comprising 14 advanced countries between 1870 and 2008, Schularick and Taylor (2009) find that "for the most part, financial crises throughout modern history can be viewed as "credit booms gone wrong" (Eichengreen and Mitchener, 2003)". The most important variable in predicting financial crises, they find, is past

fig. 4.1 US Debt to GDP from 1920

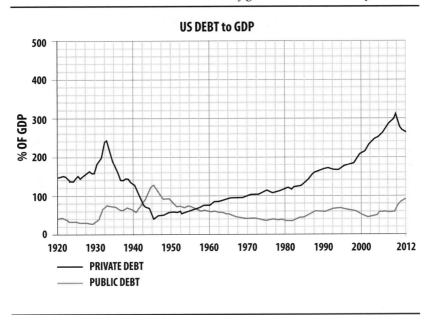

Source: Keen, 2012a

fig 4.2 UK Debt to GDP from 1987

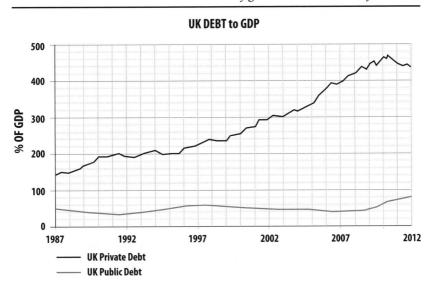

Source: Keen, 2012a

fig. 4.3 - Change in Debt and Employment since 1992

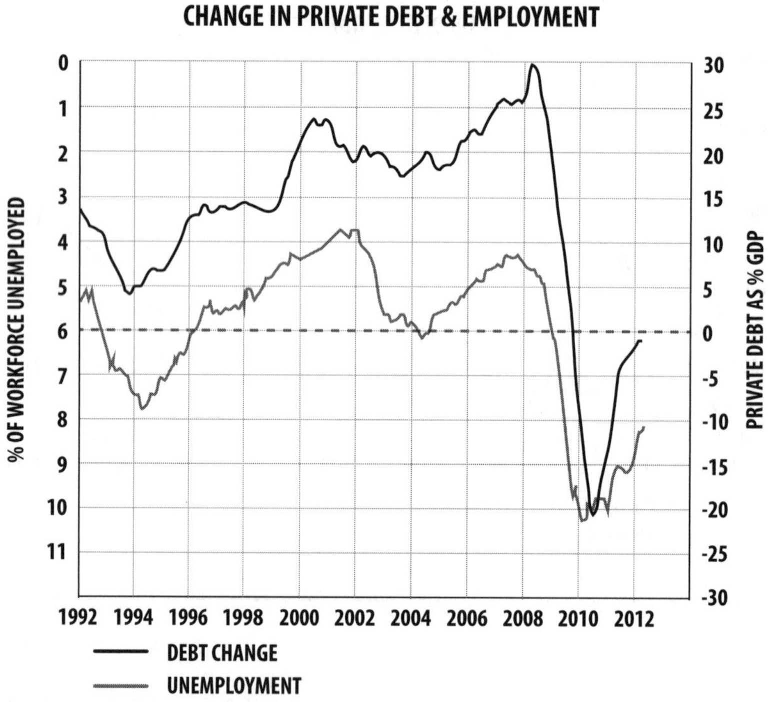

CHANGE IN PRIVATE DEBT & EMPLOYMENT

DEBT CHANGE
UNEMPLOYMENT

Source: Keen, 2012b

credit growth, a result which is robust even when they control for other key macro variables. In a separate paper Taylor (2012) goes further, stating that:

> "Over 140 years there has been no systematic correlation of financial crises with either prior current account deficits or prior growth in public debt levels. Private credit has always been the only useful and reliable predictive factor."

These results would seem to validate the theories of economists such as Minsky.

What are the effects of financial crisis on the economy? As outlined earlier, an increase in lending by banks increases purchasing power and so aggregate demand in the economy, and this leads to a boom – either directly through increases in lending to businesses or consumers, or indirectly due to the effects of lending on assets prices and therefore on wealth and consumption. As a result there is a strong causal link between increasing debt and falling

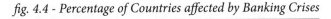

fig. 4.4 - Percentage of Countries affected by Banking Crises

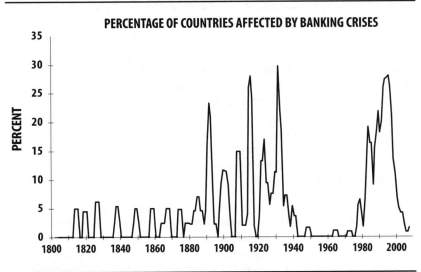

Source: Reinhart and Rogoff, 2008

unemployment. However, crucially an increase in debt beyond the earning capacity of the economy is unsustainable.

Figure 4.3 shows the data outlining the relationship in the UK between the change in private debt and unemployment since 1992. As expected, changes in debt are strongly correlated with the level of unemployment. The unproductive lending that resulted in the 2007/08 financial crisis brought about a collapse in assets prices and a sharp reduction in bank lending as banks re-evaluated their views of the future downwards. The net repayment of loans meant less money creation and therefore less spending, which lowered aggregate demand and thus increased unemployment.

Likewise, GDP also falls sharply during and after financial crises. Schularick and Taylor (2009) find that for 14 developed countries over a 140 year period, on average "in the aftermath of postwar financial crises output dropped a cumulative 6.2 percent relative to trend." These financial crisis-associated recessions tended to be around a third more costly than normal recessions and resulted in a slowdown in inflation (although since World War Two this effect has been less pronounced, possibly due to more aggressive policies by the central bank and the government to avoid debt deflation (Jordà et al.

Box 4.F - The house price bubble

In the years preceding the most recent financial crisis, bank lending created a bubble in the property market in several countries. For example, Keen (2012) calculates that 78% of the change in American house prices over the past 25 years and 60% of the change in Australian house prices over the past 30 years can be explained by the acceleration in mortgage debt. Meanwhile, in the UK house prices increased threefold between 1995 and 2007 (Nationwide, 2012). Contrary to popular belief, the increase in house prices was not fuelled by there being 'too many people and not enough houses'. As Figure 4.5 shows, between 1997 and 2007, the number of housing units grew by 8%, while the population only grew by 5%. Meanwhile mortgage lending increased by 370% over its 1997 level.

The resulting 206% increase in house prices significantly reduced the disposable income of anyone who purchased a house after 1997. As an example, if an individual on an average salary of £25,200 took out a 25 year mortgage on an average house in 2007, the repayments would account for 47% of their salary over that period (assuming the unlikely scenario that average interest rates on mortgages remain at the historically low level of 4.5%). In contrast, the same person buying the same house in 1995 would only spend 24% of their salary servicing their mortgage debt. Because of excessive money creation by the banking sector, most young people today have effectively been priced out of ever being able to own their own home.

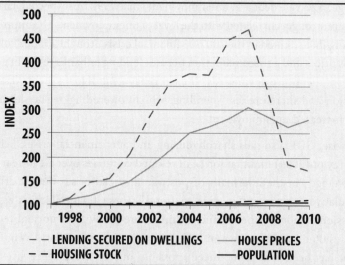

fig. 4.5 - UK property prices, 1997 – 2010 (Indexed, 1997 = 100)

Source: Nationwide house price survey 2012, Bank of England Statistical Database

> The flip side of this is people that owned or purchased property in the run up to the crisis now feel much wealthier. However for many this wealth is not accessible as it is tied up in their house. The only way to release it is to either run down their other savings, or borrow against the value of the house through housing equity withdrawal/release schemes (i.e. taking on debt secured against the value of the house). Therefore, the real beneficiaries of the housing bubble were those who purchased several properties in order to speculate on prices rising. Banks also benefitted – banks profit from debt, and higher house prices mean larger mortgage loans, longer loan durations, and more money earned in interest.
>
> The housing bubble can therefore be seen as a massive transfer of wealth, from those without property (i.e. the poor and the young), to those with property (i.e. the wealthy and the old), as well as to speculators and banks.

2010). Real investment after financial crises falls by more than 22 percent on average, which is likely to lead to a reduction in future output.

These results point to a serious problem with the current monetary system – the financial sector is perfectly capable of destroying itself and the rest of the economy on a periodic basis. Worryingly, these crises tend to occur with some regularity – in the UK there has been 12 banking crises since 1800, with 4 of those coming since 1945 (Reinhart & Rogoff, 2009). Globally the situation is similar – Figure 4.4 shows the percentage of countries in a banking crisis between 1800 and 2007 (so excluding the most recent financial crisis)

Normal recessions

Can normal recessions (i.e. those not caused by a financial crisis) also be caused by excessive credit creation by banks? Using the same 14 country 140 year dataset as Schularick and Taylor (2009), Jordà, Schularick and Taylor (2012) show "that throughout a century or more of modern economic history in advanced countries a close relationship has existed between the build-up of credit during an expansion and the severity of the subsequent recession." As Taylor (2012) explains in a subsequent paper:

> "...that credit booms matter as a financial crisis risk factor is a rather narrow conclusion, and that a more general and worrying correlation is evident. During any business cycle, whether ending in a financial crisis recession or just a normal recession, there is a very strong relationship between the growth of credit (relative to GDP) on the upswing, and the depth of the subsequent collapse in GDP on the downswing."

*fig. 4.6 - Real GDP per capita % deviation a year following a recession/
financial crisis*

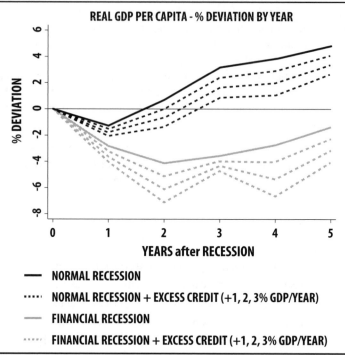

REAL GDP PER CAPITA - % DEVIATION BY YEAR

── NORMAL RECESSION

····· NORMAL RECESSION + EXCESS CREDIT (+1, 2, 3% GDP/YEAR)

── FINANCIAL RECESSION

····· FINANCIAL RECESSION + EXCESS CREDIT (+1, 2, 3% GDP/YEAR)

Source: Jordà, Schularick and Taylor, 2012

Essentially, excess credit creation by the banking sector increases the severity of any subsequent downturn, whether it results in a financial crisis or just a normal recession. Figures 4.6 and 4.7 show the path of real GDP per capita and real investment per capita from the beginning of a recession. The solid grey lines show recessions associated with a financial crisis, while the dashed grey lines show recessions associated with a financial crisis where there was 'excess' credit creation during the boom. The solid black lines show normal recessions, while the dashed black lines show normal recessions where there was 'excess' credit creation during the boom.

The charts show a clear relationship between the quantity of excess credit creation during a 'boom' and the depth and length of any subsequent 'bust'. While financial crises associated with excess credit creation stand out as particularly painful, excess credit growth also results in longer lasting and deeper recessions in general, whether or not they are accompanied by a financial crisis. As

fig. 4.7 - Real investment per capita following a recession/financial crisis

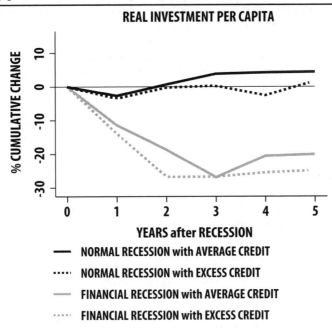

REAL INVESTMENT PER CAPITA

YEARS after RECESSION

— **NORMAL RECESSION with AVERAGE CREDIT**

····· **NORMAL RECESSION with EXCESS CREDIT**

— **FINANCIAL RECESSION with AVERAGE CREDIT**

····· **FINANCIAL RECESSION with EXCESS CREDIT**

Source: Jordà, Schularick and Taylor, 2012

Taylor (2012) notes, "economic outcomes are systematically worse the larger has been the prior credit boom".

4.4 OTHER ECONOMIC DISTORTIONS DUE TO THE CURRENT BANKING SYSTEM

As shown in Chapter 3, under the current banking system the key determinant of a bank's lending is how profitable it believes a loan will be. In a boom almost all loans are profitable and so banks create too much credit, which has the effect of amplifying the boom. This can lead to asset price bubbles and financial crises, which endanger the very banks that created the bubble in the first place. For these reasons, over the years a range of methods that attempt to control credit creation by banks have been introduced (as outlined in section 3.4), as have various regulations to protect banks and their depositors in the event of a crisis.

Box 4.G - Mal-Investment

Because credit creation increases purchasing power in the economy it can alter prices, particularly when applied to assets that have a fixed supply, such as land. Whilst credit is not a scarce resource, prices are the signalling method through which scarce resources are allocated (premises, equipment, labour etc). Money creation can therefore distort price signals, changing the returns on investment in certain sectors, whilst diverting investment away from other sectors of the economy. When the expansion of credit is reversed, so too are the price changes. Accordingly, investments that were expected to be profitable are revealed to be so only because of the effect of bank lending on prices.

A prominent example of mal-investment caused by credit creation occurred in Ireland in the run up to the financial crisis. Bank lending altered prices by so much that a fifth of the entire Irish workforce ended up employed building houses and almost a quarter of the country's GDP came from construction. This resulted in Ireland building over seven times as many new houses a year, proportional to its population, as the UK.

The house price bubble also reduced investment in pensions, as people began to see houses as a better long-term investment. Data released by the Office of National Statistics in connection with the 2006-08 Wealth and Assets Survey shows that in the UK 60% of respondents overall agreed or tended to agree that property was the best way to save for retirement, compared with 49% supporting pensions (Daffin, 2009). Comparable figures are not yet available for the 2008-10 follow-up, however preliminary analysis shows that people overestimated the value of their property in 2006-07 compared with figures from the Land Registry, Halifax and Nationwide, and underestimated the extent to which these had declined since then (Black, 2011).

It is unlikely that many, if any, of those using property investments as a way of preparing for their retirement fully understood that the rising house prices were not due to economic fundamentals, but rather due to a 370% increase in the amount of money being created by the banking sector for property purchases. In other words, those people using property as an alternative to a pension did not have the knowledge to understand why the house price inflation was an artificially fuelled bubble. Their underinvestment in other assets may be compounded if/when the bubble in the UK housing market bursts – they may find their savings (in the form of property) insufficient to cover their outgoings. An increase in the future poverty of pensioners is the likely result.

In addition, the bursting of the housing bubble will leave many with properties that are worth less than the mortgage that they took out to buy them (i.e. negative equity). Consequently, house price bubbles fuelled by banks have the effect of misleading people about their long-term interests and diverting savings away from pensions provision, with people slow to revise their beliefs appropriately when the bubbles collapses.

Finally, excess returns in the financial sector resulting from the design of the monetary system bids resources away from other, productive enterprises. As James Tobin remarked in 1984: "We are throwing more and more of our resources, including the cream of our youth, into financial activities remote from the production of goods and services, into activities that generate high private rewards disproportionate to their social productivity." As a result the economy as a whole suffers. Cecchetti and Kharroubi (2012) have found that: "Finance literally bids rocket scientists away from the satellite industry. The result is that erstwhile scientists, people who in another age dreamt of curing cancer or flying to Mars, today dream of becoming hedge fund managers."

While some of these interventions have been more successful than others, all have had unintended consequences. These are outlined below.

Problems with deposit insurance & underwriting banks

As section 3.3 showed, in a banking system with deposit insurance or banks that are 'too big to fail' there is no incentive for a bank's creditors to monitor the bank's behaviour. As Mervyn King (2010) explains:

> "Many treat loans to banks as if they were riskless. In isolation, this would be akin to a belief in alchemy – risk-free deposits can never be supported by long-term risky investments in isolation. To work, financial alchemy requires the implicit support of the tax payer ... For a society to base its financial system on alchemy is a poor advertisement for its rationality."

Instead of those that benefit from the upside of lending to banks also losing out if the loans go bad, it is the taxpayer that stands to lose – risk and reward are not aligned. Conversely, in a system without deposit insurance, depositors and bank creditors have a big incentive to monitor their bank's behaviour, to ensure it does not act in a manner which may endanger its solvency and their deposits. While they may benefit from the upside of an investment (by receiving interest on their deposits/lending), they also suffer the downside if things go wrong (i.e. they may not receive the full value of their deposit back). Risk and reward are aligned.

Deposit insurance removes a depositor's incentive to monitor bank lending decisions because they are guaranteed to receive their money back regardless of the underlying investments. This is known as moral hazard.[10] Because deposits in different banks are equally 'risky' when they are all underwritten by the government, for banks the cost of attracting central bank reserves (via customer deposits) is not affected by whether they are making high-risk or low-risk investments. With all investments via banks effectively risk-free because of government guarantees, the bank that offers the highest interest rate on its deposits will tend to find that funds flow to it from the other banks. This problem is explicitly referred to in a handbook written by the Bank of England's Centre for Central Banking Studies:

> "Bank depositors may, therefore, contribute to moral hazard if deposit insurance means that they no longer feel obliged to assess the credit risk associated with depositing money with a particular bank. In such a situation, depositors may choose banks without reference to their relative financial condition. This means that they will probably choose banks solely in accordance with the attractiveness of the interest rates they offer. Consequently, the normal impact of market forces in promoting prudent economic behaviour is reduced and unsound banks may attract additional deposits." (MacDonald, 1996)

However, any bank that wishes to attract depositors by raising the interest rate it pays on deposits will have to increase the interest rate it charges on its loans in order to maintain its spread (and therefore its profits). In general, higher rates of interest result in riskier projects being financed. Additionally, the lack of monitoring by depositors may encourage banks to make riskier loans. So, despite the fact that deposit insurance is intended to increase the stability of the banking system by preventing bank runs, it may in fact reduce stability by encouraging risky behaviour:

> "The U.S. Savings & Loan crisis of the 1980s has been widely attributed to the moral hazard created by a combination of generous deposit insurance, financial liberalization, and regulatory failure ... Thus, according to economic theory, while deposit insurance may increase bank stability by reducing self-fulfilling or information-driven depositor runs, it may

---

10.   Moral hazard is when the provision of insurance changes the behaviour of those who receive the insurance in an undesirable way. For example, if you have contents insurance on your house you may be less careful about securing it against burglary than you otherwise might be.

fig. 4.8 - Variation in the implicit subsidy

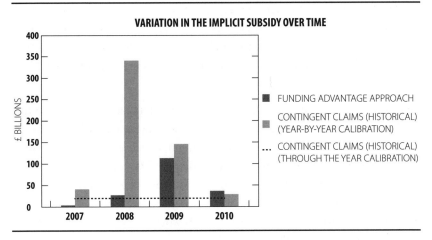

Source: Noss & Sowerbutts, 2012

decrease bank stability by encouraging risk-taking on the part of banks."
(Demirguc-Kunt & Detragiache, 2002)

Demirguc-Kunt & Detragiache go on to empirically test for whether deposit insurance increases or decreases the stability of a banking system. Based on an analysis of a large panel of countries over the years 1980 -1997 they find that:

> "explicit deposit insurance tends to be detrimental to bank stability, the more so where bank interest rates have been deregulated and where the institutional environment is weak. We interpret the latter result to mean that, where institutions are good it is more likely that an effective system of prudential regulation and supervision is in place to offset the lack of market discipline created by deposit insurance."

In conclusion, by removing incentives to monitor banks lending decisions, deposit insurance allows banks to make a greater number of loans and riskier loans than they otherwise would be able to, increasing financial instability. In addition, deposit insurance also contributes to a subsidy for the banking sector, as explained below.

Subsidising banks

As a result of deposit insurance and the negative effects of bank insolvency on the economy as a whole, some banks are seen as being too big or systemically important to fail. As we have seen, insurance has had unintended consequences, chiefly by creating 'moral hazard' – those that lend to the bank pay less attention to how their money is used because they know that the bank won't be allowed to go bust. In both cases this leads to the bank engaging in riskier behaviour than it otherwise would do – both in terms of the quantity of its lending (i.e. its leverage) and who it lends to. This makes banks more likely to need the insurance in the first place.

However, insurance also results in the banks receiving a subsidy. Those that lend to the bank (including depositors) are willing to accept lower interest rates on their loans than they otherwise might, because of the lower risk of non-repayment. Consequently the bank pays out less interest than it otherwise would have to. Instead, it is the government, and by implication the taxpayer, that underwrites the risk of the loan going bad. The Bank of England has calculated that some years this subsidy is worth in excess of £300bn (Noss & Sowerbutts, 2012) (although this figure depends on the method used to calculate the subsidy).

The subsidy tends to be higher in years where the banks are seen as more likely to need government support.[11] Noss and Sowerbutts conclude that, "despite their differences, all measures point to significant transfers of resources from the government to the banking system." (2012, p. 15)

In some years the value of the subsidy has been high enough that it is difficult to see how the banks would have been profitable without it. As well as transferring resources from the public to the banking sector, the guarantee also distorts competition between banks: the larger/more systemically important a bank is, the more likely it is to be rescued if it finds itself in distress. As a result large banks receive a bigger implicit subsidy, lowering the rate of interest they have to pay to borrow. This places large banks at a competitive advantage to smaller banks, stifling new entrants and competition. Furthermore larger banks that offer substandard products are less likely to be forced out of the market, (as they would be in other industries), reducing social welfare.

In conclusion, the inherent instability of the banking sector and the negative impacts of this instability compels the government to provide insurance, which, due to moral hazard, actually increases the risks that banks take – so increasing financial instability. On top of this it results in a subsidy to the biggest banks, which distorts the market and prevents competition, lowering

---

11.   The differing values are a result of the different methods used to calculate the subsidy, with each approach having various advantages and disadvantages.

social welfare. This subsidy increases the profits of the largest banks. Higher profits allow these banks to increase their capital, and therefore make more loans (and therefore create more money) than they otherwise would be able to.

Distortions caused by the Basel Capital Accords

Section 3.4 outlined the effect of the Basel Capital Accords on a bank's ability to make loans. To briefly recap, the second Basel Accord requires that a bank's capital is at least 8% of its risk-weighted assets. The reasons a bank is required to hold a set amount of capital are twofold. Firstly, it protects depositors if some of a bank's assets are defaulted upon. Secondly, it is thought to be able to both limit and direct a banks lending.

The Basel Accords also stipulate that a bank's assets should be 'risk weighted' when calculating capital requirements. 'Risk weighting' refers to the fact that different assets require differing amounts of capital to be held against them, reflecting the riskiness of different types of lending. When the capital requirements are calculated, the value of each type of asset on a bank's balance sheet is multiplied by its risk-weighting to give a figure for total risk-weighted assets. For example, banks are allowed to hold less capital against loans for house purchase (35% risk-weighting) than against loans they make to business (75% risk-weighting). Loans to governments have a 0% risk weighting – meaning banks don't have to hold any capital against this type of lending at all (which usually takes the form of holding bonds).

While the wisdom of allowing banks to treat government bonds as a risk free asset seems questionable in the wake of the European sovereign debt crisis, something that has received less attention is the incentive effect of allowing banks to hold lower capital against mortgage lending. At the level of an individual bank this makes perfect sense – because mortgage lending is collateralised, even in the event that the borrower defaults the bank will not make a significant loss (as long as the value of the house does not fall).

However, this also incentivises banks to favour mortgage lending over other types of bank lending, as their capital bases will support more of these types of loans (compared to business lending, for example). At the level of the entire banking industry, lower risk weights on housing may in fact increase the likelihood of a bank becoming insolvent, as they make asset price bubbles (and their associated financial crises) more likely. As we saw in section 4.1, the limited availability of land, combined with banks' ability to increase the purchasing power in an economy when making loans, makes the housing market particularly prone to asset price bubbles.

When the bubble bursts banks tend to find themselves with loans that cannot be repaid, and houses that are worth less that the loans they made against them. As a result banks may find themselves insolvent. Thus, forcing banks to risk-weight their assets may increase the potential for asset bubbles and financial crisis, and therefore increase the chances of bank insolvency – the very thing the risk weighting was meant to prevent in the first place.

CHAPTER 5

SOCIAL AND ENVIRONMENTAL IMPACTS OF THE CURRENT MONETARY SYSTEM

The previous chapter discussed the economic effects of the current monetary system, showing how through its normal functioning it could lead to booms, busts, and occasionally financial crises and depressions. In this chapter we will address some of the other impacts of the monetary system. In particular, we will look at the effect of the monetary system on inequality, public and private debt, the environment and the health of democracy.

5.1 INEQUALITY

The current economic system depends on an adequate supply of money being available for transactions between households, businesses and government. However, as section 3.2 showed, for there to be money, some people must be in debt. Even the small amount of cash which is not created by the commercial banking sector can only enter the economy in exchange for bank deposits. Consequently, in effect the non-bank sector must 'rent' the entire stock of money from commercial banks, resulting in a constant transfer of wealth from the rest of the economy to the banking sector, through interest payments.

In 2011 this rent totalled £109 billion - that is the non-banking sector paid this much in interest to the banks for the benefit of having a stock of money of roughly £2 trillion. However, this figure is artificially low due to the current historically low interest rates. For example, before the Bank of England lowered interest rates (in 2008), banks earned just over £213 billion in interest

fig. 5.1 - Banking burden on households

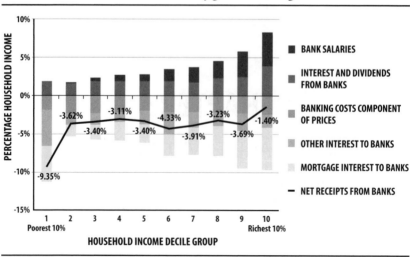

Source: Hodgson (forthcoming)

payments alone. This is a charge for something that could be provided at a much lower cost by the state.

Figure 5.1[1] shows how the banking sector transfers money towards the wealthy. On the vertical axis is the percentage of household income which is either received from or paid out to banks, while the horizontal axis splits households into deciles by income, with the poorest 10% on the left and the richest 10% on the right. The black line shows the net monetary burden/benefit of banks on each decile - that is whether the banks pay out more in interest and wages than they take in the form of interest on loans, overdrafts and credit cards. As is shown, the burden of interest payments as a percentage of household income disproportionately falls on those households in the lower deciles, while the benefits of this interest, in the form of interest payments, bank dividends and staff pay, disproportionately benefits the top decile of income earners.

---

1. The figures are drawn from analyses conducted by Positive Money combining statistics on the revenues and expenditure of UK banks (published by the Bank of England) and surveys of the finances of British households and small and medium-sized businesses commissioned by UK government and held at the UK data archive. Note the analysis only covers payments paid directly to and from banks - consequently payments made via intermediaries (e.g. pension funds) are not included. For this reason, the chart shows no net beneficiaries of bank interest payments.

Are these results surprising? In the previous chapter we saw that house prices have increased enormously since the mid 1990s, largely as a result of the surge in bank lending into the property market. Consequently, individuals have had to devote a greater percentage of their income to mortgage repayment and rent (as higher house prices tend to lead to higher rents). This implies a proportionally larger reduction in disposable income for poorer households. Meanwhile, those with more than one property, buy-to-let landlords and property speculators have all benefited from the increase in house prices. Unsurprisingly, these groups tend to be located in the higher income deciles. Higher house prices, fuelled by money creation, have therefore acted as a mechanism to transfer wealth from lower to higher income households.

Banks have benefited significantly from the increase in house prices. Higher house prices increase both the size of the average mortgage and the length of time over which it will be repaid, increasing the amount of interest paid to banks. The increase in profits produces higher levels of staff remuneration and dividend payments to bank shareholders. Because (some) bank employees tend to be very well remunerated, and because financial assets tend to be unequally distributed, the increase in bank profits also had the effect of transferring wealth towards the higher income deciles.

In addition to the large increase in lending for property, the last 20 years has seen a large increase in bank lending to the financial sector (see chart 3.4), and this has fuelled asset price inflation. This disproportionately benefited the financial sector (including investment banks), the employees of which again tend to be concentrated in the upper income deciles.

The current monetary system also tends to redistribute wealth geographically. As we have seen, the effect of charging an interest rate on every pound in existence leads to a large transfer of wealth from the rest of the economy to the banking sector. In the UK the headquarters of the major banks (and thus the high earning bank employees) are located in the London area, and this has the effect of transferring wealth towards London.

Finally, as section 4.2 showed, the banking sector periodically experiences crises when asset price bubbles (themselves created by bank lending) burst. While the initial effect of a fall in asset prices will affect mainly those who hold the assets, the subsequent bank bailouts and recession will lead to both increases in government debt and unemployment. An increase in government debt beyond a certain level tends to trigger fiscal austerity by government, resulting in cuts to the public services that are often relied upon by those on low incomes.[2]

5.2 Private debt

Under the current monetary system almost all money is created with a corresponding debt. This means that for one group of people to have a positive bank balance, another group needs to be in debt by the same amount. For there to be money, there must also be debt. Money is vital for the economy to function; without it, individuals and businesses would not be able to trade. Thus in the modern monetary system debt is not a choice: for the economy to function efficiently some people must be in debt.

Debt is also higher than it needs to be as a result of the fact that bank lending causes asset bubbles in necessities such as housing. When banks lend against assets that have a supply that cannot increase quickly (e.g. housing) or totally fixed supply (e.g. land) such lending pushes up house and land prices and often results in a bubble. Consequently individuals have to borrow more in order to purchase property, increasing the level of debt even further.

Any attempt by individuals and businesses to partially repay debts in aggregate will result in significant problems for the economy, as debt repayment leads to less new money being created and thus less new spending. In addition, a smaller stock of money, without an increase in velocity will also mean less spending and therefore less economic activity. As we have seen, this can result in recession and increased unemployment, and in the worse case, debt deflation and financial crisis.

Is it likely that an increase in velocity will offset a fall in the stock of money? Debts tend to increase in boom periods (e.g. during Minsky's 'euphoric' economy), and this tends to inflate asset prices and so feelings of wealth. Boom periods are also characterised by a reduction in 'margins of safety' as people attempt to decrease their money holdings by shifting their wealth into less liquid assets. Both the increased level of wealth and the desire to lower holdings of liquid assets (such as money) lead to an increase in spending, increasing the velocity of money.

---

2.   For example, in the EU the Maastricht Treaty requires governments to cut expenditure when the debt to GDP ratio exceeds 60%.

However, the 'bust' period is characterised by a deflation in asset prices as people attempt to pay down their debts (quicker than new loans are being made). This in itself leads to a reduction in the money stock. Likewise in the bust the perceived level of uncertainty is higher and as a result the demand for liquid assets (such as money) as a store of wealth increases. The increase in the demand for money as a store of wealth increases interest rates, lowers the percentage of money available for transactions, and lowers the velocity of circulation. As a result, any attempt to reduce debts *en masse* tends to lead to a recession. Furthermore recessions themselves can actually lead to an increase in debt amongst those on lower incomes, as the increase in unemployment and bankruptcies and the decrease in income can lead people to borrow more in order to make ends meet. This trend can be seen in the UK with the increasing prominence of payday loans and similar schemes in the wake of the financial crisis and subsequent recession.

In conclusion, as long as the majority of the money in circulation is created by banks making loans, it is very difficult for the public to significantly pay down private debt without also creating a recession.

5.3 PUBLIC DEBT, HIGHER TAXES & FEWER PUBLIC SERVICES

Seigniorage is the name given to the 'profit' that is derived by the government as a result of its ability to create money, in the form of notes and coins. However, notes and coins make up only a tiny proportion of the total money supply. Because the Bank of England (and the government) has left the responsibility for creating the majority of money to the private banking sector, it has forsaken the profit that comes on creating this money. For example, from 2002 to 2009 banks increased the amount of money in circulation by roughly £1 trillion. If the government had instead benefited from this money creation, then UK residents could have paid £1 trillion pounds less in taxes, or public services could have received £1 trillion more. Alternatively, the entirety of the UK government's national debt, which currently stands at just over £1 trillion pounds, could have been repaid.

Calculating seigniorage
In the UK the Royal Mint creates and sells coins at the cost of production (metal plus manufacturing) to HM Treasury. The coins then become assets of the Treasury, held on the balance sheet. They are then sold to banks at face

value, so that the Treasury earns the profit on the production of coins, with the profit being the difference between the cost of manufacture and the face value of the coins.

Bank notes, on the other hand, are created under the authority of the Bank of England by the specialist printer De La Rue. As is the case with coins, De La Rue is paid a fee to cover the cost of printing notes. However unlike coins, bank notes are not assets of the Treasury, but liabilities of the Bank of England. As a result, the seigniorage the Treasury receives from notes is not the face value of the notes minus the costs of printing. Instead, the seigniorage comes from the fact that unlike the other liabilities of the Bank of England, bank notes do not pay any interest (reserves, for example, pay a rate of interest, currently equal to the policy rate). For notes to enter circulation the Bank of England sells the notes to the commercial banks in exchange for central bank reserves. These reserves are in normal times borrowed from the Bank of England using repos, and, because the Bank of England pays interest on them (as well as charging banks the same rate of interest to borrow them) they are revenue neutral for the Bank (see Box 2.E). However, bank notes do not pay interest, and so the Bank of England saves the interest payable. Seigniorage is therefore the quantity of notes in circulation times the interest rate paid on reserves (currently the policy rate). Between 2000 and 2009, this came to £18 billion, and was paid directly over to the Treasury, saving the public £18 billion in taxes.

5.4 ENVIRONMENTAL IMPACTS

The following section looks at how the monetary system impacts on the environment as a consequence of the government's response to the boom-bust cycle, the funding of certain industries, and the effect of the monetary system on growth.[3]

Government responses to the boom bust cycle

As outlined in Chapter 4, the current monetary system creates an inbuilt tendency for the economy to experience temporary booms followed by recessions. This may also be followed by financial crisis when the burden of debt

---

3.   We would like to thank Beth Stratford for her input, which has greatly improved our understanding of these impacts.

becomes too large to service. While the business cycle itself has a relatively neutral effect on the environment (excluding the mal-investment effect on resource use) the same cannot be said of the government's response to these cycles, which tends to involve removing environmental regulations and reducing spending, as outlined below.

Environmental regulation in economic downturns

In a recession it is common to hear the argument that the costs of businesses are too high due to regulations which are represented as onerous, and that the relaxation of these regulations would allow businesses to hire, resulting in reduced unemployment and increased output. Although the validity of this argument is debatable, there can be no doubt that it is propagated by those who believe it to be true, by those who see the recession as an opportunity to lower their costs, and by those who did not believe the regulations were required in any case. While the benefits of environmental regulations accrue over the long-term, the government's chances of re-election usually hinge on the short-term health of the economy. As such the long-term environmental benefits of regulation often lose out to short-term political and economic considerations.

Government spending in economic downturns

Due to the volatile nature of the economic system the government periodically engages in counter-cyclical spending to mitigate downturns, prevent debt deflations, and bail out failing banks. To increase spending usually requires an increase in government debt as taxes tend to fall during recessions. Governments may also target a debt to GDP ratio below a certain level – in the EU, for example, the Maastricht Treaty requires governments to cut expenditure when its debt to GDP ratio exceeds 60%. Thus, to be able to borrow during recessions the government must ensure its debt burden does not become too large beforehand. To do so, it must not succumb to the general euphoria that is pervasive during the boom, and instead use the booming economy as an opportunity to build up budget surpluses. Needless to say, over the years governments have proved themselves unable to follow these rules, or prevent boom and bust. The majority of regulators, central bankers and academic economists, although not facing election, also appear to be incapable of resisting the prevailing consensus. Ben Bernanke, for example, famously spoke of a "great moderation" and the end of the business cycle just prior to the financial crisis.

Consequently, the government is often not in an ideal financial situation when a recession or financial crisis occurs. The most recent financial crisis is a good example of this – many governments felt the need to implement austerity measures as their debt to GDP ratios exploded due to large increases in government spending (as a result of bank bailouts and increased unemployment benefits) and reductions in tax revenues (due to the recession).

The pressure to cut spending may result in environmentally beneficial projects being cut, such as green energy subsidies or long term investments in science and technology that are not well provisioned for by the private sector.[4] After all, from a political perspective it is much easier to cut a program of primary scientific research that may or may not be beneficial at some unspecified point in the future than it is to cut public services that people rely upon in the present (such as health or education).

Funding businesses

Under the current monetary system banks acquire central bank reserves (base money) when payments are made to their customers' bank accounts. Customer deposits provide banks with a cheap source of central bank reserves, which are required to make the payments to other banks that may result from the issuing of loans. However, despite helping to fund the loans, depositors have no say and little idea over the use of 'their' money. They may therefore be unwittingly helping to fund loans to organisations that harm the environment. Because of a lack of transparency and depositor control the investment decisions of banks (and therefore of society) are driven almost exclusively by the short-term profit considerations of bank employees.[5] The effect of this is to decrease the cost of funding for certain industries over others, while ignoring society's preferences as to what is funded. This is in marked contrast to other forms of lending, where those providing the funds know what they will be used for and are able to withhold them based on this information.

---

4. The private sector is often unwilling to engage in the primary scientific research that advances scientific knowledge, due to extremely long and uncertain time periods between project implementation and fruition, the lack of certainty that anything of (marketable) value will be discovered, and the difficulties in monopolising and monetising the profits on anything that is.

5. The requirement to maximise short term shareholder value is passed on to bank staff through bonus and incentive structures.

Forced growth

Many concerned with the environment favour a steady state economy, which can be defined as:

> "… an economy with constant stocks of people and artefacts, maintained at some desired, sufficient levels by low rates of maintenance 'throughput', that is, by the lowest feasible flows of matter and energy from the first stage of production to the last stage of consumption." (Daly, 1991)

The crucial defining factor of a steady state economy is that it does not exceed the 'carrying capacity' of its natural environment. Carrying capacity can be defined as the maximum population that can be sustained indefinitely by the environment, given that the physical components of the planet (natural resources, human populations, etc.) are constrained by the laws of physics and the ecological relationships that determine their rates of renewal. This is problematic as any economy that continually grows (typically characterised by increased use of physical resources) will eventually exceed the 'carrying capacity' of its natural environment.

Is a steady state economy possible? Mainstream economics claims it is, as growth is merely one potential option for the economy. However, traditional growth models abstract from important features of the economic system which might make such an economy unsustainable in the longer term. In particular they do not include banks, money or debt. Once we allow for these institutions there are several reasons for thinking that a steady state economy may not be possible.

First, according to Duesenberry's relative-income hypothesis, individuals attempt to emulate the spending habits of their peers. However, as outlined earlier in the chapter, the current monetary system transfers wealth towards those with higher incomes. The increase in inequality leads to an increase in debt as people borrow in an attempt to 'keep up with the Joneses". The increase in debt increases inequality (through the mechanisms outlined earlier), which further increases borrowing, debt, and so on, in a self reinforcing cycle. The increase in demand and debt forces growth as firms produce more to satisfy demand and individuals work more in order to pay off higher levels of debt.

Second, borrowing from a bank requires payments to be made on fixed dates, with penalties for failing to repay on time. The requirement to repay the money borrowed plus interest within a fixed period of time incentivises the borrower (whether a business or a household) to pursue activities that provide quick returns in excess of the amount repayable. To the extent that people pay off debts by producing goods and services, higher levels of debt incentivise higher levels of growth.

Third, the monetary system facilitates asset price bubbles in essentials such as housing. More recently, speculation has been blamed for increasing food prices.[6] In order to maintain standards of living when faced with an increase in the cost of essentials, individuals must either work more in order to pay the higher prices, or borrow more to make up the difference. Both borrowing and more work increase economic growth, as outlined in the previous two paragraphs.

Fourth, the repayment of bank loans destroys money (in the form of bank deposits held by the public). If new loans are not taken out to replace the loans that are being repaid spending will be lower, and consequently, stagnation and recession may result, which can lead to debt deflation and other negative consequences. Thus the government must design policy in order to encourage individuals and businesses to become indebted, to ensure that growth is maintained and debt deflations and recessions do not occur. In the UK examples of such policies (whether deliberately designed for this purpose or not) include the recent Bank of England 'Funding for Lending Scheme' and the ability of firms to deduct interest payments against taxes.

Fifth, according to a paper by Binswanger (2009), any rate of growth below a positive threshold level will be unsustainable in the long term. Binswanger explains that banks profit from creating and lending money to firms for investment, and in return they receive a rate of interest on the loan. Firms use these loans in order to invest and increase their output. When loans are repaid the principal is destroyed, removing money from the economy, while the interest on the loan is profit for the bank. Much of this interest is recycled into the economy in the form of staff payments and dividends to shareholders; however, the bank may retain some of this interest income in order to increase its capital. The act of removing purchasing power from the economy (because money is destroyed when loans are repaid and a proportion of interest repayments goes into retained earnings) reduces the amount of money available to purchase the additional goods that the firms in question initially borrowed to produce. This represents a loss of income to firms as their payments to banks

---

6. For information about speculation on food prices see Schutter (2010) and Baffes & Haniotis (2010).

will not flow back to them. As such firms will only be able to make a profit in the aggregate if the money removed from the economy through debt servicing and the retention of bank earnings is replaced with further borrowing, which will create additional production and consequentially growth. Without the additional borrowing firms' outgoings will exceed revenue (i.e. they will make losses), which in the long run will lead to a fall in investment and bankruptcies. This will slow growth and profits further, and the whole economy will spiral downwards.

As a result, Binswanger claims that in the current monetary system there can only be a growing or shrinking economy – a zero growth economy desired by environmentalists is not possible, as it will collapse into a negative growth economy. This negative growth economy is not the one of declining resource use and sustainable lifestyles that is required to deal with the environmental and energy crises; it is one of recession, unemployment and the same pressures on government described earlier.

5.5 THE MONETARY SYSTEM AND DEMOCRACY

The following section looks at how the monetary system impacts on democracy as a result of a) the misconceptions around what it actually is banks do, b) confusion as to the benefits and costs of banking, c) the lack of depositor control over 'their' money, and d) the dependency on banks to create money.

Use of 'our' money

Banks require reserves in order to make payments to other banks (facilitating the transfer of deposits around the banking system). A bank can acquire these reserves through several channels. For a bank, the cheapest of these is to simply allow customers to deposit cash, which can then be exchanged with the central bank for reserves. Additionally, the bank allows its depositors to receive payments from the customers of other banks, which will eventually involve a transfer of reserves from the bank in question to itself (after all payments have been netted). Thus, depositors help fund bank's lending activities (although, as we have seen, banks do not require reserves in order to lend).

The absence of any control by depositors over how banks are able to use the funds they provide means that an environmentalist's deposits could be funding oil extraction and a pacifist's deposits could be funding arms manufacturers. It could be argued that environmentalists and activists should take care to bank ethically. However, as this section makes clear, a large proportion of the population are unaware that banks are not large safety deposit boxes.

Of course no one is forced to open a bank account or to keep their money in it, and members of the public could refuse to fund banks' activities by simply refusing to have a bank account and dealing only in cash. However, it is almost impossible to live in the modern world without a bank account, and most employers will not pay salaries in cash. It is also impossible for everyone to opt out. In this way people are effectively forced to fund the lending and investment decisions of banks, potentially against their own ethics and wishes.

The misconceptions around banking

There is widespread ignorance and confusion among the public about how banks actually work and what they do with the funds we provide to them. A poll conducted by ICM on behalf of the Cobden Centre found that 74% of the public thought that they were the legal owners of the money in their account (Evans, 2010). In fact, all money deposited in bank accounts is the legal property of the bank, leaving the bank free to use the money as it sees fit. Instead, of having ownership of their own money, the customer instead has a claim on the bank, which allows them to request the bank to make payments on their behalf.

Not only are many customers unaware that any money they deposit into a bank is no longer legally theirs, a significant proportion are unaware that the bank uses deposited money to help fund its loans and investments. When told that the bank does not keep their money safe in its vaults but will put at least some of it at risk, 33% most agreed with the statement: "This is wrong – I haven't given them permission to do so." (Evans, 2010)

The contrast with the pensions industry in this regard is striking. In the 1990s campaigners ensured that the Pensions Act was amended to require that the trustees of occupational pension schemes disclose "the extent (if at all) to which social, environmental or ethical considerations are taken into account in the selection, retention and realisation of investment" (The Occupational Pensions Schemes (Investment) Regulations 2005). Yet nothing even vaguely similar is on the horizon in banking.

The lack of knowledge as to what banks do has severe implications for the state of democracy. After all, how can there be a meaningful democracy without public understanding of such an important issue as what happens to your money when it is deposited in a bank account?

The power to shape the economy

The previous section showed that banks are able to use the funds that flow to them, as a result of payments made to their depositors, without the permission of the depositor. Yet the actual deposits themselves were created by banks through the process of making loans. Currently 97% of money in the hands of the public exists in the form of deposits held by banks. In contrast, only 3% was created by the government, in the form of cash.

The banks therefore have massive power to shape the UK economy. This power is even greater than that of democratically elected government, because the banking sector allocates more money via lending than the government allocates via public spending. In the five years running up to the start of the financial crisis, the banking sector's gross lending to households and individuals alone (not including lending to businesses) came to a total of £2.9 trillion. Meanwhile, total government spending during the same period was less at £2.1 trillion. Because the banks decide where to lend (for example, on housing, personal loans, car finance or investment in small businesses), they can shape much of the spending and activity in the economy. Indeed, as shown in section 4.1, if banks lend to productive business the economy will thrive. If instead they lend for speculative or non productive purposes earnings will stagnate, and rising debt will create recessions and potentially financial crises.

It is important to note that neither the quantity nor direction of bank lending is determined by 'the market'. As shown in section 3.5 (on credit rationing), the quantity of lending is not determined by the interaction of the demand for, and supply of, credit. Instead, due to the fact that the level of the interest rate alters the probability of repayment, banks limit the interest rate they charge and instead ration credit. Banks determine the quantity of lending, and therefore the quantity of money and debt in the economy.

Likewise, the allocation of new lending is not determined by the relative returns on different projects. Rather, it is determined by the likelihood of repayment, and the ability to collateralise loans to ensure that non-repayment does not result in a loss to the bank. In fact, less than 10% of all bank lending today goes to businesses that contribute to GDP – the vast majority goes towards mortgages, real estate companies, and financial intermediation. If these lending decisions had been made by local bank managers who were in touch with the local economy and knew where any investment could be most productive, then banks having greater 'spending power' than government may not be such a matter for concern. However, lending decisions are not made by local branch managers, instead they are made by senior managers at the head offices of the banks, based on a statistical analysis of the relative likelihoods of repayment. In an economy with a large number of small banks, no single bank would have any control over the direction of the economy. However, in the UK the five largest banks (HSBC, Barclays, Santander, RBS, Lloyds/HBOS) account for 85% of the current account market (2010), 61% of the savings account market (2010), 64% of the unsecured personal loan market (2009), 74% of the mortgage market (2009) and 84% of liquidity management services to small and medium-sized businesses. (Treasury, 2011)[7] As of September 2011, these five banks had just a total of 78 board members.[8]

The force driving the board members of banks is the need to maximise profit over the short term (to maximise shareholder value). However, what's profitable in the short term is likely to be bad for the bank and the economy in the longer term. In the short run banks prefer to lend to the unproductive sector: it's easier, cheaper, and appears to be safer than lending to real business. Indeed, as long as the price of the asset that collateralises the loan is increasing, the bank doesn't even need to worry about the borrower's ability to repay, as it can repossess the asset and recover the amount originally lent (the same applies if the bank can securitise the loan.) Yet in the longer term this type of lending is not sustainable, and will inevitably lead, if left long enough, to recession and possibly financial crisis. Profit maximisation by banks therefore tends to lead to government bailouts of banks, reducing the amount that governments are able to spend on programmes they were elected to pursue, and in some cases endangering the solvency of the government. As Alessandri and Haldane (2009) put it:

> "In the Middle Ages…the biggest risk to the banks was from the sovereign. Today, perhaps the biggest risk to the sovereign comes from the banks. Causality has reversed."

Why should profit maximisation by a private company reduce the ability of a democratically elected government to undertake its mandate?

---

7. For this calculation Santander is not one of the five largest providers, and as such the figure instead includes data from Alliance and Leicester.

8. RBS: 14 board members; Lloyds 12; HSBC 19; Santander 20; Barclays 13. As of September 2011.

Dependency

In 1943 Michal Kalecki argued that it was the government's reliance on big business to provide investment and jobs that gave capitalists the power to influence government:

> "Under a laissez-faire system the level of employment depends to a great extent on the so-called state of confidence. If this deteriorates, private investment declines, which results in a fall of output and employment (both directly and through the secondary effect of the fall in incomes upon consumption and investment). This gives the capitalists a powerful indirect control over government policy: everything which may shake the state of confidence must be carefully avoided because it would cause an economic crisis." (Kalecki, 1943)

Today, the government's dependence on banks gives them similar powers – for a modern economy to function money and banks are required. Small and medium sized businesses, unable to access the capital markets, rely on banks to provide funds so that they can invest and grow. These firms provide a large part of the growth and the majority of the employment in any economy, so their ability to secure financing is of crucial importance to the health of the economy – hence the government's attempts to 'get banks lending again'.[9]

Today, the banking sector regularly argues against any reform or regulations by reminding the government that they are completely reliant on the banks to provide funding to industry, as the recent comments by Josef Ackermann of Deutsche Bank AG attest:

> "There can be no doubt that reforms will produce a drag on economic recovery and this means that jobs that should be created and that need to be created may not be created. The actions by the regulatory authorities … may steer credit away from important segments of the economy, such as small and medium-sized enterprises, which are the engines of job creation in the mature economies today." (2010)

---

9.   Furthermore, the supply of money crucially depends on banks' willingness to lend at least as quickly as loans are being repaid. If banks are unwilling to do so, eventually the stock of money will shrink to zero. As a result, we are completely reliant on banks to provide the money required in order that the economy functions smoothly.

The current monetary system means we are reliant on banks to issue the nation's money and to ensure that sufficient amounts of this money reach businesses in the real economy. It is this reliance that gives banks power over governments themselves.

Confusing the benefits and costs of banking

The financial sector is often viewed as, at least in terms of tax revenue, 'the goose that laid the golden eggs', implying that we should not to be too hasty in interfering with the way these firms do business. However, the tax raised from the banking industry is only one side of the equation – the positive side. But there are also costs associated with banking: just as pollution is a cost of the oil industry, financial crises, debt, and economic instability are costs of the banking industry.

The most obvious and quantifiable of these costs is the direct cost of bailing out failed banks. Less direct costs associated with the unemployment, lost production, and lower growth that result from a banking crisis are not as easy to measure. Moreover, financial crises are not the only item on the negative side of the equation: the banking industry has long benefited from various subsidies which are often overlooked due to ignorance about how banks actually work. If our democratically elected decision-makers are led to believe that the financial sector makes a bigger net contribution to the Exchequer than it actually does, then the decisions they make regarding banking reform will be distorted in favour of banks at the expense of society as a whole.

Benefits of banking

What are the benefits of the banking sector? In 2009-2010 the government's total tax revenue was £490.6bn, of which only £2.1bn (less than half of one percent) came directly from the banks in the form of corporation tax. Another £15.2bn (around 3%) came from the banks' employees in the form of income tax and national insurance contributions. The other £473bn (roughly 97%) in taxes came from outside the banking sector. So, whilst contributing a modest percentage, the banking industry is hardly one of the biggest contributors to the government's coffers (HMRC, 2011).

Banks have also faced a one-off payroll tax (commonly known as the 'bonus tax'), and currently pay a yearly 'bank levy'. The payroll tax was a temporary one-off tax on bankers' bonuses, which totalled £2.3bn (net) in 2010-11. The bank levy was expected to raise £1.9bn in 2011-12, and £2.5bn a year from 2012-13, roughly equivalent to the revenue raised by airport taxes. However, whilst these amounts are not insignificant, they only add a fraction to the total tax bill banks will have to pay. It is worth noting that banks, unlike other industries, are exempt from paying VAT - an exemption that the Institute for Fiscal Studies has said is neither necessary nor logical (Institute for Fiscal Studies, 2011).

Since the crisis, the banking sector has contributed less tax as its taxable income has been reduced by large losses and write-downs. However, even when banks' tax payments were at their highest - £23.3bn in 2007-2008 - they were still dwarfed by tax receipts from the manufacturing sector, which totalled £63.3bn in the same period (Erturk et al., 2011).

Costs of banking

The most obvious cost associated with the banking sector is taxpayer support to the banks. Although the government's guarantees to the banks at one point totalled £1.16 trillion, this amount now stands at £456.3 billion. Over the long term it has been suggested that the total direct cost to the taxpayer will be below £20 billion (Haldane, 2012), and representatives of the banking industry have argued that the government may actually make a profit on the sale of partly nationalised banks. Viewed in this light, the financial crisis has not been that bad – in fact the tax revenue from the banking sector in 2009-10 alone may cover the bill. However, this conveniently ignores all the other costs of the financial crisis, such as the redundancies, unemployment, failed businesses and the massive rise in national debt that resulted from the recession. These costs far exceed any potential profit that the government might make on its 'investments' in RBS and Lloyds/HBOS. As Mervyn King, Governor of the Bank of England (2003 - 2013), pointed out in a recent speech:

> "The loss of world output from the financial crisis is enormous, even though such a crisis might be considered a once in a generation, or even once in a century, event. It is not difficult to see that a crisis that reduces output by between 5% and 10% for a number of years, and occurs once every fifty years, amounts to an annual cost several multiples of the revenue that will be generated by the UK bank levy." (2010)

Estimates as to these costs vary. As Haldane (2012) points out, with world GDP around 6.5% lower in 2009 than it would otherwise have been, lost output for the world economy could be as high as £2.5 trillion that year. In the UK, economic output in 2009 was about 10% lower than it would otherwise have been, corresponding to £140 billion in lost output or about £3,000 per adult. Moreover, low output is likely to persist with the present value of output losses for the world predicted to be anywhere between $60 trillion and $200 trillion and in the UK between £1.8 trillion and £7.4 trillion. For the banking sector to actually cover the costs of the crises it creates, it would need to pay a global levy of around $1.5 trillion a year (Haldane, 2012), making the UK's £2.5 billion bank levy look trivial and completely disproportionate to the real costs of the banking system.

Subsidies

We have already discussed the subsidy that the banking sector receives in section 3.3, with estimates ranging from around £20 billion a year on average, up to £350 billion plus in particular years. A further subsidy to the banking sector arises from allowing banks the power to create money when they make loans. Without this power, banks would have to attract deposits before lending. Furthermore, banks that wished to lend money would have to find depositors who would be happy to put their money into the equivalent of a 'time deposit' (a deposit that cannot be withdrawn for a certain period of time). Depositors would be likely to demand a higher interest rate on their savings to compensate them for this inconvenience, decreasing the profitability on any given loan. Huber and Robertson (2000) calculate that this special profit was worth £21bn in the year 2000. However, since then the quantity of money has been more than doubled by private bank lending. As such, this 'special' profit is also likely to have more than doubled.

To conclude, banks contribute only a small proportion of the total tax take, receive massive subsidies, levy hidden inflation taxes and periodically require bailing out at great expense to the taxpayer.

2

THE REFORMED
MONETARY SYSTEM

CHAPTER 6

PREVENTING BANKS FROM CREATING MONEY

Part One of this book critically examined the current monetary system. Chapters 1-2 began with a brief history of money and banking, before moving on to discuss the mechanics of the current system. In particular we saw that banks create money when they make loans. Chapter 3 looked at what determines the demand and supply of credit, concluding that the high demand for credit combined with ineffective regulations leaves the quantity of new lending, and therefore the amount of money in circulation, in the hands of the banks. Chapters 4 and 5 asked, given the structure of the current monetary system, what is the likely result? The normal functioning of such a system was shown to result in periodic booms, busts, and occasionally financial crises, depressions and even debt deflations, as well as serious consequences for growth, unemployment, investment, house prices, public and private debts, inequality, the environment, and democracy. With such a wide range of negative consequences, we feel obliged to ask the question first put forward by Mervyn King - of all the ways of organising money and banking, is the best really the one we have today?

In the second part of this book we describe an alternative monetary system that we believe addresses many of the weaknesses of the system we have today. Chapters 6-8 outline how the reformed banking and monetary system would work, contrasting this against the existing system, while Chapters 9-10 explain the impacts of the reformed system. In this sense the second part of this book parallels the first part: Chapters 6-8 correspond to Chapters 1-3, with Chapters 9-10 corresponding to Chapters 4-5.

In this chapter the new monetary system is introduced, beginning with the different types of bank account available to customers and the new accounts a commercial bank will hold at the central bank. A description of the mechanics of how banks will make loans is then given, to show that lending post-reform does not create new money. This is followed by a brief description of how the reformed system aligns risk and reward and allows banks to fail. The procedure for injecting new money into the economy is covered in chapter 7, while chapter 8 deals with the transition from the current system to the reformed system. A detailed explanation of the accounting structure of the new system is covered in Appendix III.

6.1 An overview

After the reform commercial banks will no longer have the ability to create money, in the form of the numbers which appear in a customer's current account. Instead, all money that can be used to make payments will be created exclusively by the central bank. Thus, unlike in the current system where two types of money circulate separately – central bank created reserves which are only used by the banking sector, and commercial bank created deposit money which is used by everyone else – in the reformed system there is no longer a split circulation of money, just one integrated quantity of money circulating among banks and non-banks alike. This money will exist in two forms – physical cash and electronic money created by the central bank.

Physical money, or cash, will be created under the authority of the Bank of England, with coins manufactured by the Royal Mint, and notes printed by specialist printer De La Rue. There is therefore no significant change from the existing arrangements.

Electronic money, created by the central bank, will be the equivalent of central bank reserves. This electronic money will exist in a computer system at the central bank, just as central bank reserves do today. However, whereas present-day central bank reserves can only be held or used by banks and the central government, after the reform the electronic money created by the central bank will belong directly to members of the public, businesses, and also to banks. This does not mean that the central bank will need to provide millions of accounts to the general public. As explained below, commercial banks will continue to administer this electronic money and the payments system on behalf of customers. The process governing the creation of this money is discussed in detail in Chapter 7.

After the reform there will be two distinct types of bank account available to businesses and members of the public:

Transaction Accounts will hold the risk-free electronic money (created by the central bank), which can be used to make payments via the usual channels. They cannot be used by the bank to fund its own lending or investments and will therefore never be put at risk. Behind the scenes, this risk-free money is actually held at the Bank of England, rather than on the bank's balance sheet, so that even if the bank becomes insolvent and fails, the money in Transaction Accounts is protected and cannot lost. Transaction Accounts, and the payment networks that allow electronic money to be transferred from one Transaction Account to another, collectively will make up the payment system.

Investment Accounts are a way for a customer to hand money to the bank on the understanding that the bank will invest or lend it – i.e. intentionally place it at risk and try to earn a rate of return for the customer. The customer placing funds into an Investment Account will have to agree to lose access to those funds for a period of time, and will also bear some of the risk of the investment.

From the perspective of a bank customer, these two account types broadly correspond to a) the present-day current/checking account, where money can be withdrawn or spent on demand, and b) savings accounts that have fixed terms or minimum notice periods. However, as explained later in this chapter, there are fundamental differences behind the scenes. Crucially, these changes mean that banks can no longer create the type of (demand) deposits that are currently used to make payments and therefore can no longer increase the total stock of money as a result of their lending activities.

The finer details of these changes are described in the pages that follow. Taken as a whole, they ensure that:

1. The payments system is separated from the lending/investing side of a bank's balance sheet (and as such is sheltered from bank failure).

2. There is a clear distinction between truly risk-free money in a bank account, and a risk-bearing investment that could lose value.

3. Banks become money brokers, rather than money creators. New lending will not create new money, but simply transfer existing money (and purchasing power) from one person to another.

4.   As bank lending will not increase the amount of money in the economy, the money supply will be stable and permanent regardless of the over or under-lending of banks.

5.   There will be risk-alignment on all investments, so that those who stand to gain from the upside of a risky investment also stand to take the downside. This eliminates 'moral hazard'.

6.   There will be different Investment Accounts for different types of loan. This will prevent banks taking large risks with funds from customers who want a low level of risk.

7.   Banks that fail will be liquidated. Customers who opted to keep their money in risk-free Transaction Accounts will have their money transferred to a healthy bank within hours and will not lose access to the payment system. There will be no need for deposit insurance or taxpayer-funded bailouts. Investment Account holders, having agreed to take risk on their investments, will become creditors to the bank and await liquidation proceedings.

Finally, with banks unable to increase or decrease the amount of money in circulation (but fully able to play the role of intermediary between savers and borrowers), the Bank of England will become solely responsible for creating new money, under the authority of a new Money Creation Committee. New money will be created only to the extent that it does not fuel inflation. The process for injecting new money into the economy is discussed in Chapter 7.

We now look at the process for restructuring the operations of banks in order to remove their ability to create money. We start by looking at the two distinct types of accounts that banks will be able to provide, the first of which will hold the state-issued currency created by the Bank of England.

6.2 CURRENT/TRANSACTION ACCOUNTS AND THE PAYMENTS SYSTEM

Present-day current accounts will be replaced by Transaction Accounts. Transaction Accounts will still:

1.   Provide cheques and ATM or debit cards.

2.   Provide electronic payment services, including for salaries and other payments.

3. Be instant access, for both electronic money transfers and cash withdrawals.

4. Provide overdrafts, if the bank sees fit (financed by Investment Accounts).

However, unlike present-day current accounts, where the safety of the deposits in a current account depends on the health of the bank's balance sheet, Transaction Accounts will be entirely risk-free and secure. This is because, while a Transaction Account holder may appear to be banking with a private commercial bank, the money in a Transaction Account is no longer a liability of the bank. Instead it actually represents electronic money, issued by the Bank of England, which belongs to the customer.

This is a crucial difference between the present and reformed system. As we saw in Chapter 1, present-day current accounts are merely promises from banks that they will use their own money at the central bank to settle payments on our behalf. These promises are only worth something as long as the bank is able to stay solvent and liquid. In contrast, Transaction Accounts will be actual money at the central bank, which banks will administer on their customers' behalf. This means that funds placed into a Transaction Account remain the legal property of the account holder, rather than becoming the property of the bank (as happens in the current system). The customer is in a sense hiring the bank to act as a middleman, whose role is to relay payment instructions between the customer and the central bank. The bank never actually takes ownership of the money, and is not allowed to instruct the central bank to transfer it without the customer's express permission.

As a result, a bank will no longer be able to use the money in Transaction Accounts for making loans or funding its own investments. Because Transaction Accounts are not held on the bank's balance sheet and are actually held in full at the Bank of England, they could be repaid in full (to all customers) at any time, without having any impact on the bank's overall financial health, and regardless of the financial health of the bank. In effect, this turns Transaction Accounts into 100% risk-free, electronic 'safe deposit boxes' for money.[1]

---

1. Despite the fact that this money is not available to private banks due to the design of the system, it would also be a legal offence for any bank to be unable to repay (i.e. transfer) the sum total of its Transaction Accounts in aggregate at any time. This requirement prevents banks from offering instant access accounts where the money is not held at the Bank of England (in the Customer Funds

With the money in Transaction Accounts safe by design, there is no longer a need for a deposit guarantee scheme. In fact, Transaction Accounts have an advantage over present-day government guaranteed bank accounts in that there is no limit to the amount that can safely be kept in them. Presently the government guarantee stands at £85,000 per account, but any amount of money could be held in a Transaction Account with zero risk of loss and no exposure to the financial health of the bank.

Account Fees for Transaction Accounts: The funds placed into Transaction Accounts will not be available to the bank to lend or invest, and therefore the bank will be unable to earn a return on these funds. However, they will still incur the costs of administering these accounts (staff wages etc.) and providing services associated with them (cheque books, ATM cards, payment system infrastructure, cash handling etc.). Consequently the banks providing these accounts will need to charge fees to customers to cover costs and make a profit.

How much would the account fees actually be? Table 6.1 give a realistic breakdown of the current yearly costs of providing a current account. The costs equate to around £5 per month (and possibly less after the one-off costs of opening a new account have been recovered), plus a mark-up for the bank's profit. These charges are already incurred by banks in the present-day banking system, and are unlikely to change under a reformed system.

The introduction of account fees may cause some objections, since nobody likes to start paying for something that is currently free. However, we should recognise that present-day current accounts only appear to be 'free'. In reality the costs of providing the service are recovered through unauthorised overdraft fines, cross-subsidisation from loans and selling of additional products (such as travel insurance, credit cards etc.). There is now a growing movement towards ending 'free' current accounts, with the Bank of England's Andrew Bailey and Paul Tucker, the FSA's Adair Turner and Sir David Walker, the new chairman of Barclays speaking out in favour of account fees that more closely resemble the costs of providing the service. It should be noted that many

---

Account). Any bank that did take customer's funds, promise repayment of the funds on demand and then lent the funds would be in breach of this law. This catch-all requirement prevents banks from offering alternative products that offer the same services as Transaction Accounts but allow the bank to use the funds for other purposes (which would effectively be a return to the current monetary system).

Table 6.1: Yearly costs of providing a current account

Cheque Book	£10 *(per book)*
Debit Card	£2
Branch	£5
Call Centre	£8
Staff	£15
Banking IT systems	£4
Customer Due Diligence *(on account opening)*	£8
MasterCard/Visa	£2
Link *(cash machine network)*	£2
BACS and other payment systems	£5
Other IT infrastructure	£2
Total	**£63**

Source: Tusmor, a consultancy firm that has been involved in setting up new banks in the UK (www.tusmor.com)

banks have already started introducing fees on current accounts and also that most businesses pay account fees as a matter of course. In reality the costs of these accounts will be many times less than the direct and indirect costs to each individual due to the instability caused by the present monetary system.

In practice, there will be significant market pressure to keep account fees low.[2] Once a customer starts banking with a bank, they are more likely to use the same bank for savings, mortgages, credit cards etc, which will likely be more profitable for the bank. Consequently, market pressure will encourage banks to lower their fees to attract new customers and grow their market share.

---

2.   One concern is that charging fees for the provision of Transaction Accounts will hurt the poor and increase financial exclusion. A solution to this problem is for the government to simply provide anyone earning below a certain threshold with a small grant which can be used to open a Transaction Account.

6.3 INVESTMENT ACCOUNTS

After the reform, the bank would need to attract the funds that it wants to use for any investment purpose (whether it is for loans, credit cards, mortgages, long term investing in stocks or short-term trading). These funds would be provided by customers, via their Investment Accounts. The Investment Account is simply a record of money that has been provided to a bank to be invested. These accounts will replace present-day savings accounts, including instant access savings accounts and fixed-term investments through a bank. The term "Investment Account" has been chosen as it more accurately describes the purpose of these accounts - as it is a risk-bearing investment rather than as a 'safe' place to 'save' money.

Investment Accounts, like present-day savings accounts, will still:

1.   Be places for individuals to earn interest on spare money (savings).

2.   Pay varying rates of interest.

3.   Be provided by normal high-street banks.

4.   Be liabilities of the bank to the customer who made the investment.

However, Investment Accounts have some significant differences from present-day savings accounts:

The Investment Account will not hold money: The Investment Account will never actually hold any money. Any money 'placed in' an Investment Account by a customer will actually be immediately transferred from the customer's Transaction Account (which represents electronic money held at the Bank of England) to the bank's 'Investment Pool' account (also held at the Bank of England and discussed in more detail below). At this point, the money will belong to the bank, rather than the Investment Account holder, and the bank will record that it owes the Investment Account holder the amount of money that they invested as a liability to the customer. In effect, Investment Accounts are simply records of investments made by customers through a bank, equivalent to a savings certificate. A step-by-step demonstration of the process of lending and investment is given later in this chapter.

Investment Accounts are illiquid: At the point of investment, customers would lose access to their money for a pre-agreed period of time. Customers would agree to either a 'maturity date' or a 'notice period' that would apply to the account. The maturity date would be a specific date on which the customer wishes to be repaid the full amount of the investment, plus any interest. The notice period refers to an agreed number of weeks' notice that the customer would give to the bank before demanding repayment.

There would no longer be any form of 'instant access' savings accounts. This prohibition on instant access savings is a necessity in order to prevent banks creating liabilities that can be used to make payments and thereby replicating the ability to create money that they have in the present system.

Investment Accounts will not be protected by government guarantee: The Financial Services Compensation Scheme would not apply to Investment Accounts. Customers who wish to keep their money completely free of risk can put their money into Transaction Accounts, which are risk-free by design, while customers who want to earn a return will be expected to take some risk (rather than having the risk passed onto the taxpayer, as currently happens).

Investment Accounts will be risk-bearing: If some borrowers fail to repay their loans, then the loss will be split between the bank and the holder of the Investment Account. This sharing of risk will ensure that incentives are aligned correctly, as problems would arise if the risk were to fall entirely on either the bank or the investor. For example, placing all the risk on the account holder will incentivise the bank to make the investments that have the highest risk and highest return possible, as the customer would take all the downside of bad investment decisions. Alternatively, if the bank takes all the risk by promising to repay the customer in full regardless of the performance of the investments, then the account holder would face no downside and would consequently only be motivated by high returns, regardless of the risk taken. This would force banks to compete by offering higher interest rates in order to attract funds, which they would then need to invest in riskier projects in order to make a profit, biasing the system towards higher levels of risk taking.

Any investor opening an Investment Account will be made fully aware of the risks at the time of the investment, and those who do not wish to take a certain level of risk will be able to opt for alternative accounts that offer lower risks and consequently lower returns. Risk and reward will therefore be aligned, while much of the moral hazard associated with the current banking system will be removed.

If the bank suffers such a large number of defaults (borrowers who are unable to repay their loans) that it becomes insolvent and fails, the bank will be closed, the remaining assets liquidated and the creditors paid off. Investment Account holders should have depositor preference, meaning that they will come first in the queue of creditors waiting to be repaid if the bank fails. Amongst all Investment Account holders, those who opted for the lowest risk accounts should be repaid before those who opted for the higher risk accounts.

Investment Accounts will have a specific purpose: At the point of opening an account, the bank would be required to inform the customer of the intended uses for the money that will be invested. Typically the broad category of investment will correspond to the level of risk taken (as discussed above), so that Investment Accounts that funded mortgages would be afforded a different risk rating than those that funded trading in commodities. The broad categories of investment will need to be set by the authorities.

This change is designed to ensure that the types of investment made by the bank (with customers' money) more closely represent the types of investments that the customers themselves would want. This is not to suggest that individuals will be making detailed decisions over how to allocate their investments across different asset classes; rather that some customers would prefer to have more information about what their funds are used for.

The Investment Account will not be money: If a bank were to provide a service whereby a customer could 'reassign' ownership of all or part of his Investment Account, then it would be possible to use Investment Accounts to make payments. For example, take the case of an individual who wished to purchase a car but whose only asset was a £1000 Investment Account that matured in 4 weeks. If the car seller was willing to accept ownership of the Investment Account in payment, the individual could pay for the car by transferring ownership of the Investment Account. This would be problematic for the system as a whole, as it would effectively give banks the ability to create money again, particularly if they made it very easy for customers to reassign Investment Account ownership. Consequently, to prevent banks being able to use their liabilities as substitutes for state-issued money, it will be necessary to ensure that ownership of Investment Accounts cannot be 'reassigned'.

6.4 ACCOUNTS AT THE BANK OF ENGLAND

Under the present-day system, all large banks have an account at the Bank of England in which they keep 'central bank reserves'. Banks use these reserves to make payments to other banks (see Chapter 2). After the reform, each bank will instead manage three distinct accounts at the Bank of England. These

fig. 6.1 - Accounts at central bank post reform

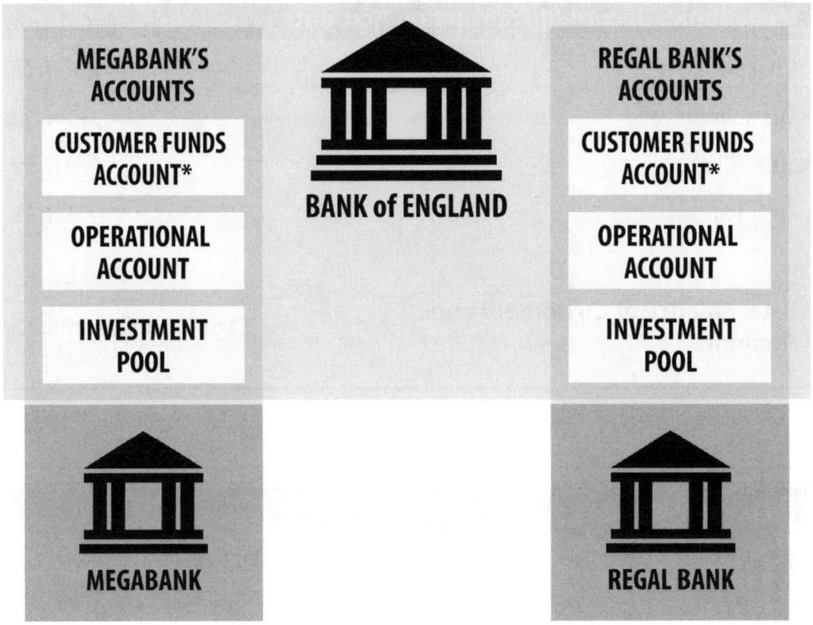

These accounts are administered by the banks but are not their property

accounts would hold electronic money that had been created exclusively by the Bank of England. The three accounts are:

The Operational Account: This is an account where the bank can hold funds for its own purposes: retained profits, new capital from shareholders, money to pay staff wages etc. In short, it is a bank's 'own money' acquired in the process of running of the bank. The money in this account is owned by the bank and the account is an asset of the bank.

The Investment Pool: This account represents the lending side of the bank's activities. It is the account that a bank will use to receive investments from customers, make loans to borrowers, receive loan repayments from borrowers and make payments back to Investment Account holders. The money in this account is both owned by and is an asset of the commercial bank.

The Customer Funds Account: This is the account in which the bank's customers' Transaction Account funds are held. The money in this account is not owned by the bank nor is the account an asset of the bank. The bank merely administers this account. When someone at another bank makes a payment

fig. 6.2 - Simplified bank internal database

MegaBank's Record of Transaction Accounts	
Customer	**Balance**
Mrs K Smith	£546.21
Mr W Riley	£1942.52
Mr J Heath	£26.78
...	...
Total Balance of Customer Funds Account:	**£168,023,163,295.72**

fig. 6.3 - Central bank internal database

Bank of England	
Bank	**Customer Funds Account Balance**
MegaBank Customer Funds Account	£168,023,163,295.72
NewBank Customer Funds Account	£156,023,123,714.52
Regal Bank Customer Funds Account	£192,923,670,202.12

to a Transaction Account holder, the balance of the Customer Funds Account will increase. When a Transaction Account holder makes a payment to someone who uses a different bank, the balance of this account will decrease.

The relationship between Transaction Accounts and a bank's Customer Funds Account

The money placed into Transaction Accounts at a bank will actually be held, in electronic form, at the Bank of England. The sum total of a bank's customer Transaction Accounts would be referred to as the Customer Funds Account administered by that bank and held at the Bank of England. However, while the bank would administer this account on behalf of its customers, it would not own any of the money within the Customer Funds Account itself. Furthermore, although the Bank of England would hold the aggregated pool of real electronic money (which it created in the first place), it need not hold any

fig. 6.4 - Relationship between Customer Funds Accounts and Transaction Accounts

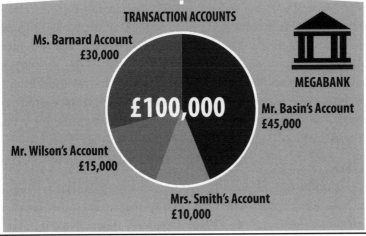

*Administered by the bank but not its property

information on individual customers or the balance of individual customer accounts, which would be the responsibility of the individual banks.

For the Customer Funds Account it administered, each bank would record the amount of this money that is owned by each and every one of its individual customers, and the transactions made in and out of each customer's account.

As a simplified example, a bank's internal database may look something like fig 6.2. Meanwhile, the Bank of England's own database will appear as shown in figure 6.3, recording the aggregate balance of the Customer Funds Account each bank administers, but no details of any individual's accounts.

6.5 POST-REFORM BALANCE SHEETS FOR BANKS AND THE BANK OF ENGLAND

Chapter 8 discusses the method for transitioning between the current and reformed monetary system in detail. For the rest of this chapter however it is assumed that the reform has been enacted and the transition is completed. The following section looks at both the commercial bank and the central bank balance sheets.

Commercial banks

After the reform, commercial banks will have the usual range of assets. Under the usual 'Cash and Cash Equivalents' will be included the bank's Operational Account and Investment Pool at the Bank of England, replacing the former entry of 'Deposits at the Bank of England' (i.e. central bank reserves). Investment Accounts are recorded as a liability, just as present-day time deposits are. However, demand deposits (current accounts) are removed from the balance sheet, converted into state-issued currency held at the central bank, and recorded on a separate register, 'Customer Funds', which shows the funds administered by Regal Bank on behalf of its customers (fig 6.5).

Central bank

The central bank's balance sheet has also lost many of its former liabilities, as these have been converted into real state-issued currency and transferred onto a custodial register (see fig 6.6).It is important to note that this is not the only way in which the accounting for a reformed system can be presented. Appendix III has an alternative treatment, in which money remains a liability of the Central Bank.

Measuring the money supply

The existing statistical measure of 'broad' money supply, M4, is calculated in a rather crude and potentially imprecise way. At the end of each month, the treasury team of each bank is required to fill in a form detailing the sum total of different types of customers' accounts. These figures are then aggregated across all banks to give the total figure for M4. This statistical measure occasionally jumps up or down - changes in the efficiency of reporting at one bank resulted in a £8 billion jump in M4 from one month to the next, whereas a

fig. 6.5 - Commercial bank's post-reform balance sheet

Commercial Bank Balance Sheet		Commercial Bank Customer Funds
Assets	**Liabilities**	*(Held in custody)*
Loans outstanding	Investment accounts	Transaction Accounts *(records of the balances of individual customers; funds actually held at Customer Funds Account at Bank of England)*
Cash	Borrowing from other banks	
Operational Account	Shareholder capital *(Equity)*	
Investment Pool		
Property & fixed assets		

fig. 6.6 - Central Bank balance sheet, post reform

Bank of England Balance Sheet		Custodial Money-Holding Accounts
Assets	**Liabilities**	*(Held in custody)*
Loans to banks	Foreign exchange bonds in issue	Customer Funds Accounts
Balances at other central banks		Operational Accounts of Banks
Bank of England's Operating Funds account	All other liabilities	Central Government Account
Securities *(Gilts, Bonds, Foreign Currency, etc.)*	Shareholder capital *(Equity)*	Investment Pools of Banks
		Bank of England's Own Funds account
All other assets *(property, etc.)*		Accounts for other central banks
		Accounts for major payment systems providers *(if necessary)*

change in the measurement procedures once resulted in a £176 billion jump! It should be recognised that M4 is simply a rough statistical measure of the total liabilities of banks to members of the public - not a precise count of the quantity of 'electronic pounds' in the economy.

In contrast, post-reform the total money supply will be much easier to count, as it is simply the total balance of all the accounts held in the Bank of England's computer system. Precisely, it is:

The sum of all Customer Funds Accounts

+

The sum of all banks' Investment Accounts

+

The sum of all banks' Operational Accounts

+

The balance of the Central Government Account

+

The balance of the Bank of England's Own Funds Account + all other balances at the Bank of England (e.g. accounts for foreign central banks)

+

Cash in circulation

The money supply figure will be a precise number, accurate to the penny, which can be calculated by the Bank of England's computer systems in a fraction of a second. This figure could be published on the Bank of England's website.

There would still need to be a manual reporting process to get the sum total of Investment Account balances from the banks, as these are not recorded at the Bank of England. In any case these would not count as part of the money supply, as they would not be available for spending until they matured.

6.6 MAKING PAYMENTS

The post-reform process of making payments is very simple. Let's look at the example from Chapter 2, where Jack wanted to pay for a van by transferring money to the van dealer, only this time in a reformed banking system.

1. Customers at the same bank

If both Jack and the van dealer have accounts at MegaBank, then the transfer can be made internally within the bank's computer systems:

fig. 6.7 - Transaction at same bank, post reform

MegaBank's Record of Transaction Accounts	
Customer	**Balance**
Jack	~~£10,000~~ → £0
Van dealer	~~£0~~ → £10,000
...	...
Total Balance of Customer Funds Account:	£168,023,163,295.72 (No change)

In effect, Jack has simply transferred his ownership of £10,000 at the Bank of England to the van dealer, although from their perspective as bank customers, they will simply see money transferred between the two Transaction Accounts. Note however that no money moves between accounts at the Bank of England, as all the money still sits in the Customer Funds Account administered by MegaBank at the Bank of England.

2. Customers at different banks

If the van dealer instead banks at Regal Bank then the £10,000 belonging to Jack, which is stored in the MegaBank administered Customer Funds Account at the Bank of England, will need to be transferred across to the Regal Bank administered Customer Funds Account, where it will become the property of the van dealer.

When Jack asks his bank to send £10,000 to the van dealer's account at Regal Bank, then MegaBank will send an instruction to the Bank of England to transfer £10,000 from the Customer Funds Account it administers to the Customer Funds Account that Regal Bank administers. As the transfer is carried out, MegaBank reduces the recorded balance of Jack's account, and Regal Bank increases the recorded balance of the van dealer's account. The transfer at the Bank of England appears as so:

fig. 6.8 - Transaction between banks, seen from central bank

Bank of England	
Bank	Customer Funds Account Balance
MegaBank Customer Funds Account	~~£168,023,110,000~~ → £168,023,100,000
Regal Bank Customer Funds Account	~~£192,923,600,000~~ → £192,923,610,000

A note on settlement in the reformed system

In Chapter 2 we saw that high value/time sensitive payments are made across reserve accounts at the Bank of England instantly, using the CHAPS payment system. Conversely, smaller value payments are not settled immediately at the Bank of England but are instead queued in one of the other payment systems, such as BACS or Faster Payments. These payments are added together and the net payment flows calculated, so that only the net debt/credit position needs to be transferred, lowering the system's need for central bank reserves.

Under the reformed system it is possible to completely do away with the smaller value payment systems that clear on a net basis and instead settle all payments in real time across the Bank of England's books, as with only one integrated quantity of money used by banks and the public alike, there is no longer any need to economise on liquidity.[3]

However, this may require a large upgrade in the capacity of the Bank of England's RTGS system in order to handle the larger flow of payments: BACS, Faster Payments and Link (the ATM network) together processed an average of 33 million transactions per day throughout 2011, whereas only 300,000 transactions a day were settled directly via the Bank of England's reserve accounts (Bank of England, 2012). As a result it is important to note that the

---

3. In addition, there will no longer be a need for the Bank of England to provide additional intraday liquidity through same day repo for securities transactions (as it currently does in CREST under a procedure known as auto-collateralisation) as due to the reforms every account will be fully liquid.

smaller value payment systems are also entirely compatible with these proposals, with no need to change any of the existing payment infrastructures.

Retaining these systems will reduce the load on the Bank of England's computer systems. In a reformed system with net settlement, instead of the end-of-day net settlement happening across central bank reserve accounts, it would take place across the Customer Funds Accounts at the Bank of England. Note that although multilateral net settlement reduces the amount of money that actually moves between banks, it does not allow banks to create money, as they do not own the Customer Funds Accounts or the money within them.

6.7 MAKING LOANS

This section explains how banks will normally make loans (including via overdrafts) under the reformed system. For the purpose of the demonstration, we will consider an example where one customer's investment of £1,000 is funding an equal loan to another individual customer. In reality, the amounts loaned may be smaller than the investment and spread across multiple customers, or alternatively, multiple investments may fund one larger loan. There does not need to be any direct link between individual savers and borrowers.

Under these proposals, in order for a bank to make a loan it must have funds on hand. Initially this requires a customer, John, who wants to make an investment using some of the funds currently in his Transaction Account. He first needs to open an Investment Account at the bank and 'fund' it with a transfer from his Transaction Account. John sees the balance of his Transaction Account fall by £1,000, and sees the balance of his new Investment Account increase by £1,000. However, in reality the money from his Transaction Account has actually moved to Regal Bank's Investment Pool at the Bank of England. The Bank of England's balance sheet has now changed (see fig 6.10).On Regal Bank's balance sheet, the funds are transferred from John's Transaction Account to the bank's Investment Pool, and the bank creates a new liability of £1,000, which is John's new Investment Account (see fig 6.11).

The money in Regal Bank's Investment Pool is then used to make a loan to a borrower, David. David signs a contract with the bank confirming that he will repay £1,000 plus interest. This legally enforceable contract represents an asset for the bank, and is recorded on the balance sheet as such. Simultaneously, money is moved from Regal Bank's Investment Pool at the Bank of England

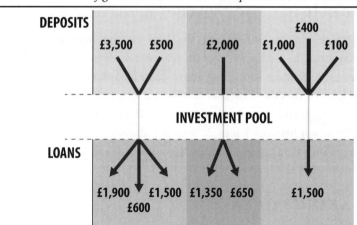

fig. 6.9 - Indirect relationship between savers and borrowers

to the Customer Funds Account administered by Regal Bank, and Regal Bank increases the value of David's Transaction Account (see fig 6.12).

The balance sheet still balances, with the Investment Account liability to John offset by the loan asset made to David. Throughout the process, electronic money in the accounts at the Bank of England has moved from the Customer Funds Account to the Investment Pool, and back to the Customer Funds Account. Ownership of the money has moved from John to David.

In summary, any money 'placed in' an Investment Account by a customer will actually be immediately transferred from that customer's Transaction Account (at the Bank of England) to the bank's 'Investment Pool' account (at the Bank of England). At this point, the money will belong to the bank, rather than the Investment Account holder, and the bank will note that it owes the Investment Account holder the amount of money that the account holder invested (i.e. the Investment Account will be recorded as a liability on the bank's balance sheet). When this money is then lent, the money will be transferred from its Investment Pool (at the Bank of England) to the borrower's Transaction Account (at the Bank of England). At no point did any money leave the Bank of England's balance sheet, and no additional deposits were created anywhere in the system. This ensures that the act of lending does not increase the level of purchasing power in the economy, as it does in the current system.

fig. 6.10 - Loan made by Regal Bank, central bank balance sheet

Bank of England Balance Sheet		Custodial Money-Holding Accounts
Assets	**Liabilities**	*(Held in custody)*
...	...	Regal Bank's Customer Funds Account £1000 → £0 *(John's Transaction A/c)*
		Regal Bank's Investment Pool £0 → £1000

fig. 6.11 - Loan made by Regal Bank, Regal Bank balance sheet i

Regal Bank Balance Sheet		Regal Bank Customer Funds
Assets	**Liabilities**	*(Held in custody)*
Investment Pool £0 → £1000	John's Investment Account £0 → £1000	John's TA £1000 → £0

fig. 6.12 - Loan made by Regal Bank, Regal Bank balance sheet ii

Regal Bank Balance Sheet		Regal Bank Customer Funds
Assets	**Liabilities**	*(Held in custody)*
Investment Pool £1000 → £0	John's Investment Account £1000	John's TA £0
New Loan to David £0 → £1000		David's TA £0 → £1000

fig. 6.13 - Diagram of flows

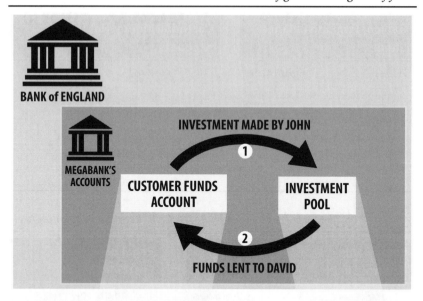

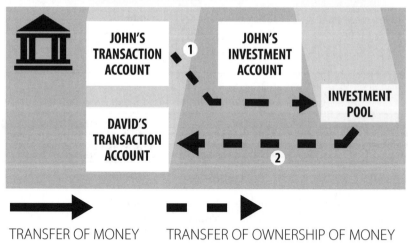

TRANSFER OF MONEY   TRANSFER OF OWNERSHIP OF MONEY

Loan repayments

To repay the loan the same process happens in reverse. After informing the Bank he wishes to repay his loan, David transfers £1,000, plus the interest he was charged, from his Transaction Account to the bank's Investment Pool. If John wishes to withdraw his Investment Account, then, on the condition that he has already given his bank the necessary amount of notice, Regal Bank will transfer £1,000 plus the interest paid on the Investment Account back

> ## Box 6.A – Maturity transformation under the reformed system
>
> A popular misconception is that the reforms proposed here prevent maturity transformation – the conversion of short-term savings into long-term loans - so that an individual wishing to borrow £250,000 over 25 years must find an individual wishing to lend £250,000 for 25 years. Obviously this would be highly inefficient. However, the proposals outlined here require neither the value of a loan, nor its maturity, to be matched by a single individual's investment. Instead, multiple individuals are able to fund single loans and withdraw their funding before the loan matures. Thus the system will operate much as the bond market does today, only with fixed maturity or redemption dates (and in general no capital gains or losses).
>
> For example, 10 people may place £1,000 each into an Investment Account, and the bank may use this £10,000 to make a loan to an individual to be paid back over 10 years. After twelve months, 2 of the 10 original Investment Account holders may wish to withdraw their investment, and as a result the bank will need to find people willing to lend a total of £2,000 to replace the money that has been removed from the account. So both maturity transformation and pooling of funds can continue. In reality thousands of loans will mature and be made every day, with each Investment Account holder funding a tiny proportion of each loan. Consequently risk will also be pooled.

into John's Transaction Account. Regal Bank's profit (the difference between the interest rate charged on the loan and the interest rate paid on the Investment Account) remains in Regal Bank's Investment Pool, and may be used to make further loans, or withdrawn to the bank's Operational Account and used to pay staff, other operating costs, or pay shareholder dividends, etc. On the other hand, if John does not wish to withdraw his Investment Account the bank will be free to use the money to make further loans. In either case loan repayment does not cause money to be destroyed, as is the case in the current monetary system. This means that the public would in aggregate be able to pay down their debts without the amount of money in circulation also falling.

6.8 How to realign risk in banking

Investment Account Guarantees

From the customer's perspective the fundamental principle of these reforms is that the customer decides how much risk they want to take with their money. Customers who wish to keep their money completely free of risk can put their money into Transaction Accounts. On the other hand, those that wish to receive a return on their money must accept a degree of risk and give up access to their money for a period of time. They will do this by placing their money into an Investment Account.

Because all the money in Transaction Accounts is held at the Bank of England, and therefore 100% safe, the Financial Services Compensation Scheme would be cancelled as it applies to bank accounts. Investment Accounts would not be guaranteed by the government or FSCS in any way, and so customers placing money into Investment Accounts will be expected to take on some risk (rather than having the risk passed onto the taxpayer through the £85,000 guarantee). This ensures that risk and reward are aligned.

However, this in itself could create new problems. For example, if the bank simply passes all the risk on to the Investment Account holder, then the bank would take all of the upside of its lending decisions but none of the downside. This would encourage the bank to use customers' money to pursue only high-risk, high-return activities. Likewise, if the bank retained all the risk on its lending, customers would be incentivised to put their money into the highest return Investment Accounts, meaning that the bank would need to make riskier investments to earn those higher returns.

Thus, in order to ensure that incentives are correctly aligned, those that stand to benefit from the upside of an investment (both the bank and the Investment Account holder) also must share in the downside if things go wrong. Therefore, in order to ensure that risk and reward are aligned the reforms will allow banks to offer the Investment Account holder a guarantee on a percentage of their initial investment. For example, as well as offering a return of 5% a year if the investments are successful, banks may guarantee that 95% of the value of an Investment Account will be repaid, with the bank covering any fall in the value of the account below 95% out of its profits from other investments. In each case, investors would have been made aware of the guarantees and made their decision to invest in a particular Investment Account, knowing the risks as well as the potential upside.

By varying the guarantees it offers on Investment Accounts according to the degree of risk in the underlying investments, banks will be able to compete by offering a variety of products that cater to different risk appetites. Investors who want a high rate of return will need to take on some of the risk themselves, while investors who are happy with a low rate of return will be able to invest with very little risk.

Of course, these guarantees will only be valid as long as the bank is solvent. If a bank becomes bankrupt, Investment Account holders would become creditors of the bank and would have to wait for normal liquidation or resolution procedures to take place to see if they will get back part of their investment. The government will not back the guarantees made by the banks.

The regulator may forbid specific guarantees

The financial regulator may need forbid an institution from offering a specific rate of return or guarantee on a particular Investment Account. The reason for this is twofold. First, 'irrational exuberance' amongst individuals and banks may lead to unrealistic returns being offered and accepted based on changes in profitability that are unsustainable in the long term. Because regulators themselves are not immune to irrational exuberance (see the belief in a 'great moderation' (Bernanke, 2004)), guarantees that promise to pay returns in excess of the average long-run historical returns should be forbidden. Furthermore, the time periods used to calculate these long-run averages must also include periods of recession, depression, and financial crisis.[4]

Second, the regulator may forbid specific guarantees or returns in order to protect individuals and bank shareholders from unscrupulous activity by bank staff. For example, assume the case (which is common) where senior bank staff are remunerated based on the bank's market share. In this situation guarantees may be offered based not on the profitability of the underlying investment, but to encourage more individuals to place their money into that bank's Investment Account instead of their competitors. While these investments may eventually lead to losses for the bank, in the meantime the senior staff will receive large payouts due to the increase in market share. Although this chain of events may seem unlikely, some commentators (for example Smith, 2010) saw just such 'looting' of banks by their staff as one of the causes of the 2007-08 financial crisis.[5]

---

4.   Offering guarantees may be problematic if the underlying investments have not existed for enough time for long run averages to be calculated. One solution would be for the regulator to disallow guarantees on these Investment Accounts. Another would be for it to allow only very conservative guarantees to be offered (i.e. low returns, a low percentage guaranteed to be repaid) and require a warning to be placed on them as to the uncertainty of their returns.

5.   For a more general discussion see Akerlof & Romer (1993).

6.9 Letting banks fail

Recall that in the current system, when a bank fails, its customers cannot access their accounts (i.e. they cannot make payments and cannot withdraw cash). In the case of the failure of Royal Bank of Scotland, this would have left millions of account holders with potentially no access to money or means of payment, especially if their only account was at RBS. As outlined in previous chapters, the resulting chaos could have led to panic and bank runs, bringing the entire payments system to a halt. In addition, as we saw in chapter 4, the existence of deposit insurance means that it will always be more expensive for the government to allow a major bank to fail than to rescue it with a capital injection.

In the reformed system, it is far easier to allow a bank to fail. If a bank made bad investment choices that lead to its insolvency, it would cease operating and the liquidation procedures would be initiated. However, holders of Transaction Accounts would not lose access to their money, because this money is held at the Bank of England – rather than on the balance sheet of the failed bank – and was never placed at risk. The electronic payments made on these accounts could continue through the normal payments system, and in time administration of these Transaction Accounts could be taken over by healthy banks (with customers selecting the bank they want to administer their accounts). Providing the IT systems are designed in the right way, banks could be allowed to fail without Transaction Account customers losing the ability to make payments for more than a few hours.

What about Investment Account holders? They made a conscious decision to place their money at risk by investing with the bank. At the point of investment they would have been made aware that the investment was not guaranteed and that, in the event of the bank failing, they would become creditors of the bank and would need to wait for the liquidation procedure to take place before they find out how much of their investment they will receive back. As the assets of the failed bank are sold off, the Investment Account holders will be repaid, although they are unlikely to receive 100% of their original investment. Those account holders who opted for the low risk Investment Accounts should have depositor preference (i.e. should be paid back earlier and in greater proportion) over those who opted for the higher-risk accounts.

Of course, if a bank is going through temporary liquidity (cashflow) problems but the Bank of England feels it is fundamentally solvent in the long term (i.e.

its assets, correctly valued, are still greater than its liabilities), then it may opt to make an emergency loan to that bank for a period of time, to allow the bank to continue to function while it looks for investors. It will be for the Bank of England to decide whether a bank in trouble is facing temporary liquidity problems or whether it is fundamentally insolvent, and to take the appropriate course of action.

CHAPTER 7

THE NEW PROCESS FOR CREATING MONEY

After the reform, banks would no longer be able to create money, in the form of bank deposits, when they make loans or buy financial assets. As a result, an alternative method for injecting (and removing) money into the economy will be required. However, before we address the question of how new money is to be created and destroyed, we must first address the questions:

1. Who should decide how much money is to be created/destroyed?

2. Who should decide how newly created money is to be used?

7.1 WHO SHOULD HAVE THE AUTHORITY TO CREATE MONEY?

The overriding principle when we are deciding who should have the authority to create/destroy money is whether or not the 'creator' can benefit personally from its creation. If the answer is yes, then there is a conflict of interest.

Banks profit from making loans, so incentivise their staff to maximise lending through sales targets, bonuses, commissions, the opportunity of promotion, etc. During periods where economic conditions are relatively benign banks and bankers profit by increasing their lending - and therefore money creation - as fast as possible. In theory the risk management department of banks should place some kind of limitation upon this increase in lending, but history has shown that risk management and prudence is often overly relaxed in the chase for profits. Besides, while the increase in money creation was most extreme in the years running up to the recent financial crisis, the average growth rate in the M4 money supply between 1970 and 2010 was still a significant 11.5% per annum. This growth in the amount of money in circulation bears no relation to the growth in GDP or the needs of the economy as a whole; instead it is driven purely by the need of banks to maximise profit.

It is also reasonable to assume that vote-seeking politicians would be little better at the job of creating new money. An important rationale for taking monetary policy away from the Treasury and handing it to the Bank of England was that it was assumed that politicians were liable to abuse this power, particularly in the run-up to elections, often leading to recurrent cycles of boom and bust (the so-called 'political business cycle'). Similarly, there would be significant temptation for the Chancellor or Prime Minister to sanction the creation of new money in order to 'buy' the goodwill of voters prior to an election.

In short, neither profit-seeking bankers nor vote-seeking politicians can be trusted with the power to create money, as the incentives both groups face will lead them to abuse this power for personal, party, or company gain. Instead, we must ensure that those that decide how much money to create do not benefit from creating it. This requires the separation of the decision on how much new money is to be created from how that newly created money is to be used.

We do this by giving these two decisions to completely separate bodies. We recommend that an independent body, the Money Creation Committee (MCC), should take decisions over how much new money should be created, while the elected government of the day should make the decision over how that money will be spent. Alternatively, the MCC may lend money to the banks to on-lend into the 'real' economy, in which case the decision over where the money is lent will be made, within broad guidelines, by the banks.

In what follows, it is important to note that the decision over who decides how much money to create need not be given to a committee at the central bank (here the MCC). The format outlined is, in our opinion, the least controversial, given that it is almost identical to the current Monetary Policy Committee. However, more radical alternatives are possible. For example, the power over money creation could be given to a committee that was independent of both parliament and the central bank. Or, the decision over money creation could be taken by the chancellor, the prime minister, or a parliamentary committee, although this will lead to the conflicts of interest outlined above. Alternatively, some argue that money creation should be decentralised to regional bodies. This is also likely to be problematic, as while each region will benefit from creating money, the costs of excessive money creation, in the form of financial instability and inflation, will be borne by all the regions.

Box 7.A - Appointments and neutrality of the MCC

The MCC must be politically independent and neutral, just as the Monetary Policy Committee (responsible for setting interest rates) is today. As well as being shielded from the influence of vote-seeking politicians, it is essential that the MCC is sheltered from conflicts of interest and lobbyists for the banking sector and other industries. Building on the rules that currently cover the Monetary Policy Committee's transparency and accountability, all increases in the money supply will be made publicly known. In addition, while the MCC will not be answerable to the Chancellor (the UK's finance minister) of the day (who will have his own political objectives to achieve), they will be accountable to a cross-party Parliamentary Group, such as the Treasury Select Committee.

If the model of the existing Monetary Policy Committee is followed, appointments to the MCC will automatically include the Governor and two Deputy Governors of the Bank of England, as is the case with the Monetary Policy Committee today. Likewise the Governor is still best placed to recommend the two internal members of the committee. However, unlike today, where the internal appointments are referred to the Chancellor for approval, under the reformed system these internal members will instead be referred to a cross party group of MPs for approval. The intention is to provide democratic oversight and scrutiny of the appointment process by Parliament whilst reducing the powers of the Chancellor as an individual. Likewise, for the same reasons, the appointment of the four external members of the MCC will also be decided by a cross party group of MPs. In total, the MCC will be made up of nine members, which, with the exception of the Governor and the Deputy Governors, will serve three-year terms.

7.2 DECIDING HOW MUCH MONEY TO CREATE: THE MONEY CREATION COMMITTEE (MCC)

The decision over how much new money to create/remove from circulation would be given to an independent body, to be known as the Money Creation Committee. As is the case today, the target of monetary policy will be the rate of inflation. However, in line with democratic principles, Parliament will have the ability to change the MCC's mandate if it considers other targets, such as economic growth or employment to be more relevant.

The MCC would aim to keep inflation at around the 2% a year target by either adding or removing money from circulation. Creation of new money by the MCC will increase the amount of spending in the economy (as it will add to government spending). Depending on the state of the economy at the time, this may push up the inflation rate (discussed in detail in Chapter 9).

Box 7.B - What measure of inflation should the MCC target?

In the current regime the Monetary Policy Committee targets a 2% inflation rate, as measured by the Consumer Price Index (CPI). However, the CPI does not include the cost of housing, even though housing is usually the greatest portion of anyone's cost of living. The absence of house prices in the measure of inflation targeted by the MPC meant that the Bank of England was able to claim in 2012 (King, 2012b), that it had successfully managed inflation over the last decade, whilst ignoring house price inflation that averaged 12% (and peaked at 18%) between 1997 and 2007 (Nationwide, 2012).

Should the Money Creation Committee be required to include house price inflation in their measure of inflation? We believe this could be problematic. Although these reforms would significantly reduce the likelihood of house-price bubbles, there will still be changes in average house prices from year to year. However, under the reformed system these price changes would be more likely to reflect changes in economic fundamentals, such as changes in the demand for housing (e.g. due to changes in population) or changes in the supply of housing (e.g. due to changes in planning laws).

Normally, a change in the price of a good owing to economic fundamentals (over and above that caused by monetary changes) is not a problem – if the price of a good in the CPI increases markedly, it is replaced with a substitute good. This makes intuitive sense – if the cost of beef doubled, people might be expected to substitute away from beef and eat more chicken instead.

However, if the cost of living somewhere doubles (either because of house prices or rents increasing) it is not possible to substitute away from the good in question – people need to live somewhere. As a result, housing would remain in the basket of goods used to calculate the inflation rate, and the recorded level of inflation would increase above target. Unable to remove housing from the basket of goods, in order to keep inflation within the target range the MCC would have to engineer either deflation or reduced inflation in the rest of the basket of goods that made up the inflation index, with potentially damaging results. Essentially the MCC would have to suppress the real economy in order to meet its inflation target, despite the fact the real economy might not be experiencing excess demand and therefore need suppressing.

In order to avoid these issues and prevent property bubbles, instead of includ-ing property prices in the targeted measure of inflation the Bank of England should be mandated to prevent bubbles (e.g. price changes caused by specu-lative behaviour), while the MCC should target the CPI measure of inflation. To prevent property bubbles the MCC would need to prevent excessive mortgage lending. This could be achieved by removing guarantees on property Invest-ment Accounts, increasing bank capital requirements for mortgage lending, or in the extreme by placing a direct cap on mortgage lending.

If inflation is above the target rate, then the MCC will likely slow or stop the rate of new money creation. Note that the MCC's decision will be based on the amount of additional money they consider necessary to meet the inflation target. Under no circumstances would they be aiming to create however much money the government needs to fulfil its election manifesto promises.

With the MCC having direct control over the amount of money in the economy, the Monetary Policy Committee (MPC) at the Bank of England would no longer be needed and could be disbanded. Currently the MPC attempts to control bank lending – and therefore the quantity of broad money in the economy – by influencing the interest rate at which banks lend to each other on the interbank market. Post-reform, central banks would have direct control over the money creation process and so there would be no need for them to set interest rates. Instead, interest rates would be determined in the markets.

The Money Creation Committee will have no control over how the newly created money is used. Whilst the way the money is used will determine to some degree its effect on inflation, giving the MCC any influence over how the money is spent would introduce a conflict of interest, whereby its members might find that their judgement is swayed by their opinion on the merit of various spending programmes. In order to prevent this conflict of interest from arising, and to ensure that the MCC does not become politicised, the decision over how much money is created and what that money is used for must be taken by separate bodies.

How the Money Creation Committee would work

Each month, the Money Creation Committee would meet and decide whether to increase, decrease, or hold constant the level of money in the economy. During their monthly meetings the MCC would decide upon two figures:

1. The amount of new money needed in order to maintain aggregate demand in line with the inflation target (similar to the setting of interest rates today), and;

2. The amount of new lending needed in order to avoid a credit crunch in the real economy and therefore a fall in output and employment (discussed in section 7.6).

Both figures would be determined, as is the case now when setting interest rates, by reference to appropriate macroeconomic data, including the Bank of England's Credit Conditions Survey (a survey of business borrowing conditions, outlined in Box 7.C). Once a conclusion had been made on the two figures mentioned above, the Money Creation Committee would authorise the creation of a specific amount of new money. This newly created money could then enter the economy in two ways:

The first (and most common) of these would be to grant the money to the government (by increasing the balance of the Central Government Account), which would then spend this money into circulation, as discussed in the next section. This process increases the amount of money in circulation without increasing the level of debt in the economy and can therefore be thought of as 'debt-free' money creation.

The second method would be for the central bank to create new money via the MCC and lend it to banks, which would then lend this money to businesses and the productive economy (but not for mortgages or financial speculation). This increases the quantity of money in circulation but simultaneously increases the level of debt, and so does not constitute debt-free money creation. This option provides a tool to ensure that businesses and the real economy do not suffer from a lack of access to credit. It will be discussed further below.

Is it possible for the Money Creation Committee to determine the 'correct' money supply?

To begin with, it is important to note that the MCC would not determine how much money the economy needs from scratch. Instead, it would decide whether to increase or decrease the stock of existing money from its existing level (which has been determined by historical events), given current levels of inflation and economic activity. This requires that the MCC take a view on the likely future path of the economy in addition to reacting to economic events. Essentially the MCC will be guided by both theory and the results of their previous decisions.

There is of course no way for the MCC to predict perfectly how much money to create. However, this is true of all monetary and political decisions – including the Monetary Policy Committee's decision to increase or decrease interest rates in the present system. The question therefore becomes one of who is most likely to supply the economy with the 'correct' amount of money: commercial banks in the current system, or an independent committee in the reformed system?

As was outlined in Chapter 2, commercial banks create money when they make loans. Bank officials therefore are not deliberately and consciously making a decision about how much money they think should be in the economy; they are instead making a decision about whether a particular loan will be profitable. This means that the stock of money is currently determined as a by-product of bank lending decisions, made in the pursuit of profit. Because the majority of banks' profits come from the interest they charge on loans, in relatively benign periods banks are incentivised to lend as much as possible, creating money in the process.

However, although the money supply is determined by the actions of companies in the private sector, it would be a mistake to believe that the stock of money is determined by market forces, for several reasons. First, the top five banks in the UK dominate almost the entire market, making it an oligopolistic market. Second, the creation of new money is not determined by the demand for money, but by the demand for credit. Third, even the market for credit is not determined by market forces – as section 3.5 showed, banks ration credit. Of course, the overall strategies of banks, and therefore their lending priorities, are determined at board level. Consequently, it is a small group of senior board members at the largest banks who determine the growth rate of lending and consequently the amount of money in the economy. As the "cash vs bank issued money" chart in the introduction showed, these incentives, combined with a lack of any meaningful constraint on bank lending, led to a doubling of the M4 money supply from 2002-2008.

Banks therefore create too much money in good times, leading to economic booms, asset bubbles and occasional financial crises. Because this money is created with an accompanying debt, eventually the economy becomes over-indebted, with a bust occurring when individuals cut back spending to repay their debts. During the bust, banks' pessimistic views as to the future state of the economy (which are magnified by disaster myopia – see Box 4.C) lead them to create too little money and as a result the economy suffers more than it needs to. The story of this type of business cycle is therefore one of banks creating too much credit, which causes a boom and eventually a bust when debt gets too high. Then, during the bust banks lend too little, worsening the downturn. In short, there is no reason to think that the level of money creation that maximises banks' profits will be the level of money creation that is best for the economy as a whole.

In contrast, under the reformed system the decision to create or destroy money will be determined by the MCC, a committee charged with creating the right amount of money for the economy as a whole. While it is unlikely that this committee will be able to get the level exactly right, history has shown that the current system rarely provides the 'right' amount of money, and more often than not gets it disastrously wrong. The choice is not therefore between a 'perfect' market-determined system on one hand and one determined by a committee on the other, but rather between leaving the nation's money at the mercy of the interests of banks or organising it squarely in the interests of the national economy. Given the above, it is difficult to imagine that the MCC could manage the creation of money more destructively than the banks have done to date.

7.3 ACCOUNTING FOR MONEY CREATION

When the Bank of England creates bank notes, these are recorded on the Bank of England's balance sheet as a liability (a promise to repay), balanced by government bonds held on the asset side of its balance sheet. This accounting convention is a throwback to the era when bank notes were exchangeable for gold and therefore an asset (the gold) had to be held to 'back' the notes in circulation. However, notes have not been redeemable for gold since 1931; as a result the current convention for accounting for the creation of money has been obsolete for more than 80 years.

Appendix III explains how this accounting process can be modernised and why there is no sound reason for the Bank of England to record notes (or, post-reform, the state-issued electronic currency) as a liability, or to hold assets against this liability. It explains that in some countries coins are accounted for differently: while they are assets of the holder, they are liabilities of no-one. It is argued that the note issuance should be modernised to be consistent with the accounting for the creation of coins and that electronic state-issued currency should also be accounted for in the same way. For the rest of this chapter it is enough simply to appreciate that electronic, state-issued money will be an asset of the holder but not a liability of the central bank or the Treasury. There is therefore no need to have any asset 'backing' the currency, since the currency gets its value from people's willingness to exchange it for goods and service, not from other financial assets held on a bank's balance sheet.

After the reforms are implemented, electronic state-issued currency will simply be a number in an account at the Bank of England. These accounts will be held off the Bank of England's balance sheet, so these numbers are not liabilities of the Bank of England. Instead, they should be seen as electronic tokens, held in custody for the owners of the money. The owners may be banks (for the Investment Pools and Operational Accounts), the government (for the Central Government Account) or members of the public (for the aggregated Customer Funds Accounts).[1]

7.4 THE MECHANICS OF CREATING NEW MONEY

When the MCC makes a decision to create new money, it will simply increase the balance of the Central Government Account at the Bank of England by that amount. This is a non-repayable grant of the new money to the government, which it will treat as additional revenue, adding to the revenue it gets from tax and borrowing. How this money enters the wider economy is discussed below. (Alternatively, the MCC may sanction the creation of money to be lent to banks to on-lend into the real economy - discussed in section 7.6).

7.5 SPENDING NEW MONEY INTO CIRCULATION

There are four ways that this newly created money can be spent into the economy:

Increasing government spending

By using the newly created money to increase government spending, the government can increase the provision or quality of public services such as education, health care or public transport, without increasing the tax burden on the public.

What if the government uses the money to increase its spending but wastes it on something that has limited benefits for society or taxpayers? First, this consideration applies to all tax revenue already. If there is a risk that the newly created money will be spent foolishly by the government, then the same risk applies to the rest of the money that the government spends each year. Second, we must avoid making the error of thinking that money can only be spent once. As an individual, you have a limited amount of money. If you spend it foolishly and 'waste' it the money is gone for good. But that money doesn't

---

1. This is not the only way in which the accounting for a reformed system can be presented. Appendix III has an alternative treatment, in which money is a liability of the Central Bank.

disappear; once you've spent it, it is in the hands of someone else and may be spent again. In the same way, even if the government wastes newly created money the money will end up in the hands of government employees and contractors, who will then go on to spend it in the real economy, where it will continue to circulate.

Cutting taxes

Rather than increasing government spending, the elected government of the day could choose to reduce the overall tax burden. This could be achieved in one of two ways:

1. Through maintaining the current tax regime but redistributing the newly created money back to the public via tax rebates (payments) after the year's taxes have been received and using the newly created money to cover the resulting shortfall. Administratively this could be very complicated, as HMRC (the UK's tax collector) does not have bank account details for the large majority of people whose taxes are paid on their behalf by their employer, and so it would rely on members of the public actually reclaiming the rebate.

2. By cancelling or reducing the rates of income tax, VAT (Value Added Tax), corporation tax, National Insurance etc., therefore collecting less money from taxation. The government would then make up the shortfall with the newly created money.

As a general principle, any government using the proceeds of this reform to reduce taxation could aim to reduce or eliminate some of the most regressive or market distorting taxes. There are however problems with this plan: while changes in tax rates are made infrequently, the amount of newly created money spent into the economy will be determined on a monthly basis. Not being able to predict or influence the decisions of the MCC will mean the government will have little idea how much new money will be created each year and therefore by how much it will be able to reduce taxes. For this reason, cancelling or reducing taxes may not be the most effective way (in terms of the government financial planning) of distributing newly created money into the economy.

Making direct payments to citizens

One alternative is for the newly created money to be shared equally between all citizens (or all adults, or all registered taxpayers). This would also mean that the newly created money is most widely distributed across the economy, rather than being concentrated in particular areas of the country or sectors of the economy as a result of large government projects, for example.

Paying down the national debt

The government could use the newly created money to retire (pay down) some of the national debt. However, one problem with this approach is that many of the bonds that make up the national debt are held by pension funds and insurance companies, which means that while some of the newly created money paid to these bondholders would end up in the hands of pensioners or insurance claimants, the majority will stay within financial markets, providing no stimulus to the real (non-financial) economy. The potential problems with using newly created money to reduce the national debt are discussed in detail in Appendix II.

Weighing up the options

The exact mix of the above will depend on the priorities and ideology of the government of the day. Since the newly created money can simply be added to the government's tax revenue, there is no need for a special process to decide how to spend it. If the public has elected a government that promises to increase public spending, then the government can justifiably use the money for this purpose. Likewise, if the public elected a government that promised to reduce the overall tax take, or pay down the national debt, then the government can use the money to these ends. Direct distribution to citizens may be a vote winner for many and would avoid many of the distortions that could be caused by funnelling even more money through government.

There will no doubt be a heated political debate about how such money could be used. However, while what the money is first spent on is important, what is more important is that the new money reaches ordinary people and the real economy, rather than getting trapped in the financial sector. For this reason it may be better that newly-created money is not used to pay down the national debt, as this money is likely to stay circulating within the financial markets, inflating these markets but doing little for the real economy.

With regards to the remaining three options, the choice must be made through a wider public debate. The analysis in Chapter 9 provides a framework for understanding the economic impacts of different methods of injecting money into the economy, and an effective government should make itself aware of these varying impacts to get the greatest economic benefit of newly created money.

Box 7.C - Determining an unmet demand for loans

Currently, as part of its work to maintain monetary and financial stability, the Bank of England conducts a quarterly survey of credit conditions in the UK. Its purpose is to monitor and 'assess trends in the demand for, and the supply of credit, including terms and conditions' (Driver, 2007). The information gathered informs the Bank of England's work in maintaining financial stability and setting interest rates, whilst helping to deconstruct the underlying drivers of bank lending and gain a richer understanding of credit conditions. The questions asked aim to assess how the demand and supply of credit to different sectors has changed over the previous three months and how these trends are expected to change in the upcoming three months.

Under these reforms the Credit Conditions Survey would gain additional importance. Because banks would only be able to lend out money that had already been deposited in Investment Accounts, a lack of customers willing to invest (perhaps due to a negative outlook for the economy) would negatively affect a bank's ability to lend, with potentially harmful effects on the economy.

The Credit Conditions Survey would help to forewarn the Bank of England if such a situation was imminent, giving it time to provide funding to banks (exclusively for lending to businesses) in order to avert a potential credit crunch.

In the longer term the Bank of England could also monitor the interest rate charged on loans to businesses. Generally speaking, a rapidly rising interest rate would suggest the need for the Bank of England to intervene to provide funding to the banks. However, there are several drawbacks to this approach. Firstly, a rising interest rate may signal either a fall in the supply of funds in Investment Accounts or a rise in the demand for loans. As Driver (2007, p. 389) notes, "if changes in the quantity of credit are associated with changes in demand from borrowers, the implications for activity and inflation can be different than if they are associated with changes in supply by lenders".

By intervening simply because market-set interest rates are rising, the Bank of England may risk intervening in a well-functioning market for lending and borrowing, causing distortions in the process. Second, if banks do set the interest rate lower than the market-clearing rate and instead ration credit, as described in Chapter 3, there is a limit to the amount that the interest rates can increase. Once the rate is at this rationed limit any rise in the demand for or reduction in the supply of money in investment accounts will not increase the interest rate, and no further information will be conveyed by them.

7.6 LENDING MONEY INTO CIRCULATION TO ENSURE ADEQUATE CREDIT FOR BUSINESSES

After the reform the Money Creation Committee will also be tasked with ensuring that businesses in the real (non-financial) economy have adequate access to credit. This may be important if there are insufficient funds being placed into investment accounts to support business activity, and is especially important in the UK, where less than 10% of all bank lending goes towards businesses that contribute to GDP (Ryan-Collins et al. 2011). For example, the MCC may decide in its monthly meetings to lend some newly created money to banks, on the condition that the banks can only lend this money to businesses that contribute to GDP (i.e. it cannot be lent for financial speculation, consumer finance or mortgages). This will mean that the new money comes into the economy not as new spending, but as new credit available for businesses. In theory this will not interfere with the MCC's inflation target, as money that is lent for productive purposes tends not to be inflationary, as discussed in Chapter 4.

This ability to make funds available for lending to business should not be used as a tool to micro-manage the economy; it should only be used to ensure that the economy does not suffer due to a lack of credit for businesses. Banks will still be responsible for deciding which businesses they lend to. This means that the Bank of England is never put in the position of 'picking winners'.

In order to lend money in this way the Bank of England will monitor the UK economy both through quantitative and qualitative methods (such as the Credit Conditions Survey). If, based on this analysis, the Bank of England concludes that banks are unable to meet demand for loans from creditworthy borrowers and businesses and this is negatively affecting the economy, then the Bank of England may make up the shortfall by lending a pre-determined amount to commercial banks, to be lent exclusively to businesses.

The allocation of loans through the lending facility may occur in any number of ways. Perhaps the most 'market orientated' of these would be to use an auction mechanism. Currently the Bank of England uses a 'uniform price' auction to allocate central bank reserves to banks in long-term repo (sale and repurchase) operations (Bank of England, 2012). Such a mechanism could be used to allocate loans to banks in a reformed banking system. This would ensure that the interest rate paid on these loans from the Bank of England

Box 7.D – Making banks lend to businesses

As explained in Box 7.C, in the event that there is not enough business lending in the economy, the Bank of England may choose to lend funds to banks on the condition this is then on lent to businesses. Banks will compete with each other for these funds in an auction. Because banks will no longer be protected from failure, they will only bid if they believe that they are able to make loans which will be repaid and therefore profitable for the bank. As a result, the better a bank is at judging the business plans of businesses that want to borrow, the higher the price it will be able to bid for funds from the Bank of England and the more likely it will be to win the auction. Because any loans made from these funds should provide a source of additional profit to banks, they will be incentivised to invest in the staff and equipment that are best at lending to businesses. This investment will encourage further lending to productive businesses by banks with alternative sources of funds (i.e. not those borrowed from the Bank of England), as their ability to assess business loan applications will be enhanced – lowering the likelihood they will make bad loans, and thereby increasing their profit from this form of lending. Essentially, banks will be incentivised to compete on their ability to make well allocated loans to businesses, with positive benefits for the economy as a whole.

would be set by what banks are willing to pay, which in turn would be determined by the demand for loans from businesses in the wider economy.

Any loans that the Bank of England makes to banks specifically for the purposes of on-lending to businesses will be funded by money created by the Bank of England. So, if for example, MegaBank were successful in securing £10 billion in loan financing from the Bank of England, its Investment Pool would be credited with £10 billion (and the money supply would therefore increase by the same amount)[2].

---

2. To prevent spikes in lending just after the Bank of England lends to the banks (due to banks wanting to lend it as quickly as possible to avoid incurring interest charges from the Bank of England on money that has not yet been lent), banks would only pay interest on these loans once the money had actually been on-lent to businesses. Then, to stop banks hoarding this money, or only borrowing in order to prevent their competitors from doing so, the borrowing banks would be required to loan this money created within a set time period or be forced to return it to the Bank of England and pay a fine (to prevent anti-competitive practices). This would prevent the situation where the MCC had to calculate how much money to create yet also had to account for a bank that had so far not lent into circulation all the money that it borrowed.

The repayment of the loan principal will occur by debiting the bank's Investment Pool and simultaneously updating the Bank of England's records (the money is destroyed upon repayment). The repayment of the interest on these loans will be credited to the Central Government Account at the Bank of England, to ensure that these interest payments – which withdraw money from the real economy – are re-circulated back into the economy through government expenditure.

7.7 REDUCING THE MONEY SUPPLY

In a growing economy it is unlikely that the MCC will ever have to destroy money, as long as the monetary growth rate is in line with growth in GDP. The Money Creation Committee should aim to be cautious in their creation of money and increase the stock of money slowly and steadily, which should ensure that there is little need for later reductions in order to correct earlier 'overshooting'. However, there may still be some circumstances where it is necessary to reduce the money supply.

As explained in the case study on Zimbabwe in Appendix I, significant inflation can be triggered when the level of goods and services circulating in the economy collapses. This may happen for a number of reasons, such as war, bad economic policies or natural disaster. Alternatively, there is the possibility that due to the environmental limits of growth being reached there will be no capacity for further growth. In a zero growth economy an increase in money creation (and therefore spending) would likely feed through into inflation. Likewise we may find we have to decrease economic output in order to live with the natural capacity of the environment. In this case to avoid inflation the amount of spending would need to shrink. Finally, it may be argued that the huge increase in money creation in the run-up to the financial crisis may need to be partially reversed as a deleveraging of debt and bank-created money occurs.

In a reformed system the Bank of England would have a number of tools by which it can remove money from circulation. These are:

- By removing money (with agreement) from the government's account at the Bank of England, directly reducing the amount of money in circulation. This effectively involves taxing money out of existence. While this would potentially be the most efficient way of decreasing the stock of money, it may also be the most difficult politically.

- By selling securities that the Bank of England already owns (such as Gilts or Treasury bonds) and removing the money received for them from circulation. Similarly, the Bank of England could remove money by issuing new bonds, such as the Bank of England bills it occasionally uses for this purpose. This method would be most likely to be used to effect temporary and reversible reductions in the money supply.

- By choosing not to roll over loans to the banking system that it had previously made. After the reform, any creation of money by the Bank of England to lend to banks (for on-lending to businesses) would increase money in circulation. Conversely, the repayment of these loans would remove money from circulation. The Bank of England could then re-inject this repaid money by re-lending it to the banks, but by choosing not to do this, the amount of money in circulation would fall. Of course, this mechanism is only useful if the Bank of England has already created some money for banks to on-lend to businesses; if this lending facility is never used, then this method of reducing the money supply will not be an option.

- By not re-circulating some of the 'Conversion Liability' to the government. As discussed in the next chapter, when the demand liabilities of banks are converted into state-issued electronic currency, they will be replaced with a new liability to the Bank of England, which is effectively a charge to the banks for the electronic state-issued currency. This 'Conversion Liability' will be repaid to the Bank of England over time as the bank's loans are repaid. Normally, this money would automatically be granted to the Treasury immediately and spent back into circulation. However, if the Bank of England needed to reduce the money supply, it could choose not to recirculate some of the funds it receives via the Conversion Liability and instead destroy this money, reducing the money supply in the process. This is probably the easiest method for permanently removing large amounts of money from circulation, although it will only apply during the transitional period.

CHAPTER 8
MAKING THE TRANSITION

This chapter explains how we make the transition between the current system and the reformed system. It is necessarily quite technical. Readers who wish to avoid the balance sheets may skip this chapter, as the following chapters assume that this process has already been completed.

An overview of the process

There are two elements of the transition to the new banking system:

1. The overnight 'switchover' on a specified date when the demand deposits of banks will be converted into state-issued currency and customers' accounts will be converted into Transaction Accounts and Investment Accounts.

2. A longer period, potentially 10-20 years following the reforms, as the consequences of the conversion of demand deposits into state-issued currency allows a significant reduction in household debt and a gradual reduction in the size of the aggregated balance sheet of the banking sector.

The economy will be operating on the basis of the reformed monetary system immediately following the switchover. However, it will take a longer period of transition to recover from the 'hangover' of debt created by the current debt-based monetary system. The monetary system cannot be considered fully reformed until this process is complete.

The balance sheets for the Bank of England, the commercial banking sector and the household sector (i.e. the non-bank sector) before, just after, and around 20 years after the reforms take place are shown at the end of this chapter. An alternative accounting treatment of the reforms and these balance sheets, in which money remains on the liabilities side of the central bank's balance sheet, can be found in Appendix III.

8.1 THE OVERNIGHT 'SWITCHOVER' TO THE NEW SYSTEM

The following steps will take place instantaneously on a specified date, known as the 'switchover' date. The balance sheets of the Bank of England, the commercial banking sector, and the household sector before this date can be found at the end of this chapter (figure 8.11). All the figures in this section are from February 2012.

Step 1: Updating the Bank of England's balance sheet

There are a number of changes that need to be made to the Bank of England's balance sheet. The first step is to accept that notes should not be recorded as liabilities of the Bank of England, for the reasons discussed in Appendix III. This immediately removes £54.9 billion (as of February 2012) from the liabilities side of the Issue Department's balance sheet. However, the assets (bonds etc.) on the Issue Department's balance sheet are so far unchanged, giving the Issue Department a net worth of £54.9bn. Figure 8.1 and 8.2 show the situation before and after this change.

fig. 8.1 - Current balance sheet of Issue Department (£m)

Bank of England Issue Department (before)	
Assets	**Liabilities**
UK Gilts £5, 749	Notes in circulation £54,921
Deposits at Banking Dept £47,562	Equity *(Net worth)* £0
Repos £1,610	
Total £54,921	**Total £54,921**

fig. 8.2 - Updated balance sheet of Issue Department (£m)

Bank of England Issue Department (after)	
Assets	**Liabilities**
UK Gilts £5, 749	Notes *(no longer liabilities)* £0
Deposits at Banking Dept £47,562	Equity *(Net worth)* £54,921
Repos £1,610	
Total £54,921	**Total £54,921**

The Bank of England keeps a separate balance sheet covering its issuance of paper bank notes, but this convention is a relic of the era when Bank of England notes were redeemable for gold, and is no longer necessary in this reformed monetary system. We therefore merge the two balance sheets of the Bank of England – the Issue Department and the Banking Department.

The balance sheet of the Bank of England's Banking Department initially appears as shown overleaf (from the Bank of England's 2012 Annual Report).

fig. 8.3 - Current balance sheet of Banking Department (£m)

Bank of England Banking Department (before)	
Assets	**Liabilities**
Balances at other central banks £372	Deposits from other central banks £14,806
Loans to banks £15,157	Deposits from banks £217,623
Securities (incl. foreign currency) £4,782	Deposit from Issue Dept £47,562
Derivatives £461	Public Deposits £1,234
	Other deposits £21,367
QE (Asset Purchase Facility Fund) £286,579	Forex bonds in issue £5,104
Securities available for sale £5,340	All other liabilities £4,839
All other assets (property, pension fund etc) £2,781	Equity (Net Worth) £2,937
Total £315,472	**Total £315,472**

When merging the two balance sheets, the Banking Department's deposit from the Issue Department, (a liability), is cancelled out by the Issue Department's deposit at the Banking Department (an asset). These items become zero and are removed from the balance sheet. The equity of the Issue Department, at £54.9bn is added to the £2.9bn positive equity of the Banking Department, giving the merged balance sheets net worth of £57.9bn (shown opposite).

fig. 8.4 - Merged Bank of England balance sheet (£m)

Bank of England Balance Sheet (after)	
Assets	**Liabilities**
	Deposits from other central banks
FROM ISSUE DEPT:	£14,806
UK Gilts	Deposits from banks
£5,749	£217,623
Deposit at Banking Dept	Deposit from Issue Dept
£0	£0
Repos	Public Deposits
£1,610	£1,234
	Other deposits
FROM BANKING DEPT:	£21,367
Balances at other central banks	Forex bonds in issue
£372	£5,104
Loans to banks	All other liabilities
£15,157	£4,839
Securities (incl. foreign currency)	
£4,782	
Derivatives	
£461	
QE (Asset Purchase Facility Fund)	
£286,579	
Securities available for sale	
£5,340	
All other assets (property, pension fund etc)	Equity (Net Worth)
£2,781	£57,858
Total	**Total**
£322,831	**£322,831**

Next we convert the liabilities of the Bank of England that are effectively electronic money, and remove them from the balance sheet, onto a record of Funds Held in Custody, as follows (shown in figure 8.5).

- Deposits from banks, which represent the present-day central bank reserve accounts, are converted into state-issued electronic currency and become the new Operational Accounts. The original liability becomes zero and can be removed from the balance sheet.

- Public deposits, which would include the Consolidated Fund (the government's account at the Bank of England) are converted into the new Central Government Account (and again is removed from the liabilities side of the Bank of England's balance sheet).

- Deposits from other central banks would be converted into accounts for those central banks.

- We can also add the Investment Pools of the commercial banks. These accounts will initially have zero balances. We will look at how these accounts are 'funded' in section 8.2.

With the reserve accounts and other deposits now converted into electronic state-issued money rather than being liabilities of the Bank of England, the Bank of England will have positive net worth of £312.9 billion. This net worth has come from the purchases of government bonds through issuing bank notes, and the purchase of government bonds through the creation of central bank reserves through the Quantitative Easing scheme. In effect, this £313 billion is seigniorage which has been earned from the creation of money, but which has only been recognised as a result of the fact that this reform does not require backing assets to be held against the state-issued currency (for the reasons discussed in Appendix III). We now need to complete our changes to the balance sheet of the Bank of England by converting the demand deposits of banks into state-issued currency held at the Bank of England.

fig. 8.5 - Final Bank of England balance sheet with funds held in custody (£m)

Bank of England Balance Sheet		Funds Held in Custody
Assets	**Liabilities**	
UK Gilts £5,749	~~Deposits from other central banks~~ → £0	Deposits from other central banks £14,806
Repos £1,610	~~Deposits from banks~~ → £0	Operational Accounts of Banks £217,623
Balances at other central banks £372	~~Public Deposits~~ → £0	Central Govt Account (Public Deposits) £1,234
Loans to banks £15,157	~~All other deposits~~ → £0	All other deposits £21,367
Securities (inc foreign currency) £4,782	Forex bonds in issue £5,104	Investment Pools of Banks £0
Derivatives £461	All other liabilities £4,839	
QE (Asset Purchase Facility Fund) £286,579		
Securities available for sale £5,340		
All other assets (property, pension fund etc) £2,781		
	Equity (Net Worth) £312,888	
Total £322,831	**Total £322,831**	**Total £255,030**

Box 8.A - Dealing with the bonds purchased through Quantitative Easing

Quantitative Easing was a scheme set up in response to the financial crisis. One effect of QE was to boost the broad money supply, or at least negate the contraction in the money supply which arose when banks stopped lending but people continued paying down their debts. The scheme was undertaken by buying government bonds from pension funds and other non-bank investors. Pension funds received bank deposits in exchange for the bonds, and the pension funds' banks received new central bank reserves in their accounts at the Bank of England. As well as creating new bank deposits, this boosted the level of central bank reserves from a pre-crisis level of around £20bn to over £217bn, meaning that there was less need for banks to lend to each other in order to acquire the reserves needed to settle payments.

In theory, the Bank of England will reverse this process once the economy has recovered, by selling the bonds back into the market, so reducing the stock of central bank reserves back to their pre-QE level. However, the likelihood of the reversal occurring is questionable. One of the most obvious obstacles is that, by selling the government bonds that it bought back into the market, the Bank of England will actually be competing with the government's own issuance of bonds. Therefore, it would need to wait until a time when the government is borrowing very little and consequently issuing a very low level of bonds.

With that in mind, there are two ways that the Bank of England could handle the government bonds that it owns. First, it could continue to hold them to maturity, with the government paying interest to the Bank of England and the Bank of England recording this interest as profit and returning it straight back to the government. This would, in effect, make this portion of the national debt interest free for the government (because all the interest is returned). As the individual bonds mature, the government could pay the Bank of England the face value of the bonds.

The second option is to simply accept the reality that these bonds were purchased through the creation of money, by the QE scheme or note issuance, and for the bonds to be cancelled. This will lower the national debt significantly. It does constitute monetising the debt (printing money to pay the government's debts), which is generally considered to be poor economic policy, but in reality this has already happened as a result of the actions of the Bank of England and government in response to the financial crisis.

Step 2: Converting the liabilities of banks into electronic state-issued money

With the Bank of England's balance sheets consolidated and existing central bank reserves converted into new electronic money held off the Bank of England's balance sheet, we are now ready to convert the demand deposits of commercial banks into electronic state-issued money.

The first step is to calculate each bank's total amount of pound sterling demand liabilities to individuals, businesses and public sector organisations. Each bank has this data readily available. As a worked example, let's assume that MegaBank has demand liabilities of £300bn.

*fig. 8.6 - Conversion of Liabilities into State-Issued Money **i***

MegaBank	
Assets	**Liabilities**
All assets ...	Demand liabilities £300 billion All other liabilities ...

Next, the total aggregate demand liability of each bank is removed from its balance sheet, and an equal amount of new state-issued currency is created and added to the Customer Funds Account that the bank administers. For example, the Customer Funds Account administered by MegaBank would now be £300bn whereas its demand liabilities would now be zero.

*fig. 8.7 - Conversion of Liabilities into State-Issued Money **ii***

MegaBank Balance Sheet – Loans		Customer Funds
Assets	**Liabilities**	*(Held in custody)*
	Demand liabilities £300 bn → £0 All other liabilities ...	Customer Funds Account £0 → £300 bn

This is state-issued currency, held at the Bank of England, which belongs to the customers of MegaBank. For actual UK figures, the total stock of demand liabilities is approximately half of M4, at around £1,041bn (as of September 2012, according to Table B1.4 of the Bank of England's BankStats publication), so the total quantity of money in all the Customer Funds Accounts combined would be £1,041bn on the day of the switchover (shown in figure 8.8).

In effect, the Bank of England has 'extinguished' the banks' demand liabilities to their customers by creating new state-issued electronic currency and transferring ownership of that currency to the customers in question. Customers of banks now have either a) electronic money in their Transaction Account, with the actual money being held at the central bank, and which can be used to make payments on demand, or b) a claim on a bank, via their Investment Account, which has a maturity date or notice period and which is still a liability of the bank, to be paid in the future. Each bank would no longer have any demand deposits at all, and the only accounts held on its balance sheet would be Investment Accounts, with fixed notice periods.

Would the creation of £1,041 billion of electronic currency be inflationary? No, for the simple reason that this 'creation' is simply converting bank-issued money into state-issued money, and the process neither increases nor reduces the amount of money in circulation. However, this money has already had an effect on demand (and therefore prices), but at the point when it was initially created by the banking sector's loan making activity.

Other Changes

Simultaneously with the changes above, each bank will convert its fixed-term and fixed-notice savings accounts into Investment Accounts. These Investment Accounts will still be recorded on the balance sheet as liabilities of the bank to the customer. Current accounts will be converted into Transaction Accounts, and the new legal custodial relationship will start to apply to these accounts.

Step 3: The creation of the 'Conversion Liability' from banks to the Bank of England

If removing the demand liabilities from bank balance sheets were the end of the process, then the UK banking sector in aggregate would have lost around £1,041bn of liabilities. With their assets unchanged, this would have increased their collective net worth and shareholder equity by £1,041bn. This would

fig. 8.8 - Conversion of Liabilities into State-Issued Money (£m) **iii**

Bank of England Balance Sheet		Funds Held in Custody
Assets	**Liabilities**	
UK Gilts £5,749	Deposits from other central banks £0	Deposits from other central banks £14,806
Repos £1,610	Deposits from banks £0	Operational Accounts of Banks £217,623
Balances at other central banks £372	Public Deposits £0	Central Govt Account (Public Deposits) £1,234
Loans to banks £15,157	Other deposits £0	All Other deposits £21,367
Securities (inc. foreign currency) £4,782	Forex bonds in issue £5,104	Investment Pools of Banks £0
Derivatives £461	All other liabilities £4,839	Customer Funds Accounts £1,041,000
QE (Asset Purchase Facility Fund) £286,579		
Securities available for sale £5,340		
All other assets (property, pension fund etc.) £2,781		
	Equity (Net Worth) £312,888	
Total £322,831	**Total** £322,831	**Total** £1,296,030

represent a huge paper profit for banks and their shareholders. To negate this effect, we replace the old demand liability to the customers with a new liability, the 'Conversion Liability', which is to the Bank of England. This means that the net worth and balance sheet of the banks is completely unchanged, as the aggregate balance sheet for the banking sector shows below. The assets side is also unchanged, as reserve accounts – deposits of banks at the Bank of England – have simply been converted into the new Operational Accounts, which are still held as an asset of the commercial bank.

fig. 8.9 - Aggregated Balance Sheet for Banking Sector Post-Switchover

Aggregate Balance Sheet of Banking Sector	
Assets	**Liabilities**
Reserve accounts at Bank of England £217.6bn → £0	Demand liabilities £1,041bn → £0
Replaced with Operational Accounts at Bank of England £0 → £217.6bn	**Replaced with** Conversion Liability £0 → £1,041bn

This liability to the Bank of England would in effect be a charge, at face value, for the state-issued money that the Bank of England created to extinguish the bank's demand liabilities to customers. The liability would be repayable to the Bank of England at a schedule that matches the maturity profile of the bank's assets (i.e. as the bank's loans to businesses and the public are gradually repaid, the bank will repay the Bank of England).

Under normal circumstances the Bank of England will be required to automatically grant the money paid to it as a result of the Conversion Liability to the Treasury to be spent back into the economy. This means that repayment of the Conversion Liability will not reduce the amount of money circulating in the economy.

At this point the balance sheets of the economy will appear as they do in figure 8.12. The large increase in equity at the Bank of England is a direct result of removing money from both banks and the central bank's balance sheet. This increase in equity is in effect a reclaiming of the seigniorage revenue from the banking sector to be repaid to the government as the commercial banks' assets mature, from where it will be spent back into the economy.

8.2 ENSURING BANKS WILL BE ABLE TO PROVIDE ADEQUATE CREDIT IMMEDIATELY AFTER THE SWITCHOVER

From the changes made in the previous section, we can see that on the morning immediately following the switchover, the Investment Pools of banks will have balances of zero, implying that banks would be unable to lend until they had first acquired funds from elsewhere. This section looks at where this funding for lending could come from.

Funds from customers

There are two sources of money that the banks will be able to lend from as a matter of routine:

1. From new Investment Accounts opened by customers. On any particular day, there will be a number of customers who wish to put money aside to earn some interest. Upon opening Investment Accounts they will provide funds for lending.

2. From loan repayments from existing borrowers. The money from these borrowers, if it is not needed to repay Investment Account holders (many of whom will typically roll over their investments) can be re-lent. On any particular day, significant sums of money will be collected from borrowers in loan repayments, much of which could be re-lent.

These two sources of funding alone suggest that banks should have little shortage of funds to lend immediately after the reform is implemented. However, there are two additional sources of funds to ensure that banks are able to lend sufficient amounts to support the economy immediately after the switchover. We will consider these two sources below.

Lending the money created through quantitative easing

In much of the press, Quantitative Easing was described as 'printing money and lending it to banks so that they can lend it to businesses and the public'. This description is highly inaccurate; banks could not lend the reserves that were created through QE to the public, as central bank reserves can only be held by organisations that can hold accounts at the Bank of England (i.e. banks and central government).

However, as discussed above, during the overnight switchover the reserve accounts at the Bank of England (which hold liabilities of the Bank of England) are converted into Operational Accounts, which will hold state-issued electronic currency. Crucially, unlike central bank reserves, this state-issued currency can be lent to members of the public.

This means that on the morning after the switchover, there will be £217.6bn of state-issued currency in the bank's Operational Accounts. This sum is far beyond what the banks would need for actual operating funds (i.e. to cover staff, salaries, rent and other operating costs) and so they would probably wish to use a significant proportion of these funds for lending. For that reason, there is unlikely to be any shortage of funds available for lending by banks on the day after the switchover.

In fact, the danger immediately after the reform may not be that there is a shortage of lendable funds, but that there is a glut of funds due to the large balances in these Operational Accounts, and as a result an incentive for banks to lend too much too quickly. For that reason, the Bank of England may want to restrict bank lending (through a temporary regulation) for a brief period immediately after the overnight switchover, or take steps to actually reduce the amount of central bank reserves before the switchover, to avoid the risk of a potential lending boom.

Providing funds to the banks via auctions

Box 8.A explained that it is highly unlikely that the QE scheme will be reversed in the near future. However, in the unlikely scenario that it is reversed and the banks only have enough funds in their central bank Operational Accounts to cover their own operations, but not to fund lending, what will be the result?

In this case, the Bank of England could use the auction mechanism discussed in section 7.6 to lend funds to banks, which the banks could then lend on to businesses and members of the public. There would need to be some strings attached to these funds (for example, the funds should not be used for speculative purposes).

The banks would enter the auction for funds the day before the switchover, bidding for the amount of funds they wish to borrow. (The Bank of England already runs auctions in this way as a matter of routine). Banks would then find that these funds have been placed into their Investment Pools on the morning after the switchover.

The four sources of funds described above show that there is no real risk of a credit crunch immediately after the switchover.

8.3 THE LONGER-TERM TRANSITION

Repayment of the Conversion Liability

Figure 8.13 details the balance sheets of the economy after the transition is complete. As discussed earlier, when the demand liabilities of banks are converted into state-issued electronic currency, the banks lose those demand liabilities but acquire a new, equal-value Conversion Liability to the Bank of England. This Conversion Liability will be repaid as the bank's loans are gradually repaid. The exact rate of repayment will be agreed between the bank in question and the Bank of England, to ensure that the repayments are spread fairly evenly over a number of years and that the rate of repayment does not reduce the bank's ability to provide a useful level of lending throughout the transition.

The repayment of the Conversion Liability converts one asset held by the Bank of England (the Conversion Liability) to another – electronic money held in the Bank of England's own account – as funds are transferred from the commercial banks to the central bank. Then the transfer of this money to the Treasury reduces the equity of the Bank of England while at the same time reducing its assets. The Treasury then spends the money back into the economy via any of the mechanisms outlined in Chapter 7, giving the government an additional £1,041 billion in what is essentially seigniorage revenue over a period of around 20 years.

This seigniorage revenue is non-inflationary, as it does not increase the money supply; it is simply the recycling of loan repayments from businesses and households back into the economy via spending rather than new lending.

Allowing deleveraging by reducing household debt

There is a crucial difference between loan repayments made by borrowers in the reformed and current monetary systems. Within the current system, when loans are repaid, the bank reduces both its assets (the loan) and its liabilities (the borrower's bank account balance) in tandem (See section 2.5). For the money supply to be restored to its previous level requires that someone else borrows, increasing the overall level of debt. This precludes any significant reductions of the level of household debt, as the lower levels of spending associated with lower levels of lending tend to increase the likelihood of recession.

In contrast, after the reform, debt repayments do not affect the money supply, as debt repayment involves the transfer of an asset (state-issued electronic currency) from the borrower's Transaction Account to the bank's Investment Pool. From the bank's Investment Pool the money will be used to a) make further loans, b) repay Investment Account holders, or c) pay staff and dividends (via the Operational Account). During the transitional period, it may also be used to repay the bank's Conversion Liability to the Treasury. Thus the repayment of the conversion liability will transfer money to the government's bank account, from where it will be spent back into the economy. As a result, the stock of money will be maintained, although because the money is spent and not lent into circulation, it is possible for debt to be lower than it otherwise would be. The reforms therefore introduce a fundamental and profound change in the monetary system.

It is important to remember that while the Conversion Liability requires banks to pay £1,041bn to the Bank of England, it does not require there to be £1,041bn in circulation; the same units of state-issued currency, when recycled through the system, can be used to repay debts numerous times. Consequently, just £50bn of currency, transferred through the Conversion Liability each year, could clear the entire Conversion Liability in around 20 years. Each time that it is spent back into the economy, it will provide further debt-free money to the economy and allow individuals and households to further reduce their debts.

It is also crucially important to recognise that repayment of the Conversion Liability does not drain £1,041bn from the banking system. When the money received by Treasury is spent back into the economy (or distributed back to citizens) it will be transferred back to the Customer Funds Accounts administered by the banks. Banks will then be able to encourage customers to transfer some of this money into Investment Accounts to fund their own lending.

Forcing a deleveraging of the household sector

The extent to which the Conversion Liability leads to a reduction in household debt depends entirely on what the people who receive this money do with it (after it has been spent by the Treasury). If those who receive the money decide to spend it rather than pay down debts, then there will be no significant deleveraging in the short term.

fig. 8.10 - Flow of loan repayment profits post reform

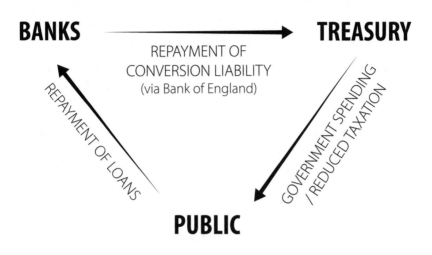

However, over time it is likely that the repayment of the Conversion Liability will lead to a significant deleveraging, especially given the indebtedness of the household sector and the desire of many people to reduce their current levels of debt. It is also possible to force a deleveraging of households and a reduction in the size of the aggregate banking sector's balance sheet. This can be done as follows:

1. As repayments are made on the Conversion Liability, the Treasury must distribute this money directly to citizens in equal proportions (i.e. divided equally by every eligible adult).

2. If a citizen receiving the money has debts, the payment must be used to pay down those debts.

3. Citizens who have no debts can use the funds as they wish (e.g. to spend, to place into an Investment Account or to invest in other assets).

As most individuals and households have at least some debt, this will ensure that most of the repayments on the Conversion Liability are recycled into paying down the debts of the household sector.

There are significant benefits to this approach:

1. The deleveraging would reduce the size of the banking sector's balance sheet in absolute terms and relative to GDP. This would reduce the risk

that banks pose to the economy through their failure. Whilst after the reform bank failures would not cause a contraction in the amount of money in circulation there are still significant implications if a bank that had a large market share of say, business lending, were to fail.

2. The resulting reduction in household debt would leave households with higher disposable income (because less has to be spent on debt servicing), which should increase economic growth overall.

3. A reduction in the debt of the household sector is by definition an increase in the net wealth of households. Higher net wealth of households should reduce dependency on the state (reducing the demands placed on government expenditure), and allow households to put more income into preparations for retirement.

Deleveraging is possible even if the MCC never increases the money supply

The recycling effect of repayments on the Conversion Liability means that deleveraging (a reduction in household debt) of up to £1,041 billion is possible even if the Money Creation Committee chose never to increase the money supply (and therefore does not create any additional new debt-free money). This ensures that regardless of the decisions of the MCC, the economy will be transformed from one that is dependent on bank-issued, debt-based money, to one that has a money supply that is independent of the amount of debt and the lending decisions of banks.

fig 8.11 - Balance sheets: the current system

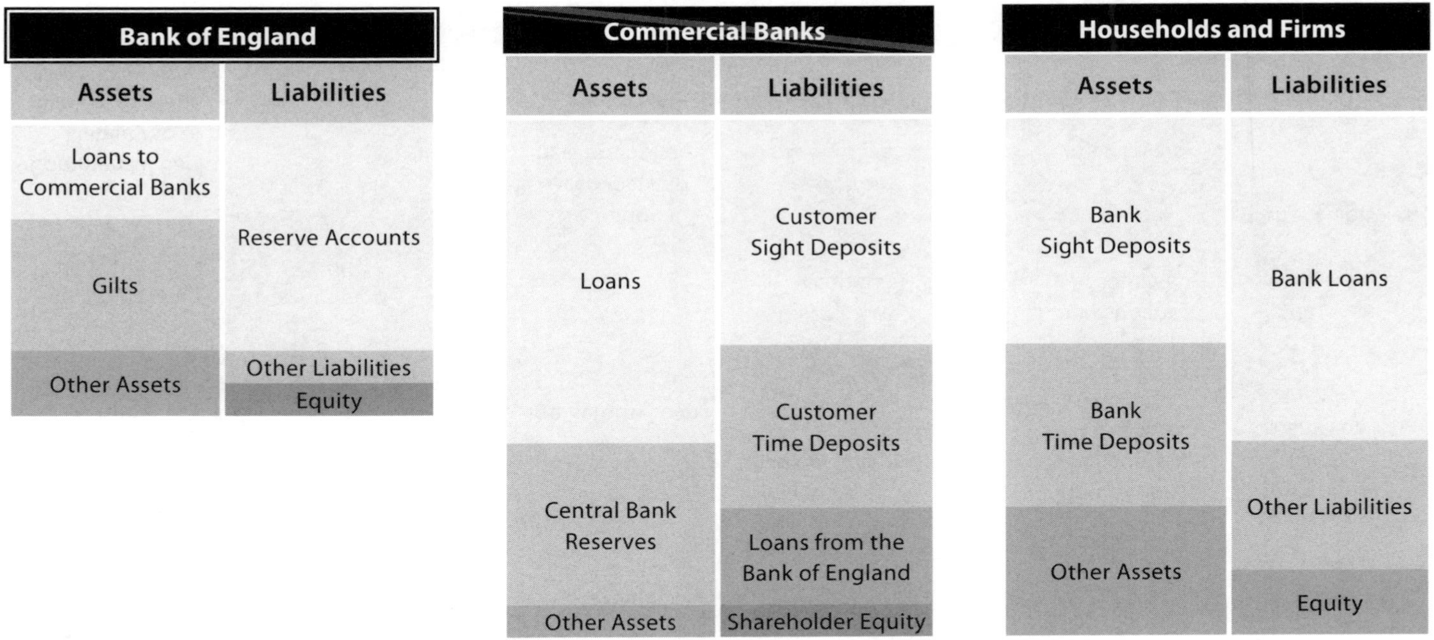

Bank of England

Assets	Liabilities
Loans to Commercial Banks	Reserve Accounts
Gilts	
Other Assets	Other Liabilities
	Equity

Commercial Banks

Assets	Liabilities
Loans	Customer Sight Deposits
Central Bank Reserves	Customer Time Deposits
	Loans from the Bank of England
Other Assets	Shareholder Equity

Households and Firms

Assets	Liabilities
Bank Sight Deposits	Bank Loans
Bank Time Deposits	
Other Assets	Other Liabilities
	Equity

That deposits exceed bank lending reflects the fact that during QE the Bank of England purchased bonds from non-banks. This led to an increase in deposits and reserves one for one.

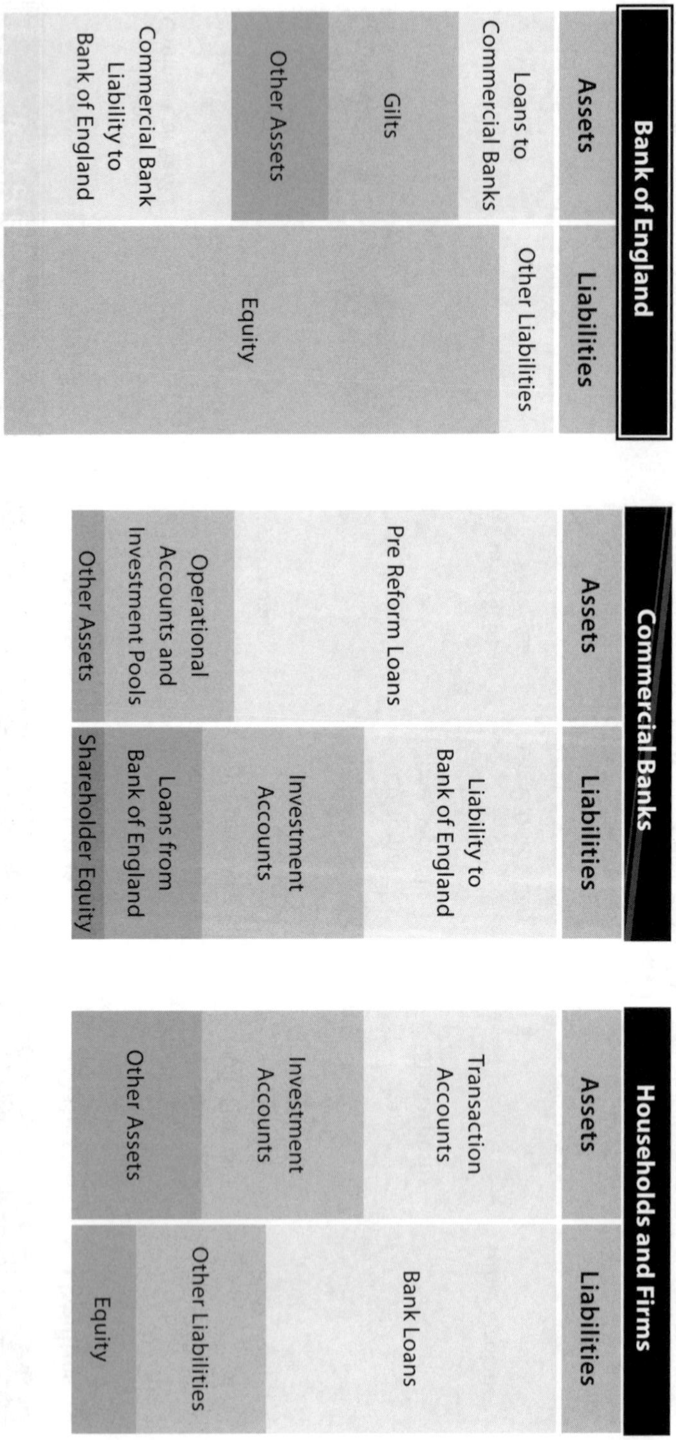

fig 8.12 - Balance sheets: one day after the switchover

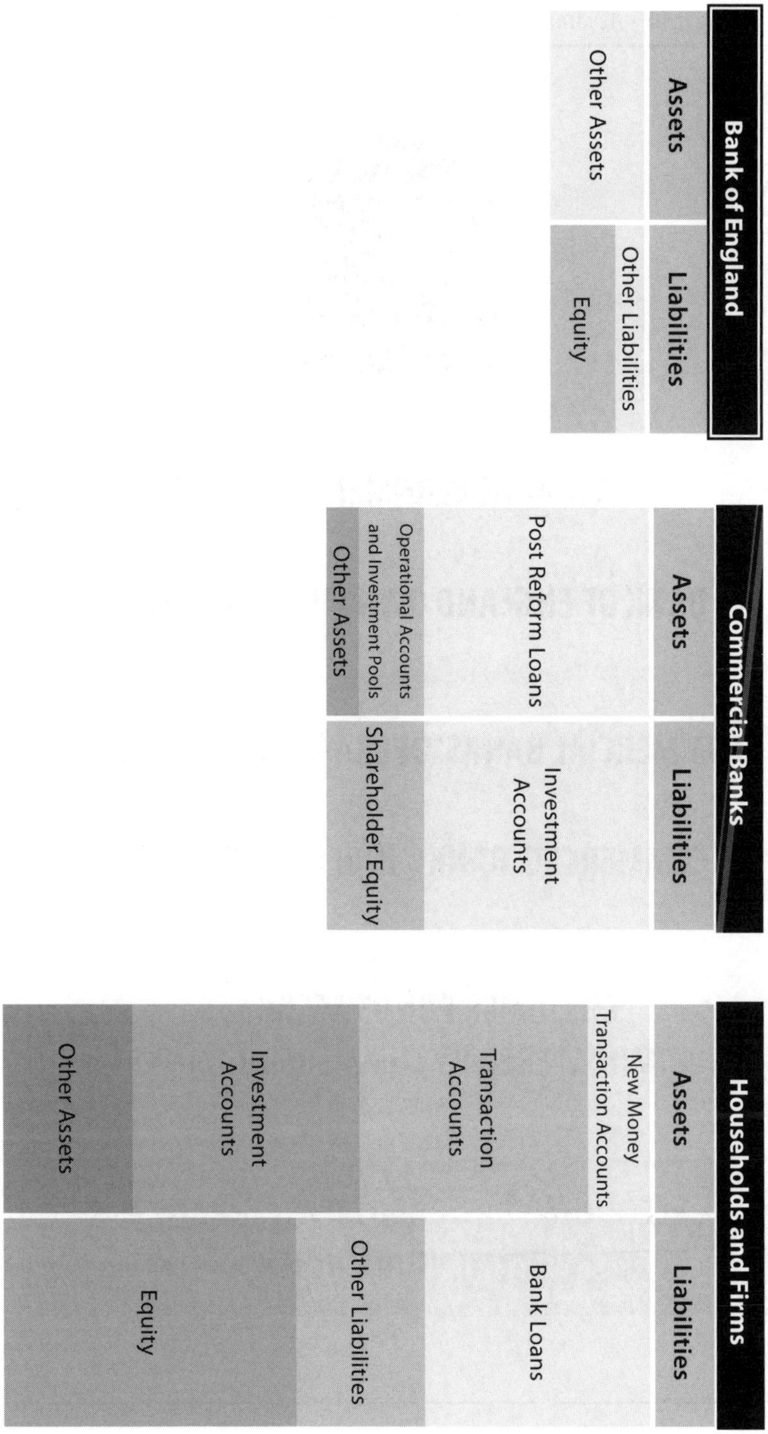

fig 8.13 - Balance sheets: Approx. 20 years after switchover

fig. 8.14 - Accounts held in custody at the Bank of England post-reform

BANK of ENGLAND

CENTRAL GOVERNMENT ACCOUNT

BANK OF ENGLAND OWN FUNDS ACCOUNT

COMMERCIAL BANKS' OPERATIONAL ACCOUNTS

COMMERCIAL BANKS' INVESTMENT POOLS

**CUSTOMER FUNDS ACCOUNTS
ADMINISTERED BY COMMERCIAL BANKS**

**ACCOUNTS FOR OTHER CENTRAL BANKS
& PAYMENT PROVIDERS**

CHAPTER 9

UNDERSTANDING THE IMPACTS OF THE REFORMS

This chapter looks at the economic impacts of a monetary system where money is issued solely by the state and injected into the economy through the various mechanisms outlined in Chapter 7. We begin by briefly summarising a few key differences between the current monetary system and the reformed system. We then look at the likely impact of bank lending and central bank money creation in a reformed system, before addressing the reform's impact on financial stability and asset price bubbles. Finally, we address the environmental and social impacts of a reformed monetary system.

9.1 DIFFERENCES BETWEEN THE CURRENT & REFORMED MONETARY SYSTEMS

There are a few key differences between the current monetary system and the reformed system outlined in Chapters 7 and 8. In essence the rules of the monetary system have changed and this will change the dynamics of the economic system. The key differences are shown in the table overleaf.

9.2 EFFECTS OF NEWLY CREATED MONEY ON INFLATION AND OUTPUT

What will be the economic effects (in the short run) of money creation in a reformed monetary system? In short, the effect of money creation will depend largely on what the new money is created for. In the following section we look at the effect of money creation under four different scenarios:

1. Distributing newly created money to citizens via a 'citizen's dividend'

2. Using newly created money to increase government spending

3. Using newly created money to cut taxes

4. Lending newly created money to banks to on-lend to businesses that contribute to GDP

For consistency with chapter 4, we reapply the quantity equation to show the effect of money creation and bank lending on output and prices. To recap, M stands for the quantity of money in circulation, V for the velocity of money (the number of times the same unit of money is used for a transaction in a given time period), T for the number of transactions in a period, and P for the average price level of the transactions. The left hand side (MV) of this equation represents the total amount of spending for a given time period, whereas the right hand side (PT) shows the total value in monetary terms of the number of transactions for the same time period. In all of the examples that follow for purposes of intuition it will help to imagine that the economy in question is initially in a steady state.[1]

Distributing newly created money to citizens via a 'citizen's dividend'

Let us first take the simplest case where the newly created money is granted directly to citizens, via a form of citizen's dividend. In this case the new money increases the purchasing power of the citizens that receive the dividend (and purchasing power in the economy as a whole). If this money is spent on consumer spending and the economy is near full capacity, then with no corresponding increase in the level of output (Y), we would expect to see inflation:

(1)
$$(\uparrow M_{CR}) V_R = (\uparrow P_R) Y$$

Subscript I stands for investment, C for consumption, R for real economy, F for financial economy, $\uparrow$ stands for increase in

At full capacity, an increase in money in the real economy x constant velocity leads to an increase in prices but no change in output.

1. By this, we mean that the levels of output, prices and employment are neither falling nor rising. Just enough loans are being provided, through Investment Accounts, to support production and prices at their current levels. Consumer prices are stable as the amount of money circulating (via Transaction Accounts, assuming velocity stays constant) is balanced with the level of production in the economy. Obviously a situation in which all key variables are static and unchanging is unrealistic, however it is useful as an aid to our understanding and intuition.

Differences between the current & reformed monetary systems

Current System	Reformed System
Money and purchasing power is created by banks when they make loans	Money and purchasing power is created by the state in response to decisions made by the Money Creation Committee
Loans create new purchasing power	Loans transfer purchasing power between savers and borrowers
Loans increase the money supply	Loans have no impact on the money supply
Loan repayments decrease the money supply	Loan repayments have no impact on the money supply
New money is created in tandem with an equal amount of debt	New money is created free of any corresponding debt
An increase in bank investment in one part of the economy does not require a reduction in spending elsewhere	An increase in bank lending in one part of the economy requires a reduction (or 'deferment') of spending elsewhere in the economy: purchasing power is transferred from a saver to a borrower
Banks can lend as and when they find a creditworthy borrower, and can find any necessary central bank reserves after the loan has been made	Banks must first raise funds from Investment Account holders and other investors before they can make a loan

Alternatively, if the economy is significantly below full capacity (as in a recession) then the increase in spending would likely lead to a rise in output of goods and services, as firms use machines that were laying idle and hire the unemployed and underemployed:

(2)
$$(\uparrow M_{CR}) \, V_R = P_R \, (\uparrow Y)$$

Below full capacity, an increase in money for consumption in the real economy x constant velocity leads to increases in output but no inflation.

However, it is highly unlikely that all citizens who receive the dividend would spend it entirely on consumer goods and services. Some of this money would be used to pay down debt and some would be invested via Investment Accounts. In these cases the effect of the newly created money will depend on how the money that is invested is used, as described subsequently.

Using newly created money to increase government spending
Alternatively, the government may decide to use the newly created money it receives from the Money Creation Committee to increase government spending. As with a citizen's dividend, what the money is spent on will determine the effects. If the money is distributed via transfer payments such as the state pension, tax credits and benefits, then the effect will be the same as with a citizen's dividend, with the difference that it will initially be a narrower group of people spending the newly created money. If they spend this money purely on consumer goods and services and the economy is near full capacity then this may lead to consumer price inflation. If the economy were below full capacity then the additional spending would be expected to lead to additional output (i.e. growth in GDP) but without inflation. However, as before, if those who receive the money then invest it via Investment Accounts, the effect will depend on how that money is invested.

Alternatively, the government may decide to spend the newly created money on something that increases the productive capacity of the economy (for example, transport infrastructure, improving the quality of the broadband network, etc.). In this case both the stock of money and the productive capacity of the economy will increase, as in equation 2. For that reason, we would expect output to increase, but with no significant changes in prices (in the long run, although in the short run there may be temporary effects on prices). That said, if the improvements in infrastructure were significant, it could actually lower costs to businesses and so be deflationary or disinflationary.

However, newly created money will likely be spent more than once; when it is spent by the government it will be transferred to the accounts of government employees and employees of companies working on government contracts. What these people do with the money they receive will also have an effect on inflation and output, just as with a citizen's dividend (see section 9.4).

Using newly created money to cut taxes
Alternatively, the government may decide that it will use the newly created money to decrease taxes. If it decreases taxes on individuals (using

newly-created money to cover the resulting shortfall in tax revenue), the effect will be exactly the same as with the citizen's dividend – the citizens that received the tax cut will have more disposable income, increasing purchasing power in the economy while not changing the economy's productive capacity. If all of this extra disposable income is spent on consumer goods and services and the economy is near full capacity, then we might expect inflation. If the economy is below full capacity we could expect output (i.e. GDP) to increase with no change in prices. However, if some of this extra income is invested, then the effect may be inflationary or disinflationary (a slowing rate of positive inflation), depending on how that money is used.

If the government decreases taxes on business instead, then this may also lead to inflation if the businesses that received the tax cuts use the additional money to raise wages or distribute profits and the recipients of this money (staff and shareholders) use this money for further spending on consumer goods and services). However, if businesses used the proceeds to invest in increasing their productive capacity, then the newly created money will have exactly the same effect as when the central bank lends to banks to on-lend to productive businesses (discussed in the next section); the money supply, M, will increase, leading, via investment, to an increase in the productive capacity of the economy and output, Y (without a significant change in prices):

(3)
$$(\uparrow M_R)\, V_R = P_R\, (\uparrow Y)$$

Lending newly created money to banks to on-lend to productive businesses
As described in section 7.6, the Money Creation Committee may choose to create and lend money to banks, on the condition that the banks then on-lend this money to businesses in the real, non-financial economy.

The economic effects of this type of money creation are identical to the effects of credit creation by banks for investment purposes in the current system. As the loans are made new money is created (so M increases). Because the loans are made for investment in the productive sector of the economy investment increases and with it the productive capacity of the economy. Consequently we would not expect to see any inflation in this scenario. The effect of the increase in M will be to increase GDP:

(4)
$$(\uparrow M_{IR})\, V_R = P_R\, (\uparrow Y)$$

9.3 EFFECTS OF LENDING PRE-EXISTING MONEY VIA INVESTMENT ACCOUNTS

We will now look at the effects of different types of bank lending after the reform. Under a reformed banking system, bank lending will simply transfer existing money (and therefore purchasing power) from lender to borrower, without altering the stock of money in circulation. For example, post-reform a person placing their money in an Investment Account will see their purchasing power fall, as they will not be able to access the money for a period of time (although they will gain an asset, the Investment Account, in exchange). The money they placed in the account will then be transferred to the Transaction Account of the borrower (via the bank's Investment Pool). Conversely, in the current system bank loans do not require a reduction in anyone else's account.

Lending pre-existing money for productive purposes

Take the case of a business borrowing to invest. By investing the business increases the productive capacity of the economy. However, in making the loan the bank does not create new money, instead money is simply transferred around the system. Looking at equation 5, increases in (MI R) increase investment spending, and this has the effect of increasing output (Y).

(5)
$$(\uparrow M_{I\,R})\,V_R + M_{CR}\,V_R = P\,(\uparrow Y)$$

Increased investment in the real economy leads to an increase in output.

However, this is not the end of the story. The money for the loan initially came from someone else's Transaction Account, i.e. the initial investor has deferred consumption (in order to invest in the account) and, this should decrease the upward pressure on prices. In addition, the increase in production arising from the investment will lead to there being more goods and services in the economy. The deferment of spending and increase in productive capacity should have a counter-inflationary effect. As a result prices are likely to rise less quickly than they would otherwise.

(6)
$$(\uparrow M_{I\,R})\,V_R + (\downarrow M_{CR})\,V_R = (\downarrow P_R)\,(\uparrow Y)$$

In addition to equation 5, the decrease in money spent on goods and the larger number of goods leads to lower prices ($\downarrow$ stands for 'decrease in')

It is important to note that in a system where money is created debt-free, falling prices (deflation) is not as problematic as it can be in the current system (see section 9.5). However, low inflation may still be more desirable than deflation, so any deflationary pressure will lead to an injection of money by the MCC in order to hit its 2% inflation target. Thus increased investment by businesses as a result of bank lending may need to be offset by the MCC granting newly created money to government to be spent into circulation.[2]

However, in the real world the effect on prices and output are unlikely to be instantaneous. Investment takes time, and therefore the deflationary impacts of the additional production will not be felt until later. Also, money will circulate several times each period. Thus any money lent for productive investment will be used to pay staff (e.g. in the investing firm). Any consumption spending by these staff is likely to have an inflationary effect, countering the deflationary effect of the investment.

Lending pre-existing money for house purchases and unproductive purposes

What about an increase in non-productive lending, such as loans made to purchase existing property? In this situation the quantity of money in circulation does not change, but property purchases increase. This increases the demand for property without increasing its supply. As a result, property prices increase. Likewise an increase in spending on pre-existing financial assets will not increase the number of financial assets in circulation (at least in the short run) so price will increase:

(7)
$$(\uparrow M_F)\, V_F = (\uparrow P_F)\, T_F$$

Increased spending on financial assets leads to rising prices of those assets, given the same supply of assets (Subscript F for financial)

However this increase in lending for property must be funded by someone choosing to invest, rather than spend, some of their income. This reduction in potential consumer spending may have some deflationary effect on consumer prices (assuming a constant velocity).

---

2. The MCC needs to be aware that the money it creates and grants to government may also allow an asset price bubble to continue for longer than it could otherwise (see footnote 4 for more details).

(8)
$$M_{IR} V_R + (\downarrow M_{CR}) V_R = (\downarrow P_R) Y$$

In addition to equation 7, the decrease in consumption spending leads to lower prices.

Alternatively, if the money is diverted from Investment Accounts that were funding investment in the real economy, the productive capacity of the economy will grow less slowly than it otherwise could, leading to (future) inflation in the consumer goods markets, as investments will not be made and (future) production will therefore not increase by as much as it would otherwise.

(9)
$$(\downarrow M_{IR}) V_R + M_{CR} V_R = (\uparrow P_R) (\downarrow Y)$$

In addition to equation 7, the decrease in investment and the lower quantity of goods leads to lower prices.

Regardless of where the money is diverted from, house price inflation is not sustainable in the long-term as it requires money to be transferred away from the purchase or the production of consumer goods, which will lead to a decrease in demand and output.[3] This is in contrast to the current system where the rest of the economy is not impaired by asset prices bubbles until after they burst, allowing them to continue for far longer than they otherwise would be able to. This makes house price bubbles more likely to be self correcting in a reformed system: increased investment in housing would imply less investment in the productive economy, less spending on consumer goods, less economic activity and therefore a lower ability for the economy to service higher house prices. As a consequence house prices would be likely to quickly revert to an affordable level.[4]

---

3. Neither process is sustainable in the long term with a fixed stock of money, as both lead to a decrease in the production of consumer goods, either due to lower demand, or directly by decreasing investment and therefore output. As the economy enters a downturn the ability of individuals to purchase houses at increased prices is impaired, leading to a fall in borrowing for house purchases and a reduction in prices.

4. If the central bank increased money creation (and therefore spending) to compensate for the decrease in demand then the bubble could continue. As a result the central bank will be obliged to act to prevent bubbles in land and property. It is pertinent to note that the newly established Financial Policy Committee

As Chapter 3 showed, under the current monetary system the economy periodically suffers from booms and busts, as a result of banks' credit creation activities. Entrepreneurs and businesses are harmed by both the boom and the bust in the current system. In the boom, easy access to credit and inflated feelings of wealth pushes many into entrepreneurial activities that are unsustainable in the bust, leaving them with debts that cannot be repaid (damaging their ability to be entrepreneurial in the future). Meanwhile, in the bust entrepreneurs cannot secure credit even for good ideas, as banks now have a negative view of the future and are also attempting to rebuild their balance sheets.

In a reformed monetary system the situation will be rather different, as bank lending will no longer expand the stock of bank deposits. Accordingly, the propensity for the economy to experience asset price bubbles, recessions and depressions should be greatly reduced. Instead of banks lending pro-cyclically, their lending decisions will instead reflect the long term savings preferences of the public. Entrepreneurs and businesses should be incentivised to invest, safe in the knowledge that there is a much lower likelihood of events outside their control - such as financial crises and recessions which lead to a fall in demand for their products and therefore bankruptcy.

There is also a lower chance of mal-investment in a reformed monetary system. In the current system, mal-investment is created as a result of banks' lending (and increasing purchasing power) against assets with an inelastic or wholly fixed supply. This affects prices and in so doing alters the relative returns on different investments, dragging people into otherwise unprofitable or socially useless activities (see for example box 4.F). As the previous section made clear, the likelihood of such asset bubbles and the mal investment that goes with them occurring in a reformed system is much lower than is the case today.

Lending pre-existing money for consumer spending

In addition to lending for asset purchases, unproductive lending by banks also includes loans made for the purchase of consumer goods. If the money for this lending comes from a transfer of money from Transaction Accounts to Investment Accounts the quantity of money spent on consumer goods and services remains the same, as money has been transferred from an individual or organisation that wishes to delay their consumption to an individual or organisation that wishes to consume now. Both output and prices are unaffected.

---

at the Bank of England already has the power to curb lending by placing limits on the public's access to mortgages.

9.4 LIMITATIONS IN PREDICTING THE EFFECTS ON INFLATION AND OUTPUT

It should be clear from the scenarios in the preceding two sections that the effect of money creation on the economy depends on a wide range of different factors and the individual choices taken by a large number of people. This makes predictions about the exact effect on inflation and output very difficult. Some broad principles will help although even these are not hard and fast rules:

1. If pre-existing money is lent and this increases the productive capacity of the economy (such as loans to businesses in the real, non-financial economy or investment in boosting national infrastructure), then this is unlikely to create inflation, and could even have a deflationary or disinflationary effect. However, any deflation will be immediately offset by the central bank creating new money which will be granted to the government to be spent into circulation (if the central bank is targeting inflation).

2. If newly created money is allocated towards spending on goods and services while the economy is significantly below 'full capacity', then we would expect to see output (i.e. GDP) increasing without a corresponding increase in inflation.

3. If the economy is close to full capacity, then additional money creation that feeds through into consumer spending could be inflationary.

It should be noted that rather than the simplistic 'all money creation creates inflation' argument that is often heard, the reality is much more complicated, and the deflationary impacts of certain uses of newly created money could balance out the effect of the increases in demand.

It should also be remembered that the models presented here are simply devices for aiding our intuition. In reality the effects of any actions by central or commercial banks are far more complex than the simple mechanical process displayed here. Individuals and organisations will alter their behaviour and adapt to the new circumstances brought about by the initial action, setting off further series of events into the future.

Box 9.B - Interest rates

Post-reform, the interest rate will normally be determined by the market, rather than the central bank. The interest rate on bank loans will be determined by the demand for borrowing and the supply of funds placed in investment accounts. The supply of funds placed into investment accounts will be determined by society's liquidity preference: if people wish on aggregate to hold more liquid assets (e.g. money), they will place less of their money into Investment Accounts. The demand for borrowing, on the other hand, will be determined by a number of factors. For example, the demand for business borrowing will be influenced by the expected profitability of an investment which itself will depend on expectations of future economic conditions. Taking both the supply of money and the quantity of investment accounts as given (i.e. looking at the short run), the interest rate on investment accounts in general will be set by an interaction between the liquidity preference of society and the demand for borrowing.

Changes in interest rates will therefore represent either changes in liquidity preference or changes in the demand for loans. Both factors are liable to change in response to expectations of future economic conditions. However, expectations, as they are largely based on conventions rather than fundamentals, are prone to sudden changes. Consequently, the interest rate may become volatile in some circumstances, with negative effects on businesses. In this situation the central bank may wish to lend to banks to stabilise fluctuations in interest rates caused by changes in liquidity preference.

9.5 POSSIBLE FINANCIAL INSTABILITY IN A REFORMED SYSTEM

Chapter 4 outlined Hyman Minsky's Financial Instability Hypothesis. To sum up, the essence of Minsky's hypothesis is that booms and busts, asset price bubbles, financial crises, depressions, and even debt deflations all occur in the normal functioning of a capitalist economy. What is more, periods of relative stability increase the likelihood of instability and crises by increasing returns and thus the desirability of leverage. The banking sector, with its ability to create credit, facilitates this desire for leverage, which sets in train a series of events that culminate in recession and in some cases a financial crisis and depression. In short, Minsky considered the capitalist system to be inherently unstable. In this section we discuss the likelihood of financial instability in a reformed banking system.

In the current monetary system, when a bank makes a loan the quantity of broad money increases. When this new money is used to purchase an asset whose supply is inelastic (i.e. an asset that's supply does not increase in response to an increase in price), the price of the asset increases. Under a reformed system bank lending will be limited to the amount that individuals are willing to place into Investment Accounts, and so the ability of banks to inflate asset bubbles will be reduced. However, although bank lending will not create new money, it may shift money that would have been spent in one sector to another sector. If money is moved to sectors where the supply of goods is inelastic, the price of the goods will rise. Therefore bank lending may still have an ability to fuel asset price bubbles, although to a lesser extent than is currently the case.

A reduced possibility of asset price bubbles

In order for bank lending to inflate an asset price bubble (for example in property) under a reformed system, banks would have to continually increase the flow of money from either Transaction Accounts or other Investment Accounts to Investment Accounts that fund mortgages.

To see why this process is unsustainable in the long term, let us first examine the case where the money to finance the increase in mortgage lending comes from people transferring money from their Transaction Accounts to Investment Accounts. As individuals invest more of their money via Investment Accounts, purchases of consumer goods will have to decrease (assuming the velocity of circulation does not change). This will temporarily lower demand for goods and services, in theory lowering prices and leading to lower growth and output. The more money that is diverted from immediate spending to fund mortgage lending, the more demand will decrease. If lower prices do not tempt people to spend more, then eventually the lower demand will lead to lower output and increased unemployment. Due to a lower level of income those already with a house (and a mortgage) will find their ability to repay reduced. Faced with the possibility of default, many will be forced to bring their property to market in order to repay their outstanding debts. Likewise, in a weaker economy individuals will be discouraged by the higher property prices and weaker economic conditions, and banks will be less willing to lend. All this will cause an increase in the supply of houses brought to market and lower the demand for them. In addition, individuals who are struggling to service their mortgages may start to default. This in turn should lead to a reduction in house prices. Banks are likely to react by lowering the returns on Investment Accounts that fund mortgages, lowering their attractiveness to investors and limiting the extent of the bubble.

Box 9.C - Unemployment

The fact that asset price bubbles will be less likely to occur (and smaller when they do) means that the risk of financial crises will be far lower. Financial crises tend to be associated with large recessions and even depressions, which themselves are associated with increased levels of unemployment. Financial crises also tend to necessitate large government bailouts of failing banks, which along with higher levels of unemployment and lower tax revenues, lead to increases in government debt. Whilst potentially undesirable in the long term, high levels of government debt can also be used in the short term to justify the removal of spending on socially beneficial schemes, such as health, education, law and order etc. that are not well provisioned for by the private sector. The removal of asset price bubbles will therefore see less of a push to lower government spending on socially beneficial schemes. Furthermore unemployment that arises from economic downturns caused by the credit cycle should be reduced. Both of these factors should have socially beneficial effects.

Alternatively, if the money to fund these mortgages is diverted from Investment Accounts that were being used to fund productive investments then investment will fall. Output will fall accordingly, which will lead to a fall in demand and employment. The more money that is diverted into mortgage lending and away from profitable investment in this way the more the economy will suffer. Again, lower growth and higher unemployment will make it more difficult for those who have borrowed to repay their mortgages and this may force many who have unaffordable mortgages to try to sell their houses. In addition, in a weaker economy new borrowers will be discouraged from borrowing, and banks will be less willing to lend. The supply of houses to market will therefore increase and the demand for them will fall, leading to a reduction in their price. Again, banks are likely to respond by lowering the returns on mortgage investment accounts, lowering their attractiveness to investors and limiting the extent of the bubble.

We should compare these outcomes with those that occur in the current monetary system. In the current system, when a bank makes a loan it does not require anyone else to give up access to their money – purchasing power is not reduced when additional money is created (by lending). In fact the economy may appear to benefit in the short term – people feel richer and for that reason start to spend more. Speculative booms can therefore go on much longer unchecked. The longer the bubble lasts, the greater is the proportion of buyers that will have shifted into 'ponzi' and 'speculative' positions. Thus when problems do materialise they are much more intractable than if they had been spotted early on. Essentially the current monetary system makes the economy highly pro-cyclical. In contrast, under a reformed system it is much more difficult for house price bubbles to continue unchecked; instead they are naturally self-limiting.

Other factors limiting bubbles

In addition to the above, there are other factors that may prevent a bubble from forming in the first place. First, removing money from those Investment Accounts that fund businesses, and putting it into Investment Accounts that fund mortgages will alter the interest rates offered on the two accounts. With businesses still looking for funds to borrow, interest rates offered on Investment Accounts that invest in business should increase, which should slow or reverse the outflow of money from them.

Second, under a reformed banking system risk and reward will be aligned. With no deposit insurance on Investment Accounts, account holders bear a proportion of the risk on the investment. As shown in section 4.4, by ensuring depositors get their money back no matter what, deposit insurance removes the incentive for depositors to monitor their bank's lending decisions. However, in a reformed system both the customer and the bank share the risk of the bank's loans failing. This eliminates moral hazard, and incentivises account holders to monitor their bank's investment decisions. This should make them wary of returns on investment accounts that appear 'too good to be true'. Banks should also be less willing to continue investing funds in potential bubbles as they will share in any losses that arise from their investments, with no option of being bailed out by government.

In conclusion, it appears that asset bubbles under the post-reform monetary system will still be possible, but will be much less likely to get out of control. The effects outlined above ensure that there are a number of feedback loops that make asset bubbles self-limiting, whereas in the current system asset price bubbles are self-reinforcing.

Central bank intervention in asset bubbles

The above discussion assumed that the central bank did not intervene to attempt to stop the asset bubble forming. Under the reform proposals the central bank could be required to step in to try to prevent asset price bubbles in housing, since housing (whether bought or rented) is a necessity. It may also wish to try to prevent asset bubbles in other financial assets if it appears that the asset bubbles may harm ordinary people rather than just speculators.

Box 9.D - House prices

Section 4.2, showed how house prices are heavily determined by the amount of money created by banks via mortgages. As well as creating affordability problems for people wishing to purchase a house, it also results in a transfer of wealth from those without houses to those with them. This has the effect of increasing inequality.

Under a reformed system, banks would have to borrow money before lending, and as a result the propensity for bubbles to occur in the housing market would be greatly reduced. Because house prices would be far more stable, they would no longer be seen as 'investments' and so speculation on house prices would cease to be profitable. In addition, with house prices increasing more slowly (if at all) people will be less likely to treat houses as a substitute for other forms of saving for retirement.

The social effects of lower house prices would be enormous – as mentioned earlier, if a person on an average salary bought an average house today, over the next 25 years they would end up spending almost half their salary on mortgage repayments. In comparison, in 1995 mortgage repayments would have accounted for around a quarter of their salary. Reducing the likelihood of house price bubbles will therefore lower the cost of living, with obvious social benefits. This lower cost of living should also reduce demands for higher salaries, and leave consumers with more disposable income, with significant potential benefits for businesses and employment.

Currently the central bank already performs this role through the new Financial Policy Committee, which is charged with "monitoring and taking action to remove or reduce systemic risks with a view to protecting and enhancing the resilience of the UK financial system" (Bank of England website). Its powers include the ability to limit bank lending to prevent asset bubbles. Under the reformed system, the Bank of England would have similar powers. If, based on its research and monitoring of the economy, it believed there to be an asset price bubble developing, it would be obliged to intervene. For example, if it was worried that a bubble was forming in the housing market it could oblige the banks to reduce or remove the guarantees on their mortgage Investment Accounts (see section 6.8). Other things being equal this should discourage investors from placing money in them. If this didn't work, or if the bubble was more advanced, the central bank could increase the percentage of capital banks had to hold against new mortgages. In the extreme case it could even place an upper limit on mortgage lending for each bank, in line with their current market share. Banks would then have to limit mortgage Investment Accounts and instead direct money placed into Investment Accounts to other sectors of the economy. Lending for property would then fall, and this should deflate the bubble. Once prices have deflated to a satisfactory level, the central bank could remove the restrictions on bank lending.

When an asset bubble bursts

The previous section discussed why asset price bubbles are less likely to occur under a reformed banking system, as well as why those that do occur are likely to be significantly smaller and last for a shorter duration than in the current system. Nevertheless, asset price bubbles are still possible. What would happen when such a bubble eventually burst? The next section contrasts the bursting of a bubble under the current monetary system with the likely outcome in a reformed monetary system.

Deflation – without government intervention

Irving Fisher's debt deflation theory of depressions (see section 4.2) shows how the bursting of an asset bubble could lead to debt deflation and recession. In his theory banks play a crucial role: they lend money to those who wish to buy into the bubble, increasing debt in the process. Because bank lending increases purchasing power, the act of lending for the purchase of assets helps facilitate asset price rises. Fisher's analysis begins in an over-indebted economy. This leads to step 1 of his theory: "Debt liquidation leads to distress[ed] selling", followed by step 2: "Contraction of deposit currency, as bank loans are paid off, and to a slowing down of velocity of circulation" (1933).

However, unlike in the current system in a reformed system bank deposits would not contract, as loan repayments would not destroy money - instead repayment would transfer state-issued currency from the borrower to the bank, and then back to the investment account holder. In addition, as shown in section 10.1, although banks that go bust will not be rescued, the funds of Transaction Account customers will continue to exist and will be transferred to other banks, meaning that the failure of a bank in a reformed system will not lead to a damaging contraction in the stock of bank deposits.

However, the velocity of circulation of money may still slow down. With loan repayments not altering the quantity of currency in circulation step 3, "A fall in the level of prices", step 4, "A still greater fall in the net worths of business, precipitating bankruptcies", step 5, "A like fall in profits", step 6, "A reduction in output, in trade and in employment of labor" and step 7 "Pessimism and loss of confidence" will only occur due to the decrease in velocity rather than because of a shrinking stock of deposits, and as such will be smaller than otherwise (Fisher, 1933, p. 342). However, if the central bank was targeting an inflation rate, the fall in prices caused by the fall in velocity would be met with an injection of newly created money, offsetting the effect of the velocity decline and therefore the deflationary effect of the velocity decline.

Even if the central bank does not inject new money, the effect of falling prices that comes about from a slower velocity of money may be cancelled out by what is known as the Pigou-Patinkin effect. This implies that falling prices will make those with money feel wealthier (as they can buy more with the money they have), which should lead to an increase in spending, automatically stabilising prices and output. This dynamic does not occur in the current monetary system, because while those who hold positive money balances do indeed see the value of their money increase in real terms during a deflation, those who are in debt see the value of their debts increase in real terms (because their debts do not fall in value when prices fall). Because in the current system deposits are created by banks' lending, each pound of deposits is matched by a pound of debt, and so the positive wealth effect and the negative debt effect cancel each other out. Conversely, under post-reform banking the stock of money (state-issued currency, which replaces deposits) exists independently of the stock of loans. As such if deflation occurs the Pigou-Patinkin effect is likely to be positive in aggregate, which should act as an automatic stabiliser, increasing demand when prices fall.

Deflation - with government intervention

The above analysis shows what might happen if the government and central bank did not intervene in the market. In reality, both the central bank and government are likely to intervene. In response to a deflation in consumer prices (due to hoarding or a slowdown in velocity) the central bank is likely to inject money into the real economy via government spending (in order to hit its inflation target). The increase in spending will counteract the decrease in the velocity of circulation/hoarding of currency in Transaction Accounts. Consequently, when the asset bubble pops those sections of society that were not directly engaged in the bubble will be protected from the negative spill-over effects caused by a lower velocity of circulation.

Likewise the government may increase its spending to counteract any downturn in demand. Unlike in the current system its ability to engage in counter-cyclical spending will be aided by the fact that it will not have to provide funds to bail out banks. In addition, the government will likely have lower debts to begin with due to it gaining a source of revenue from money creation.

Box 9.E - Bank failures

Under a reformed system bank failure will no longer require government bail-outs. Consequently there will be no increase in government debt (due to bail-outs) after a bank fails and therefore no need for the government to increase taxes/borrowing or decrease spending. No longer too important to fail, banks will be more wary about lending into perceived asset bubbles and individuals will be more cautious about which banks they lend to. This will decrease moral hazard and thus decrease the likelihood of asset bubbles and bank failure.

Additionally, because banks will no longer need to be bailed out by the government, if there is a recession or depression the government will be in a better financial situation to counteract the downturn through countercyclical spending. Conversely, in the current system the financial crisis was associated with large bank bailouts which limited (politically) the ability of the government to borrow to engage in countercyclical spending, with negative effects for the economy as a whole (see Taylor, 2012).

Long term effects of government actions

Section 4.2 outlined how, in the longer term, inflation may be engineered by governments to reduce the real value of debt and in so doing prevent debt deflations, financial crises and depressions. For example, in the 2007-08 crisis the central bank slashed interest rates and directly purchased assets. These actions prevented financial assets from falling in value (and in fact may have increased their price). In effect a floor was set under the price of certain assets, which legitimised previous investment and lending decisions and protected some financial market participants from losses.

Although these actions prevented an even worse financial crisis from developing, in the long run they imparted an inflationary tendency to the economy. Not suffering from the downsides of their investment decisions, banks are more willing to extend credit and borrowers are more willing to invest in assets they believe to be 'protected'. Furthermore, the implicit insurance the government has provided is likely to lead to an increase in the risky behaviour (due to moral hazard) that led to the crisis in the first place, setting the stage for an even bigger crisis in the future.

Conversely, under the reformed system, banks would be allowed to fail. The government and central bank would be under no obligation to intervene in the market and in so doing validate risky behaviour. This will lower moral hazard, as banks will now face the full downside of their investment decisions. This should decrease their willingness to participate in asset price bubbles. As

> **Box 9.F - An additional source of wealth**
>
> Because money will be created by the central bank free of any corresponding debt, money will now be a source of wealth for the private sector in aggregate. Currently, with almost all money created as debt, money cannot be a source of wealth for everyone – for one person to have a positive money balance another must have a debt. With debt-free money circulating, the economy as a whole will be able to pay down its debts, without corresponding reductions in the stock of money. As a result debt is less likely to be required for the everyday running of business, small expansions, and everyday purchases by individuals. However, whilst those starting businesses or those businesses undergoing a rapid expansion are still likely to require debt financing, the proportion of financing through own funds should be higher than is currently the case.
>
> The increases in wealth will likely lead to a reduction in the interest rates banks charge businesses. As Bernanke and Gertler (1989) explain:
>
>> "the greater is the borrower's net worth – defined operationally as the sum of her liquid assets and marketable collateral – the lower the external finance premium should be. Intuitively, a stronger financial position (greater net worth) enables a borrower to reduce her potential conflict of interest with the lender, either by self-financing a greater share of her investment project or purchase or by offering more collateral to guarantee the liabilities she does issue."
>
> With money a source of wealth in aggregate, and the economy as a whole able to pay down its debts, the balance sheets of the entire economy should improve. Stronger balance sheets will 'lower the external finance premium' and increase the ability of businesses to self-finance.

a consequence the tendency for asset price inflation due to risky bank behaviour should be lower. Also, the need for the government to use consumer price inflation in order to reduce the real value of debt will be decreased.

9.6 DEBT

Because 97% of the money in the hands of the public consists of bank deposits, in order for there to be money, normally someone must be in debt. In the current system, the absence of a state-issued, debt-free electronic money means that the money needed for the economy to function must be borrowed from the banking sector. In addition, any attempt by the public to repay debt in any significant amount has the effect of lowering spending, potentially triggering recession, which makes it difficult to further reduce debt.

In contrast, the reforms would introduce a permanent, debt-free, stable, state-issued supply of money that is not dependent on banks lending. The recycling of money through the Conversion Liability (see section 8.3) would make it possible to significantly reduce the debt burden of the public without reducing spending, money creation (and the stock of money) and therefore triggering recession. As explained in Chapter 8, during the conversion to the new system, the bank's demand liabilities would be converted into state-issued currency and the bank would acquire a new Conversion Liability to the Bank of England, effectively as a charge, at face value, for the state-issued currency used to convert the demand liabilities into real money. As banks use the money from loan repayments to pay down their liabilities to the central bank, the money will be granted to the government by the Bank of England to be spent back into the economy. There is no change in the amount of money in circulation, as measured by the total stock of state-issued currency at the Bank of England. When the state-issued currency is injected into the economy via government spending, tax rebates or simply by a citizen's dividend, there is no debt corresponding to the newly-issued money. In effect the money is 'debt-free'. Through this recycling of money, it is possible to pay down over £1 trillion of household, consumer and business debt over a period of 10 to 30 years.

9.7 INEQUALITY

Under the current system, money used to repay bank lending sinks without trace - the economy can only continue to function if money is continually borrowed back into existence. Within the reformed system the amount of money in circulation will exist independently of bank lending decisions. What is more, under the reformed system money will predominantly be spent into the economy 'debt-free'. Thus, money will exist without a corresponding private debt – there will no longer be a need for the rest of the economy to 'rent' the medium of exchange from the banking sector. Instead, the money the economy needs to function will be provided to the economy by the central bank for essentially zero cost.

Of course, banks will still lend in the reformed system, and this will result in payments to the bank as a result of the interest that they charge on loans. Likewise people will still need to borrow. However, unlike in the current system the quantity of loans will exist independently of the money creation, and thus the gross quantity of interest payments to banks will likely be lower. Additionally, in order to lend banks will first need to acquire funds from Investment

Account holders. Because these accounts will carry risk, Investment Account holders will demand a higher rate of return than they currently do on their bank deposits (which are riskless due to deposit insurance). Both factors will lead to lower bank profits, lower staff wages, and as long as Investment Account holders are not overly concentrated in one area, an increase in the geographical dispersion of interest payments.

In the longer term a lower propensity for asset price bubbles will stabilise asset prices, particularly in the housing market. Stable property prices will lower the attractiveness of housing as a vehicle for speculation, increasing its affordability particularly for the lowest earners. In addition, the removal of credit driven asset price cycles should lower the risk of banking/financial crises, and remove the need for bank bailouts should one occur. No bank bailouts mean lower government debt, negating the need for cuts in public spending (which disproportionately affect the poor) during recessions.

9.8 ENVIRONMENT

As section 5.4 showed, the current monetary system negatively impacts on the environment in several ways. First, it creates a business cycle where recessions are positively correlated with the removal of regulation protecting the environment. In addition, the increase in government debt associated with large recessions and financial crises can eventually lead to cuts in government spending, which may include investments in technologies that may benefit the environment. Furthermore, banking is undemocratic, and this can lead to individuals helping to fund lending to industries they would otherwise not wish to. Finally the current monetary system may create a growth imperative which makes the steady state economy desired by some environmentalists impossible.

Under a reformed system, a major cause of the boom-bust cycle – the creation of money by banks when making loans – will be removed. Hence the economy should be far more stable, with fewer and smaller recessions. Consequently, there should be less pressure on government to remove regulations that protect the environment during downturns. Smaller booms and busts will lower the need for the government to engage in countercyclical spending, or bail out banks in a financial crisis. This should free up money, which could be used to increase spending on the research and development of green technologies.

Another aspect of the reforms that would benefit the environment is the directed nature of the Investment Accounts. Individuals and organisations would have a choice over how the money that they save is to be used. For example, each bank would provide a range of Investment Accounts with different interest rates and risks attached to them. Each account would fund a different broad sector of the economy. So, a typical bank might offer a variety of Investment Accounts, one of which funds mortgage lending, another that funds small and medium sized businesses, a third that funds consumer lending, etc. Banks could even market accounts based on their 'greenness'. For example, a bank could offer an account that funded only 'green' businesses, and excluded big energy companies, or companies with a history of pollution. In reality the possibilities are endless. Crucially, individuals would no longer be unwittingly funding activities that they disagreed with. As a result, the investment decisions of banks would start to reflect the investment priorities of society.

In addition, the act of choosing not to put money in certain types of Investment Account (e.g. one that funds companies that damage the environment) will decrease the amount of funds that banks have available to lend to a particular sector. Other things being equal this should lower the quantity of lending and increase the interest rate on any loans to that sector. This will lead to an increase in costs for these companies, potentially making any new investments unprofitable. Alternatively, the increase in costs may be passed on to the consumer, which will lower demand for goods from companies that damage the environment. Likewise, an increase in the money placed into Investment Accounts funding green companies will lower the cost of funding to these companies. Again, this benefit could be passed on to the consumer or reinvested. This will change relative prices, altering the demand for the products and creating a market mechanism that will lead people to favour products produced by environmentally responsible companies on price grounds.

A further aspect of the reforms that could benefit the environment is the removal of the growth imperative in capitalist economies (as described in section 5.4). This would make possible the kind of steady state economy favoured by many environmentalists. Indeed, one of CASSE's (the Centre for the Advancement of Steady State Economics) fifteen policies for achieving a steady state economy is to "Overhaul banking regulations, starting with gradual elimination of fractional reserve banking, such that the monetary system moves away from a debt structure that requires continuous economic growth."

Why does a reformed system lessen the growth imperative? First, in a reformed system inequality should be lower as 'rent' is no longer being paid on the entire stock of money. Lower inequality should lower borrowing and working hours by people previously attempting to 'keep up with the Joneses'. Second, in a reformed system continuous borrowing is no longer required merely to maintain the level of spending Accordingly governments need not fear the effects of a credit contraction (although they will want to maintain a certain level of lending for other reasons) and so can remove any incentives that promote excessive indebtedness and as a result economic growth. Third, as bank lending no longer increases the level of purchasing power in an economy, asset price bubbles in essentials should be less likely. A low propensity for asset price inflation should lower the required levels of borrowing in order to purchase a house, which pushes people to work harder. Fifth, any increase in a bank's capital will not remove money from circulation, and loan repayments will not destroy money. Consequently the growth imperative which applies to the current system (as postulated by Binswanger (2009)) will not apply. Even if some economic actors choose to hoard money in their accounts (effectively taking it out of circulation) the central bank can easily offset any negative effects by increasing the quantity of money spent into circulation.

9.9 DEMOCRACY

As section 5.5 showed, the current monetary system impacts upon democracy in several ways. First, there are problems due to the lack of understanding as to what banks actually do. Second, the power to create and allocate money gives a small number of banks a huge amount of power over the future direction of the economy. Third, the government is reliant on banks to lend to small businesses and entrepreneurs to ensure the level of investment and therefore growth and employment is maintained. Fourth, the complex nature of the monetary and banking system disguises from the general public and government the banks' true fiscal contribution to society.

Under a reformed system, Investment Accounts would allow people to choose what broad sector of the economy their money goes to. Furthermore, because Investment Accounts require people to give up access to their money for a period of time and accept a degree of risk, people would be more likely to understand what banks actually did. Likewise, the removal of deposit insurance and the ability to let banks fail would remove the 'too big to fail' subsidy.

Thus politicians and the general public could be able to better assess the contribution of the banking sector to society.

Likewise in a reformed system the power to create money would be removed from banks altogether. While banks would still determine which firms to grant loans to and the interest rates on those loans, this lending would no longer create new purchasing power. Instead, the amount of money in the economy would be determined by a body that was transparent and accountable to society as a whole.

Finally, the decisions on what sectors of the economy would receive funding would be much more democratic. If individuals didn't want the bank to lend their money, then the bank wouldn't be able to. However, if an individual wanted to lend some of their money then they would actually have some control over how their money was to be used – unlike today. While banks could still choose which firms within a sector receive funding, the quantity of funds available to each sector would be determined by the saving decisions of the population as a whole. Banks could still attempt to influence individuals' choices by altering the returns on different Investment Accounts, based on how profitable they found it to lend to different sectors. However, if the population were truly averse to lending to a particular sector, then less money would go into those Investment Accounts, and as a result the banks' lending to these sectors would be considerably lower. Essentially individuals would have some control over what their money is used for. In terms of how the funds are allocated, it would be similar to a stock market tracker or exchange traded fund – the investor decides on the broad sector they want to invest in, with the bank picking the specific companies to lend to within that sector.

CHAPTER 10
IMPACTS ON THE BANKING SECTOR

10.1 IMPACTS ON COMMERCIAL BANKS

The reforms earlier have both advantages and disadvantages for the banking and financial sector. These effects are discussed below.

Banks will need to acquire funds before lending

As we saw in Chapter 2, currently when a bank makes a loan it creates new deposits for those who have borrowed the money. After the reform, this will no longer be the case, although banks will still be able to make loans using funds that customers have provided specifically for this purpose via Investment Accounts. Banks will no longer be able to make loans first (by making an accounting entry) and 'go looking for the reserves later', as they do in the current system. Instead, they will have to find the money they need to make loans before they make them. Banks will thus become true intermediaries, merely transferring pre-existing purchasing power from savers to borrowers.

It is difficult to predict how individuals will allocate their funds between Investment and Transaction Accounts after the reform. However, the current ratio of money in sight deposits (which are similar to Transaction Accounts) to time deposits (which are similar to Investment Accounts) may give us a clue.

Currently the balance of time deposits to sight deposits is £1.5 trillion to £1.1 trillion (58% in time deposits vs. 42% in sight deposits).[1] Whether this ratio

---

1. These figures were arrived at by adding together all sight deposit categories (MFIs, public sector, private sector and non-residents – Bank of England codes: RPMB3GL, RPMB3MM, RPMB3NM, RPMB3OM) and all time deposit categories

remains the same after the reform depends on several factors. On one hand, people will have an incentive to place their money into Investment Accounts. For one, banks will pay no interest on Transaction Accounts, and will also charge a small monthly or annual fee to cover their administration costs. Second, because Transaction Accounts pay no interest, a positive inflation rate implies a negative real interest rate on Transaction Accounts. Assuming the Bank of England retains its two percent inflation target, the real interest rate on Transaction Accounts would equal minus 2%.[2] Other things being equal, this should incentivise people to place money they are not spending into Investment Accounts. Conversely, the fact that Investment Accounts will carry an element of risk is likely to counteract this affect somewhat.[3] Which affect dominates will depend upon a function of individuals' risk aversion and the interest rate and level of risk offered on each type of Investment Accounts.

Market forces should go a long way to making sure that the appropriate level of funds are available for investment. Banks are unlikely to passively wait for money to come in, particularly if they feel they are missing out on profitable opportunities to lend. Under the reformed system the central bank will decide on the quantity, or growth rate, of money. The price of money – the interest rate – will be set by the market. By ceding control of the interest rate, the central bank gives commercial banks a tool to attract money into Investment Accounts. For example, in a situation where a bank had a profitable lending opportunity but no money in its Investment Pool it could seek to attract more

---

(MFIs, public sector, private sector and non-residents – Bank of England codes: RPMB3PM, RPMB3QM, RPMB3TM, RPMB3HL) for the 30th September 2011.

2.   The real interest rate is the interest rate after inflation has been taken into account. If inflation is at 2% and the interest rate is at 5%, then the real interest rate will be 3%. So, the real interest rate (at low levels of inflation and interest) is approximately nominal interest minus the expected inflation rate. If the interest rate on Transaction Accounts is 0% and expected inflation is at 2% then 0-2 = minus 2% real interest rate. At this rate of inflation, in real terms the purchasing power of the money in the account will fall by 2% each year.

3.   In the current system, time deposits are guaranteed by government via deposit insurance (See section 3.3). However, the risk of loss under the reformed system is likely to be relatively small, as long as the probability of default on the loans is uncorrelated and the bank's loan book is of sufficient size to ensure adequate pooling of risk.

funds by changing the interest rate it offers on its Investment Accounts.[4] An increase in the offered rate would attract money into its Investment Accounts. Conversely interest rates could be lowered if the supply of funds outweighed demand from eligible and creditworthy borrowers. Banks could also seek to alter the funds in Investment Accounts through non-interest rate measures, such as altering any guarantees provided on the accounts. By doing so (e.g. by guaranteeing 90% of the value of an account rather than 80%) the bank alters the risk-adjusted return which – other things equal – will affect the attractiveness of the investment and the amount of funds put into such an Investment Account.

If a bank did wish to attract money into Investment Accounts by raising interest rates, it would need to either increase the interest rates it charged on loans in order to maintain profits (the 'spread') or accept a lower margin. However, it is important to note that any increase in the interest rate banks charge on loans is limited in scope. Beyond a certain point higher interest rates eventually lead to lower profits (for banks), as higher rates lead to riskier projects being funded and riskier behaviour by borrowers (see section 3.4 for more details).

The impact on the availability of lending

A common criticism of proposals that seek to remove the ability of banks to create money is that it would cause a reduction in the level of lending in the economy. For example, the Independent Commission on Banking wrote that reforms of this nature "would drastically curtail the lending capacity of the UK banking system, reducing the amount of credit available to households and businesses" (2011, p. 98). In response to requests, the Commission would not clarify what they meant by the word 'drastic', why they thought lending would fall, or disclose whether they had done any calculations to reach such a conclusion. However, despite the lack of evidence for such an assertion, it is still a common argument and therefore requires investigation.

The basic premise of this argument is that removing the banking sector's ability to create money will reduce its capacity to make loans, and as a result the economy will suffer. However, this ignores several crucial issues.

---

4.   Equally, if the bank had too many funds it could reduce the interest rate offered on Investment Accounts, or lend the excess funds to other banks.

First, the implicit assumption is that more lending is always better. This is in turn based on the assumption that bank lending primarily funds productive investment. However, as fig. 3.4 showed, the most desirable form of lending, from an economic point of view, accounts for less than 10% of total lending. The rest does not contribute to GDP, and much of it may in fact be harmful to the economy - unconstrained lending for property was a prime cause of the housing bubble that triggered the 2007-08 financial crisis.[5]

Second, a further implicit assumption is that under the current system there will never be a shortage of banks that are willing to lend, and that banks will always satisfy the demand for credit. Yet nothing could be further from the truth. As Chapter 4 showed, banks lend too much in the good times (particularly for unproductive purposes), which creates a boom and often a bubble. However, when the bubble bursts banks cut back their lending, harming businesses. Bank lending is therefore highly pro-cyclical and the banks' initial over-lending sows the seeds for their later reverse. As Mark Twain famously said: "A banker is a fellow who lends you his umbrella when the sun is shining, but wants it back the minute it begins to rain."

Third, under the reformed system banks do not need to wait passively for funds to come into the bank. They will instead raise the interest rates they offer to attract more funds from customers. Market mechanisms will therefore ensure that any shortage of credit will push up the interest rate, attracting new funds from savers.

Fourth, any bank faced with a shortage of funds to invest could approach other banks to enquire about any excess funds they might be holding and borrow from these banks. If there were a shortage of funds across the entire banking system, particularly for lending to businesses that contribute to GDP, the Bank of England would possibly opt to auction newly created money to the banks, on the provision they are on-lent into the real economy (i.e. to non-financial businesses, see section 8.2 for more details).

Fifth, the argument that the reforms would 'drastically curtail' lending seems in part to be based on viewing bank lending as a one-shot game, rather than a cyclical ongoing process. This assumes that money can either be a) in a Transaction Account, where it is available for spending, or b) in an Investment Account, where it is tied up for a period of time. While it may appear this way

---

5.   This is not to say that lending to non-productive purposes should be stopped, merely that an excessive level can result in asset price inflation and financial crisis.

from the perspective of each individual (they may see, for example, £1,000 in a Transaction Account and £4,000 as their Investment Account balance), it is not how the economy as a whole works. Money, in terms of state-issued electronic currency, is never actually 'held' in an Investment Account. As described in Chapter 6 the Investment Account is simply a record of money that has been provided to a bank to be invested. Through the process of making a loan the bank moves money from its Investment Pool to the borrower's Transaction Account. As a result the money 'in' Investment Accounts is almost always in another customer's Transaction Account. From here the Transaction Account owner can, if they so choose, place this money into an Investment Account. Consequently all money in Transaction Accounts is potentially available for lending. Therefore it is a logical error to think that there will be a shortage of funds available for Investment Accounts - if money lent to a borrower is spent and ends up with someone who does not need it at the time, they may place it back into an Investment Account, where it can be used for lending again. In other words, the same money, when circulating around the economy, can be re-lent multiple times.

In conclusion, concerns about the impact of these reforms on the level of lending provided by banks are overstated. Much of current bank lending serves no useful purpose and could be lost without any impact on the performance of the economy. Indeed, a large proportion of bank lending is actually harmful to the health of the economy, as the last few years have clearly shown. Therefore, a reduction in bank lending need not be harmful to the economy, particularly as under a reformed system it will not mean a reduction in new money creation or spending and the adverse macroeconomic conditions this brings. As a result of the factors outlined here, bank lending is unlikely to fall 'drastically', and if it does, the Bank of England will be able to step in to ensure that funds are available for the banks to on-lend into the economy.

Banks will be allowed to fail

As described in Chapter 6, the proposals mean that banks can be allowed to fail. They can no longer rely on government bailouts if they become insolvent. This will mean that they should, in theory, improve their risk-management and take fewer risks that could threaten the solvency of the whole bank. Whether this change in bank behaviour will actually happen is not guaranteed, but regardless, banks that become insolvent will be allowed to fail, rather than being rescued by the taxpayer.

The 'too big to fail' subsidy is removed

Since it is possible to allow banks to fail under the reformed system, the banking sector will lose its 'too big to fail' subsidy. This subsidy was partly a consequence of the implicit guarantee that the government would rescue any banks that failed, due to the fact that within the current system it is more expensive for the government to allow a bank to fail than to rescue it.

The 'too big to fail' subsidy also arose as a direct result of deposit insurance. Deposit insurance effectively makes lending to a bank risk-free for the depositor, lowering the interest rates that banks need to pay to depositors and on their other borrowings. This resulted in "significant transfers of resources from the government to the banking system." (Noss & Sowerbutts, 2012, p. 15)

Of course, the loss of the subsidy will make banks less profitable. When a bank borrows money, the interest rate it pays will be higher to account for the risk that the loan will not be repaid. While this will increase the costs to the bank, it also increases the returns to the person lending to the bank (i.e. the Investment Account holder).

Lobbyists for the banking sector have argued that this subsidy to banking is beneficial for bank customers as it lowers the cost of borrowing. Yet this fails to take into account the lower interest rate paid on deposits, and the increase in the risk of financial crises such insurance brings about (Demirguc-Kunt & Detragiache, 2002). Furthermore, the question of why a highly profitable industry should receive a subsidy from the taxpayer is not clear. Subsidies should be reserved for businesses that have positive externalities (benefits that they cannot be rewarded for directly through the price of their products). With the current financial crisis costing the world economy anywhere between $60 trillion and $200 trillion in lost output (Haldane, 2010), it is quite clear that banks' negative externalities far outweigh any positive contribution they may make. Indeed in a recent speech Andrew Haldane, the Executive Director of Financial Stability at the Bank of England, went much further:

> "Assuming that a [financial] crisis occurs every 20 years, the systemic levy needed to recoup these crisis costs would be in excess of $1.5 trillion per year. The total market capitalisation of the largest global banks is currently only around $1.2 trillion. Fully internalising the output costs of financial crises would risk putting banks on the same trajectory as the dinosaurs, with the levy playing the role of the meteorite." (2010)

The need for debt is reduced, shrinking the banking sector's balance sheet

As discussed in section 9.6, these reforms significantly reduce the systemic need for debt that exists in the current system, because money is currently only created when someone takes on debt. In addition, the injection by the Money Creation Committee of new debt-free money into the economy, along with the recycling of repaid loans through the banking sector's new Conversion Liability to the Bank of England (see section 8.3), means that overtime the overall level of private debt will fall significantly.

This will naturally have a significant impact on the banking sector. Debt is the main 'product' that banks sell, and these reforms reduce the need for their products. The banking sector's aggregate balance sheet, over the 10-30 years after the reforms, will shrink considerably as both a percentage of GDP and in absolute terms. While this will obviously be threatening to the banking sector, it is an advantage for society and the economy as a whole. A lower burden of debt means less income is spent on servicing debt, and therefore more will be spent in the real economy. By reducing the size of the banking sector and the burden of household debt, we allow the real economy to grow.

Basel Capital Adequacy Ratios could be simplified

The 'Capital Adequacy Ratios', set by the Basel committee, are intended to ensure that banks keep a sufficient 'capital buffer' to absorb losses on bad loans. The fear is that if a bank's capital buffer is too low, it will quickly become insolvent in the event of defaults, and will then turn to the government (and therefore taxpayers) for a bailout or other support. This is because, within the current system, most banks cannot be allowed to fail.

Under a reformed system the central bank and government would no longer need to bail out banks if they became insolvent, as the insolvency of a bank would not reduce the amount of money held by the public, or have severe negative economic consequences. However, the retention of minimum capital requirements is important to prevent senior management 'looting' the bank: i.e. running the bank in a highly risky way to maximise short term profits (and therefore their remuneration) at the expense of the long-term interests of shareholders (Akerlof & Romer, 1993).

Nevertheless, regulators may wish to remove Basel II's requirement to apply risk weights to lending to different asset classes, as it exacerbates a systemic bias against lending to business, which when multiplied across all banks can increase the risk of financial crisis. Banks have to hold less capital against mortgage lending than they do against small business lending and as a result can make more loans to mortgages. This gives banks a strong, systemic bias away from lending to businesses and towards lending to property. Thus regulation adds to the bank's pre-existing bias to prefer to lend for property, as unlike a mortgage secured on a house, a small business will rarely have significant assets that can be repossessed and sold if the borrower defaults.

However, while lending for property lowers the risk of loss for an individual bank in the short term, it increases the risk of losses for the banking sector as a whole. If the banking sector directs most of its lending to mortgages and away from business lending, then house prices will inflate and become increasingly unaffordable, while the real economy stagnates from a lack of investment. With a stagnant real economy expected to pay salaries that will cover increasingly unaffordable housing costs, house price inflation eventually results in defaults on mortgages, which could bring down the entire banking sector. The Basel Accords may therefore make asset price bubbles, banking and financial crises more rather than less likely. Given that risk weighting probably does more harm than good, it may be desirable to remove it.

Easier for banks to manage cashflow and liquidity

After the reform, all loans made by a bank will be funded using funds from Investment Accounts. As every Investment Account has a defined repayment date (or a maturity date), the amounts that the bank will need to repay on any one day will be statistically far more predictable than under the current system. For Investment Accounts with maturity dates, the bank will know the exact amount that must be repaid on any particular date. It will also know, from experience, what percentage of customers with maturing accounts will ask for the investment to be rolled over for another period (in other words, what percentage of accounts will not need to be repaid on that date). With regards to minimum notice periods, it will know – from analysis of its own data – the statistical likelihood of an account being redeemed within the next 'x' days. This means that its outgoings are far more predictable.

In addition, incoming funds are also highly predictable because the bank has a collection of contracts with specified monthly repayment dates and amounts on the assets side of its balance sheet (as it does today). This means that it knows almost exactly how much money it will receive on any particular date (allowing for a small degree of variance due to defaults and late payments).

Consequently the banks' computer systems will easily be able to forecast cash flow (money coming in and out) and identify any future shortfalls with a much greater degree of certainty than under the present system. These shortfalls could be prepared for by scaling back loan making activity and building up a buffer. At the same time, it will be able to identify periods when the money coming in will be greater than the repayments due to customers, and therefore increase loan-making activity to soak up the surplus.

Reducing the 'liquidity gap'

Banks within the current system tend to have a significant amount of their liabilities redeemable on demand (i.e. the current account balances that we presently use as money). However, their assets tend to mature (i.e. be repaid) over a much longer period of time. Consequently, there is a significant 'liquidity gap' between their liabilities and their assets, with liabilities being short-term and liquid, and assets being long-term and much more illiquid.

These proposals significantly reduce this liquidity gap. As described in section 8.1, when the conversion is made between the current and reformed systems, banks' demand liabilities are removed from the balance sheet and converted into state-issued currency held at the Bank of England. In place of this demand liability the banks receive a new liability, which is a Conversion Liability to the Bank of England. This Conversion Liability will be repaid over a schedule that corresponds to the maturity profile of the bank's assets i.e. as the bank's loans are repaid, the bank will repay its liability to the Bank of England. As a result the maturity mismatch between the assets and liabilities that corresponded to their sight deposits will be reduced to zero. This radically reduces the liquidity gap of every bank that is affected by the reforms. Instead of having half its liabilities repayable on demand, it will now have no on-demand liabilities and its remaining liabilities (the Conversion Liability, plus its Investment Accounts) will have a maturity profile that is much more closely matched with that of its assets. This will make the banks far more secure and much less vulnerable to liquidity crises.

10.2 IMPACTS ON THE CENTRAL BANK

Direct control of money supply

In Chapter 3 we argued that the Bank of England has little ability to manage money creation by banks as its tools are weak, indirect and ineffective. This argument appears to be supported by comments made by the Bank's Governor in 2010:

> "The Bank of England's key role has always been to ensure that the economy is supplied with the right quantity of money – neither too much nor too little. For fifty years, my predecessors struggled to prevent there being too much, so leading to inflation. I find myself in the opposite situation having to explain that there is too little money in the economy." (King, 2010)

The suggestion that one of the most powerful banking institutions in the world 'struggled' to control private bank money creation points either to inadequate tools, or to a monetary system that can't be controlled.

In contrast, these reforms give the Bank of England direct control over the money creation (through the Money Creation Committee), with the ability to increase or decrease the stock of money by precise amounts, without relying on a complex series of uncertain connections which are themselves subject to long and uncertain lags (e.g. see fig. 3.2).

No need to manipulate interest rates

With the ability to control money creation directly, there is no longer any need for the Bank of England to set interest rates as a means of influencing aggregate demand (although as discussed in box 9.B, the central bank may wish to intervene to prevent large fluctuations in interest rates). This should benefit the economy, since in addition to being an ineffective tool, the manipulation of interest rates can also negatively impact on pensioners when rates are lowered and young borrowers or first-time buyers when rates are raised.

A slimmed down operation at the Bank of England

Post-reform, the central bank would have two essential functions, as now:

1. To maintain monetary stability, that is, to keep inflation at a low and steady rate as determined by the government. This would be primarily achieved by its control over money creation via the Money Creation Committee.

2. To maintain financial stability. This would include:

- Providing the payments system in which all electronic state-issued currency is held, and the means for banks and other payments systems (e.g. BACS, Visa) to interface with this.

- Overseeing the liquidation or resolution of banks that fail and ensuring that Transaction Accounts are transferred to healthy banks quickly with minimal loss of service.

- Monitoring the financial system for weakness, including potential asset price bubbles.

Recent changes in the UK mean that the Bank of England will have a wide range of responsibilities beyond this and will serve as the chief regulator of banks. However, when it comes to making the monetary system work, the following aspects, programmes and functions of the Bank of England will no longer be required:

- Open Market Operations

- The Cash Ratio Deposits Scheme

- The Discount Window Facility

- The Special Liquidity Scheme

- 'Funding for lending' – although the proposals do replace this with a facility to provide funding to banks to be on-lent to businesses

- Quantitative Easing

It is quite possible that this could allow for a much more streamlined functional operation at the Bank of England.

10.3 IMPACTS ON THE UK IN AN INTERNATIONAL CONTEXT

The UK as a safe haven for money

To the best of our knowledge, Transaction Accounts would be the only type of account worldwide where a member of the public can hold their money at the central bank with zero risk of loss. Whilst anyone with deposits at a bank is exposed to the risk of that bank failing (even allowing for the £85,000 government guarantee), a holder of a Transaction Account has zero risk of loss, regardless of the amount of money they hold in that account. For this reason, a UK banking system providing Transaction Accounts may find that it becomes a 'safe haven' for people wanting to hold money without risk, whilst still having the convenience of debit cards, cheque books and internet banking.

Pound sterling would hold its value better than other currencies

The UK M4 money supply has increased by an average of 11.5% a year over the last 40 years. Similar patterns are followed around the world. In contrast, a reformed system would put the control of money creation in the hands of an independent, transparent body which will be tasked with maintaining a low and stable inflation rate. The Money Creation Committee would announce, on a monthly basis, exactly how much money would be created, providing greater transparency than is available with any other currency.

It is highly unlikely that the MCC will ever create money as quickly as the banking sector has done over the last 40 years. This means that prices are more likely to be the result of fundamentals rather than due to credit bubbles. The greater stability and transparency of the money creation process could make the UK an attractive place to hold money and the pound sterling an attractive currency to hold.

In fact, this increased attractiveness of pound sterling as a 'safe haven' currency could raise foreign demand for the currency and cause sterling to appreciate against other currencies. However, if this happens to a significant extent, the process would eventually self-correct: an appreciating currency makes foreign goods cheaper in terms of the domestic currency, with cheaper imports then feeding into lower inflation. The MCC response to falling prices would be to increase money creation. This would lead to more spending and therefore more imports, thus increasing the supply of pounds on the foreign exchange market. An increased supply of currency should lower its price in terms of other currencies - reversing the initial appreciation.

The above factors mean that if the exchange rate does change as a result of these reforms, it is likely to appreciate, rather than depreciate. However, at the same time the self-balancing mechanism outlined above ensures that any appreciation would be checked.

No implications for international currency exchange

Because of the structure of the payments systems that handle currency exchanges between countries, these reforms have no practical implications for trade between the UK and the rest of the world. Currently, international currency exchanges are settled over the banks' accounts at the central bank for each of the respective currencies (e.g. the Bank of England for pound sterling, the Fed for US dollars, the Bank of Japan for Yen). Post-reform, these trades will settle over the equivalent accounts (i.e. the banks' Operational Accounts at the Bank of England). For international banks wishing to buy or sell sterling, they will notice no difference at all in the way the process works, even if the UK switches to a reformed system whilst other countries continue to allow commercial banks to create money.

Would speculators attack the currency before the changeover?

Traders in financial markets have a tendency to react to the news announcement first, and then think and analyse once the first reaction is over. So whenever a country announces a decision to switch to a new system, it is possible that there will be a short-term depreciation (fall) in that currency. However, speculators are always over-ruled, sooner or later, by the economic fundamentals. As the reforms would make the UK a fundamentally stronger economy, with less private household debt, less exposure to banking crises, and a currency that will not be debased by the profit-seeking lending activities of commercial banks, there is no reason why any fall in the currency (as a result of panic) would be more than temporary.

10.4 IMPACTS ON THE PAYMENT SYSTEM

National security

The stability and resilience of the payments system is a matter of national security. The former Chairman of the Federal Reserve Board, Alan Greenspan, has commented that:

> "We'd always thought that if you wanted to cripple the US economy, you'd take out the payment systems. Banks would be forced to fall back on inefficient physical transfers of money. Businesses would resort to barter and IOUs; the level of economic activity across the country would drop like a rock." (Greenspan, 2007)

A couple of high-profile bank failures might be sufficient to lead most shop-keepers and businesses to accept cash only as payment (because they could not be guaranteed that they would ever get the money if they were paid electronically). We do not wish to dwell on the potential consequences of a collapse in the payment system, but in a country that relies mainly on just-in-time food distribution, with only a few day's supply of food on supermarket shelves at any one time, the potential impact of the large supermarkets being unable to make payments to their foreign suppliers is sobering.

However, since these proposals allow banks to fail with no interruption to the payments system, they significantly increase the resilience of the economy and nation. Under these proposals, a bank the size of RBS could have been allowed to fail, yet its current account customers would have been able to continue to make and receive payments. Rather than bank failures becoming a threat to social order, they would become a temporary inconvenience.

Opening the door to competition among Transaction Account providers

The reforms also open the way for a new type of bank that only provides Transaction Accounts. This bank would do no lending or investment; it would only administer accounts on behalf of customers. Its income and profits would come from account fees, and it would compete with other banks on the grounds of customer service and price. Because there is no risk of this service failing due to bad investments (because there are no investments), there is a hugely reduced need for this type of payments-only bank to be regulated. As a result, the costs to regulators would be significantly lower (these costs are discussed in section 6.2). Providing that the Bank of England was committed to increasing choice and fostering competition among Transaction Account providers, the Bank of England could design its IT systems in such a way that it would be very cost effective for a new entrant to 'plug into' the payments system and start providing services.

By opening the door to this type of bank, it is possible to increase the level of competition within the banking sector, which should force the larger UK banks to be more innovative with regards to their payment services.

CONCLUSION

"When you start printing money, you create some value for yourself. If you can issue a thousand pounds-worth of IOUs to everybody, you've got a thousand pounds for nothing. And so we do restrict the ability of people to create their own [bank] notes ... We're protecting you from charlatans."

PAUL FISHER[1]

Executive Director, Bank of England

There is a curious contradiction at the heart of the contemporary monetary system. While one agency of the state – the police – spend considerable time and resources trying to prevent the private creation of paper money (commonly referred to as 'counterfeiting'), another agency of state – the Bank of England – spends significantly more time enabling and facilitating the private creation of money by the corporations that we know as banks. Banks are able to create money because their IOUs (liabilities) can be used, via a sophisticated electronic payment system, as a substitute for the paper money issued by the state. These privately-issued IOUs now make up 97% of all the money in the UK economy.

Yet as Paul Fisher's quote attests, the Bank of England is clearly aware that the ability to issue "a thousand pounds-worth of IOUs" gives the issuer "something for nothing". In the last decade alone, UK banks have issued more than a trillion pounds of additional IOUs. The value that they got for "nothing" was a trillion pounds-worth of interest bearing assets in the form of debt contracts secured on the property and future labour of the British public. No other business is able to obtain value for itself in this way.

---

1. Speaking to BBC Radio 4 "Analysis – What Is Money?", 1st April 2012.

As a result, personal and household debt is at its highest level in history, causing hardship and stress for millions. The bias of banks towards lending for property over investing in business has ensured that housing has become unaffordable for an entire generation, while the real economy has become weak and stagnant, starved of investment by the banks whose core purpose is allegedly to invest in business and help the economy grow.

Some take this as proof that markets, left to their own devices, are inefficient and prone to failure. Yet the reality is that there is perhaps no industry in the world that conforms less to the principles of capitalism than banking. No other industry has its creditors reimbursed by the government if it is unable to do so[2]. No other industry has the monopoly privilege of issuing the money that everyone else must use in order to trade and do business. No high-street shop or restaurant will be rescued by the government in the event of financial mismanagement or bad business practice. And in no other industry would the failure of one firm threaten to bring down the entire UK economy. Yet banks are able to continue in business whilst contravening almost every principle of capitalism in the process.

The privileged, protected and subsidised position that banks hold is not a law of nature or economics. Banks only exist in the form they do today because of countless government interventions throughout history to save them from their own worst excesses. With each failure the banks have benefitted from some new guarantee or concession designed to patch up the system and get back to business as usual, be it deposit insurance after the crisis of the 1930s, the lender of last resort function after the Overend Gurney panic in 1866, bailouts in 2008 or Quantitative Easing in 2009. Each crisis thus strengthens the remaining banks and protects them from their previous excesses, setting the stage for even bigger crises in the future.

The current system cannot be fixed by subjecting it to ever more rules and regulations; houses built on sand will eventually collapse no matter how many rules the occupants are asked to abide by. The issue that must be addressed is the ability of the banking sector to create money. For decades, such concerns have been sidelined. Yet these concerns are becoming more widespread that ever before, with even the chief economics commentator for the Financial Times, Martin Wolf, expressing the view that:

---

2.   With the exception of certain other financial businesses, such as insurance, pension and endowment providers.

"It is the normal monetary system, in which the 'printing' of money is delegated to commercial banks, that needs defending. This delegates a core public function - the creation of money - to a private and often irresponsible commercial oligopoly." (Wolf, 2012)

This core public function is one upon which the stability of the entire economy depends. As a result instability and fragility are built into the current monetary system.

Despite the destructiveness of the current monetary system, there are still those who defend it. One reason for this is a deep level of ignorance of how the monetary system actually works. Most of the population (and most politicians) are under the impression that only the state has the authority to create money. Many of those who do understand that most money is created by banks believe this happens through the limited and predictable 'money multiplier' model of money creation, which places control of the money supply firmly in the hands of the central bank. As the evidence and analysis in this book has made clear, the Bank of England does not have that level of control. In fact, Sir Mervyn King's admission (section 10.2) that for half a century the Bank of England has "struggled" to control money creation by banks suggests that this is not a system that can be controlled.

The reforms outlined in this book would bring the creation of money under democratic control. By removing the power to create money from banks and returning it to an independent but accountable public body, which may only sanction its creation during periods when inflation is low and stable, the creation of money can be made to benefit the real economy. Instead of new money being allocated where it is of greatest benefit to the banks, it would instead be allocated where it would most benefit the population as a whole – in the real economy, through increases in government spending, tax rebates and reductions, or via direct payments to citizens. In doing so it returns the privilege and benefits of money creation to the people.

As banks lose their power to create money, they would also lose their power to excessively shape the future direction of the economy. A requirement for banks to inform their customers exactly what will be done with the money they put into Investment Accounts will ensure that, to a reasonable extent, the investment priorities of banks start to reflect the investment priorities of society as a whole.

By removing the power of banks to create money, these reforms address many of the problems of the current economic system at their source. They also turn banks back into ordinary businesses whose failure poses no threat to the wider economic system.

But would these changes bankrupt the banks? Would we lose the UK's most profitable industry? A few issues need to be considered here. First, an industry that can only be profitable thanks to permanent taxpayer-funded subsidies is not profitable in any real sense. Second, much of the profits of the banking sector come from its monopoly on the creation of money and the fact that – with the exception of cash – all of the money needed in the economy must be borrowed from them. This significantly overstates the true profitability of banking. Third, banking itself (as opposed to the wider financial sector) employs only one out of every 53 workers in the UK (ONS, 2012), yet the consequences of the current design of this banking system causes instability, insecurity and the risk of unemployment for the other 98% of the workforce. Some reduction in the size of the banking sector would be a fair price to pay for greater stability, investment and employment in the real, non-financial economy.

However, the most powerful argument to suggest that these changes would not be harmful is that the reforms simply require banks to work the way that the rest of the investment industry already operates. With the exception of banks, the rest of the investment sector must acquire funds from savers first before they can lend. If these companies can be profitable without the ability to create money, there is no reason that well-run banks could not be too.

The Next 40 Years

> *"Our problems are man-made, therefore they may be solved by man. No problem of human destiny is beyond human beings."*

> **John F Kennedy**
> **35th President of the United States**

Without doubt, the changes outlined here will be bitterly opposed by the banks and their lobbyists. There is a natural desire on behalf of banks to get back to 'business as usual' as quickly as possible. But the reality is that will be no more business as usual – the levels of personal and household debt are simply too high to allow for another lending boom. There is also a high probability that many of the largest banks worldwide are bankrupt in a strict accounting sense, although few governments would force a strict audit of bank assets when they would be forced to pick up the tab for any bank insolvency.

If we keep the current monetary system, financial crises will continue to occur, with the costs passed onto ordinary people and businesses. There is no justification for this when the changes that need to be made are both beneficial and relatively simple to enact.

The monetary system, being man-made and little more than a collection of rules and computer systems, is easy to fix, once the political will is there and opposition from vested interests is overcome. The real challenges which face us over the next 40 years, such as how to provide for a growing global population, a changing climate, and increasingly scarce natural resources, require a monetary system that works for society and the economy as a whole. For that reason, our current system is no longer fit for purpose and must be reformed. This book has provided a detailed and workable proposal that would address the deepest flaws in the current monetary system and allow us to move on to dealing with the other issues facing society and the world. The challenge now is to ensure that these changes are made so that we can all start to reap the benefits of a monetary system that works for society rather than against it.

3

APPENDICES

APPENDIX I

EXAMPLES OF MONEY CREATION BY THE STATE: ZIMBABWE VS. PENNSYLVANIA

The common response to the idea of allowing the state to issue money and spend it into the economy is that such an approach would be highly inflationary. The examples of the hyperinflation in Zimbabwe or Weimar Republic Germany are often mentioned as a reason why states cannot be trusted to issue currency. However, those making these claims rarely have any in-depth understanding of what happened in Zimbabwe, Germany or any of the other hyperinflationary periods. In reality, each period of hyperinflation happens due to a unique set of circumstances that are completely inapplicable to the UK or any of the countries where these reforms are likely to be implemented.

In this appendix we look first at the Zimbabwean experience between 2007 and 2008, as this is the most recent example of hyperinflation. We also briefly look at the period of hyperinflation in Weimar Republic Germany.

We then look at a Pennsylvanian money system in the 1720s, to show that if managed properly, money creation can lead to a prosperous and low inflation economy. Unfortunately there are few contemporary examples of responsible state-issued currency; every country world-wide runs on some variant of the banking system outlined in Chapter 2, and as a result has suffered significant inflation and indebtedness (whether at a household or government level, or both). In many cases, countries under the current system can only attempt to keep inflation low by raising interest rates, which can stifle beneficial investment (Chang, 2007) and harm the economy.

Zimbabwe

While inflation can be described as a general increase in the price level, or equivalently a fall in the purchasing power of a currency, hyperinflation is a different phenomenon entirely. Although definitions are in general rather arbitrary, many economists distinguish hyperinflation from merely high inflation by defining it as a price level increase of at least 50% per month (Cagen, 1956). This is in contrast with 'normal' inflation, which many countries, including the UK, target at 2% a year. Fortunately, hyperinflations tend to be rare, with around 56 occurrences in modern economic history. The latest of these took place in Zimbabwe under President Mugabe.

After gaining independence in 1980, Zimbabwe was on its way to prosperity, with an average GDP growth rate of 4.3 percent a year. For about two decades it experienced sustained growth, which was only occasionally interrupted.[1] The country is endowed with rich resources and mineral reserves, possessing huge deposits of diamonds, gold, nickel, iron, platinum, coal and other natural goods. Compared to other African countries, it had a sophisticated industry manufacturing textiles, cement, chemicals, steel, wood and other products. Agricultural production, the mainstay of its economy, is supported by 10,747 dams (out of 12,430 water dams in the entire Southern African region) (Sugunan, 1997). The tobacco industry was Zimbabwe's most successful generator of foreign exchange, earning about US$600 million in 2000. Zimbabwe was also a popular tourist destination. Perhaps most important to Zimbabwe was its strong banking sector and a well-functioning property rights system, which "allowed owners to use the equity in their land to develop and build new businesses, or expand their old ones." (Richardson, 2005, p. 1)

However, by the end of the 1990s Zimbabwe's economic progress came to a halt and the country's economy entered into a depression. What caused this turnaround? Media reports often simplistically imply that the printing of money was the cause of Zimbabwe's economic collapse. However, in reality the economic collapse came first, and the mass printing of money came as a consequence of this.

Zimbabwe's president, Robert Mugabe, and other members of the leading party ZANU-PF, have been eager to blame the economic decay on the continuous years of drought and the targeted sanctions of Western countries. Yet these

---

1. For example, in 1992 GDP dropped by nine percent due to the worst drought in 50 years (Richardson, 2005).

claims are easily refuted: sanctions on top government officials only came into effect in 2002. Empirical research questions the claim that drought is to blame: "The historically close relationship between rainfall and GDP growth ended in 2000 – the first years after the land reforms." (Coltart, 2008, p. 10)

So what were the real reasons for Zimbabwe's decline? In the mid 90s, about 4,500 white families owned most of the commercial farms, employing 350,000 black workers and often providing financial support for local infrastructure, hospitals and schools. Simultaneously about 8,500 black farmers ran small-scale commercial farms that were able to access credit from Zimbabwean banks and vitally contributed to the agricultural production (Richardson, 2005). However, the prevalence of white farmers in agricultural production – commonly viewed as a heritage of colonialism – sparked negative sentiment, and fuelled calls by Mugabe and others to return the fertile 'stolen lands' to black Zimbabweans (Hill, 2003, p. 102).[2]

Nevertheless, these conflicts did not constrain the growth of the economy until the rhetoric was acted on. The 'point of no return', according to Coltart (2008), took place in 1997 with three crucial developments. The first was that the war veterans, who fought for independence and had traditionally been loyal to the ZANU-PF, became ever more disgruntled with the ruling elite's growing wealth and began demanding a bigger stake. In response, Mugabe committed to increase pension payments and other forms of benefits. Secondly, Mugabe ordered an expensive deployment of the Zimbabwean military in the Democratic Republic of Congo (which lasted until 2003), in order to support the regime of Laurent Kabila, and in so doing protect the mining investments made by members of the Zimbabwean ruling elite. Thirdly, and probably most crucially, the Zimbabwean government finally began to make good on its threats to acquire vast tracts of land that were owned by the white commercial farmers.

Whilst the first two events increased government spending, the third lowered production and exports, which reduced tax revenues. This rise in government spending and fall in government income was "the beginning of the Zimbabwean economy's downward spiral." (Coltart, 2008, p. 14) The effect of the

---

2. While these political tensions were present before Zimbabwe's independence, the election of Robert Mugabe increased the hostile rhetoric.

land redistribution policy was several-fold.[3] Firstly, foreign investors fled, fearing their assets could be seized next. By 2001 foreign direct investment in Zimbabwe fell to zero, whilst the World Bank's risk premium on foreign investment rose from 4% to 20%. Secondly, the non-enforcement of land titles removed a major source of collateral for bank loans. As a result lending to farmers dried up, and investment in agriculture plummeted. Thirdly, those farmers who were evicted found themselves unable to pay back their loans. This, combined with the loss of income from farm loans, lead to dozens of banks collapsing, with massive negative repercussions for Zimbabwean businesses. Fourthly, the land redistribution, although supposedly meant to benefit the poorest Zimbabweans, actually largely benefited the ruling elites who cherry picked the most fertile farmlands. With the commercial farmers deserting Zimbabwe, crop yields collapsed and famine ensued.[4] Fifth, land values collapsed due to the removal of property rights, and with it much of Zimbabwe's wealth (Richardson, 2005).

With such a large loss in output, tax revenue also fell dramatically. Combined with the increase in spending, the government's budget came under severe pressure. This was exacerbated in 2001 when the government defaulted on the servicing of its loan from the International Monetary Fund (IMF). In response, the IMF refused to make any concessions (such as refinancing or loan forgiveness) to punish the government for its policies, most significantly the land reform measures. With reduced food production due to the land reforms, the government had to buy food from abroad to try to prevent mass starvation. But, because of the default on the IMF loan, Zimbabwe's creditworthiness was effectively ruined, making it impossible to get loans elsewhere. As a result, the Zimbabwe government started to issue its own national currency

---

3.   In fact, the Reserve Bank of Zimbabwe predicted such a response in early 2000. As Richardson (2005) states: "In early 2000, Mugabe was handed a confidential memo from the Reserve Bank of Zimbabwe, the country's central bank. The memo predicted that going forward with farmland seizures would result in a pullout of foreign investment, defaults on farm bank loans, and a massive decline in agricultural production."

4.   Although there is no reliable data displaying the financial costs of land reform, economists have estimated the aggregated agricultural industry's output falling from 4.3 million tons in 2000 (worth, at today's prices US$3.35 billion) to just 1.4 million tons in 2009 (worth some US$1 billion), a decline of more than two thirds in overall volume and value. Smallholder farmers' production suffered similar losses, with output decreasing some 73 percent in the same period.

and used the money to buy U.S. dollars on the foreign-exchange market. The attempt by the government to plug the increasing deficit between spending and revenue through the creation of money increased the purchasing power in the economy, just as the fall in output in the agricultural and manufacturing sector decreased the amount of goods available to purchase. The result was the classic case of 'too much money chasing too few goods'. High inflation ensued, with annual rates above 100% from 2001. By 2003 the value of the Zimbabwe dollar had deteriorated to such an extent that it was costing the government more to issue the notes and coins than they were worth at face value. In light of this the government began issuing time-limited 'bearer checks' in very high denominations.

After defaulting on the IMF loan, the situation in Zimbabwe rapidly deterio-rated, with each new political measure from ZANU-PF aimed solely at keep-ing a hold on power. It achieved this goal by shuffling aside any opposition, and by appropriating the country's resources through the confiscation and redistribution of privately owned assets. This included killing representatives of the opposition and several white farmers in order to occupy their lands.[5] The intimidation of not only the political opposition and the judiciary but the whole population became crucial to maintain political and economic power. For example, in 2004 human rights groups reported that about 90 percent of the opposition members suffered from criminal violation, 24 percent had been subjected to potentially lethal attacks and 42 percent had been tortured.

By 2005, economic conditions had grown particularly bad. More than 80 percent of the Zimbabwean population was officially unemployed. The infor-mal sector of the economy, which accounted for less than 10% of the total in 1980, was by 2005 the main source of income for the majority of Zimbabwe-ans: more than 3 million people worked in the informal economy compared to only 1.3 million in the formal sector (Tibaijuka, 2005). With economic condi-tions rapidly worsening, the government resorted to extreme measures to both

---

5.   In response both the opposition and the Commercial Farmers Union (CFU) took legal action. Although initially approved by the Supreme Court, which challenged the legality of the land reform programme, the Chief Justice Antony Gubbay was subsequently threatened with physical violence and forced to resign. He was immediately replaced by a judge sympathetic to the government. In 2005 the government completely removed any remaining right of commercial farmers to have the courts adjudicate on the confiscation of their properties (Constitu-tional Amendment no.17).

bolster its position and get the economy under control. For example, in 2005 the government implemented a law which required exporters to sell up to 30 percent of their foreign exchange earnings to the Zimbabwe Reserve Bank at an artificially low exchange rate. This immediately imposed a huge cost on the manufacturing sector, which was exacerbated when the Zimbabwean dollar was strengthened due to foreign aid (as the price of their exports, in terms of other currencies, increased while the price of imports decreased). With costs also rapidly increasing (particularly interest rates) local manufacturers were struggling to survive (Coltart, 2008).[6]

Further pressure was placed on the economy through government attempts to control inflation. However, inflation continued to rise, with price rises reaching the 50% a month necessary to be classified as hyperinflation by mid to late 2007 (McIndoe, 2009). The government continued to attempt to restrict inflation, including through direct price control mechanisms in 2007 yet with little success. Prices continued to increase, and every economic indicator markedly worsened.

To help cover the shortfall on the Zimbabwean government's shrinking income, the Reserve Bank of Zimbabwe increased the amount of currency in circulation at an alarming rate after 2003, leading to the introduction of the second Zimbabwe dollar in 2006, at a value of 1000 old Zimbabwe dollars and devalued 60% against the US dollar. This was followed by a further devaluation of 92% in 2007. The third Zimbabwe dollar was introduced in 2008 at 10 billion times the second Zimbabwe dollar (Noko, 2011).

By November 2008, the rate of inflation in Zimbabwe had peaked at 79.6 billion percent per month (Hanke & Kwok, 2009). In the build up to the inflationary peak, prices were revised upwards at an ever faster pace, in daily, hourly or within even shorter periods. The prices of goods in Zimbabwean dollars were updated vis-à-vis the exchange rate of foreign currencies, which were exchanged in a currency black-market in the streets, shops and backyards where people tried 'to get rid of their Zimbabwean dollars' as soon as they got them (The Economist, 2008). With the value of the Zimbabwean dollar decreasing vis-à-vis other currencies at an ever-increasing rate, 'dollarisation'[7]

---

6.   The manufacturing sector's output had already shrunk by more than 47 percent between 1998 and 2006 (Coltart, 2008).

7.   The term 'dollarisation' can be defined as when the inhabitants of a country use a foreign currency (usually the US dollar) for everyday transactions. The

fig. I.1 - One hundred trillion Zimbawean dollar note

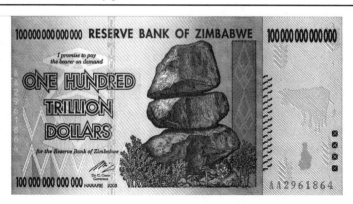

– the use of US dollars instead of the local currency – became widespread as "people simply refused to use the Zimbabwe dollar" (Hanke & Kwok, 2009, p. 354). By February 2009 the authorities officially recognised the demise of the Zimbabwean dollar, and a 'multi-currency system' was adopted.[8] This brought to an end ten years of high inflation and two years of hyperinflation. As a result the price level (in US dollars) stabilised, and the economy started to recover. Bank accounts denominated in Zimbabwe dollars were suspended at the current exchange rate of Z$35 quadrillion to US$1 (IMF, 2010).

In the end, the damage done to the Zimbabwean economy was staggering. Between 2000 and 2008 output contracted by 40 percent, while the government's budget revenue fell from more than 28 percent of GDP (in 1998) to less than 5 percent (in 2008). This resulted in the:

> "almost total collapse in public services. By the end of 2008, most schools and many hospitals had closed, transport and electricity networks were

---

foreign currency can either replace or simply operate alongside the domestic currency.

8. As reported by the IMF: "Under this system, transactions in hard foreign currencies are authorized, payments of taxes are mandatory in foreign exchange, and the exchange system largely is liberalized. Since the abolition of all surrender requirements on foreign exchange proceeds on March 19, 2009, there has not been a functioning foreign exchange market for Zimbabwe dollars. Bank accounts denominated in Zimbabwe dollars (equivalent to about US$6 million at the exchange rate of Z$35 quadrillion per US$1) are dormant. Use of the Zimbabwe dollar as domestic currency has been discontinued until 2012. While five foreign currencies have been granted official status, the U.S. dollar has become the principal currency." (IMF, 2010)

severely compromised, and a water-borne cholera epidemic had claimed more than 4,000 lives." (IMF, 2010, p. 51)

In conclusion, it was the struggle to maintain political power that led the Mugabe regime to implement policies that caused a significant fall in the productive capacity of what had been a prosperous and growing economy. This fall in output, and the consequent fall in tax revenues (combined with some expensive military forays) squeezed government revenues further. The expropriation of farmland in order to appease political allies destroyed Zimbabwe's agricultural sector, with subsequent detrimental knock-on effects on other economic sectors. Consequently tax revenues fell dramatically, and with government expenditures increasing (again to appease political allies) the government, via its control of the Reserve Bank of Zimbabwe (and therefore political control of money creation) was forced to turn to the printing of money to fill the gap.

So, while the hyperinflation was made possible by the printing of money, it is not the case that money printing always leads to high or hyper-inflations. Rather, it was the printing of money to finance expenditure, with no regard for the inflationary consequences, and following a collapse in the productive capacity of the economy, which pushed Zimbabwe into hyperinflation. Had Zimbabwe's central bank been independent of politicians, and focused on price stability rather than facilitating government spending (with more careful control over money creation), the hyperinflation would have been impossible.

Two conclusions can be drawn from the Zimbabwe experience:

1. There is a danger when those with the power to create money can also benefit from its creation. This is the basis for our argument that neither vote-seeking politicians nor profit-seeking bankers should be given the ability to create money. Instead, this power should be with an independent body whose remit is to keep inflation low and steady.

2. Hyperinflations do not happen simply because of an increase in money creation; there must also be a collapse in the productive capacity of the economy to start the inflationary pressure.

Table 1 – Inflation rates in Zimbabwe		
Date	Month-on-month inflation rate (%)	Year-over-year inflation rate (%)
April 2007	100.7	3,713
June 2007	86.2	7,251
August 2007	11.8	6,592
October 2007	135.6	14,840
December 2007	240.0	66,212
January 2008	120.8	100,580
February 2008	125.8	164,900
March 2008	281.2	417,823
April 2008	212.5	650,599
May 2008	433.4	2,233,713
June 2008	839.3	11,268,758
July 2008	2,600.2	231,150,888
August 2008	3,190.0	9,690,000,000
September 2008	12,400.0	471,000,000,000
October 2008	690,000,000.0	3,840,000,000,000,000,000
November 2008	79,600,000,000.0	89,700,000,000,000,000,000,000

Source: Hanke & Kwok, 2009

Other hyperinflations

Germany's hyperinflation of 1923 is also typically held up as an example of the dangers of money creation by governments. A recent working paper by economists at the IMF unpicks this common interpretation of events:

> "The Reichsbank president at the time, Hjalmar Schacht, put the record straight on the real causes of that episode in Schacht (1967). Specifically, in May 1922 the Allies insisted on granting total private control over the Reichsbank. This private institution then allowed private banks to issue massive amounts of currency, until half the money in circulation was private bank money that the Reichsbank readily exchanged for Reichsmarks on demand. The private Reichsbank also enabled speculators to short-sell the currency, which was already under severe pressure due to the transfer problem of the reparations payments pointed out by Keynes (1929). It did so by granting lavish Reichsmark loans to speculators on demand, which they could exchange for foreign currency when forward sales of Reichsmarks matured. When Schacht was appointed, in late 1923, he stopped converting private monies to Reichsmark on demand, he stopped granting Reichsmark loans on demand, and furthermore he made the new Rentenmark non-convertible against foreign currencies. The result was that speculators were crushed and the hyperinflation was stopped. Further support for the currency came from the Dawes plan that significantly reduced unrealistically high reparations payments." (Benes & Kumhof, 2012)

The authors of the working paper conclude that, "this episode can therefore clearly not be blamed on excessive money printing by a government-run central bank, but rather on a combination of excessive reparations claims and of massive money creation by private speculators, aided and abetted by a private central bank."

Another working paper from the Cato Institute (Hanke & Krus, 2012) analyzed all 56 episodes of hyperinflation around the world. As a Reuters journalist summarized the findings:

> "By looking down the list you can see what isn't there — and, strikingly, what you don't see are any instances of central banks gone mad in other-wise-productive economies...[H]yperinflation is caused by many things, such as losing a war, or regime collapse, or a massive drop in domestic

production. But one thing is clear: it's not caused by technocrats going mad or bad." (Salmon, 2012)

The empirical reality, both when looking at quantitative data and qualitative descriptions of what actually happens in hyperinflations shows that they are not the results of well-governed states abusing the money creation process.

Pennsylvania

One of the defining aspects of early American history is the use of money, by Britain, in order to maintain its power over the American colonies. By restricting the colonies' ability to create their own money, which they needed in order to trade with each other, the colonies were forced to deliver resources and materials to Great Britain to earn foreign currency, which they could then use to purchase goods elsewhere (Middleton, 2002). This relegated the colonies to mere providers of raw materials, allowing Britain to preserve its hegemony.

Nevertheless, the northern colonies of New England started to establish production and processing industries and by the 1750s they became the New World's centre for processing, transportation, storage, distribution, marketing and mercantile services (Rousseau & Stroup, 2011). However, the colonies were still in "dire need for a monetary system" (Zarlenga, 2002, p. 364) or as a Pennsylvania merchant wrote to a correspondent in London, they required "some proper medium for Currency without which Commerce is a perplexing Employment." (Lester R. , 1938) In fact, the colonial merchants at that time were quite inventive regarding the trade and exchange of goods, even using some goods as means of payment,[9] including tobacco, rice, sugar, beaver skins, wampum, 'country pay'[10] and others. Yet these methods of payment suffered from various weaknesses, and as such did not last for long. As a result trade within the colonial territories remained weak.

So, without an adequate means of payment for day-to-day transactions, merchants, traders and producers used a variety of substitutes such as barter,

---

9.   This method of payment is distinct from barter trade for two reasons. Firstly, the monetary value of these products was fixed by law in different times and regions. Secondly, debtors were "permitted by statute to pay certain debts with their choice of these commodities at nominal values set by the colonial legislature." (Michener, 2010)

10.   Country pay consisted of various agricultural products that had been monetised by law.

commodity monies, shop notes, book credit, and bills of exchange. However, each of these alternatives created transaction frictions because trades could not be completed until a double coincidence of wants was identified (Baxter, 1945). Trade within towns was often coordinated by shopkeepers who, in addition to supplying finished goods, also kept transactions records for the residents. But shop notes, which were issued by shopkeepers in exchange for goods and were in turn often paid out by employers to labourers for redemption at the store, tended to limit consumption to items that a particular shopkeeper had on hand (Davis, 1900). Book credit, a close relative of shop notes, could remain unused for months until a shopkeeper or customer presented an item for exchange that the other desired (Rousseau & Stroup, 2011).

With the means of payment in general a poor substitute for money, the colonies continued to experiment:

- In 1652 John Hull set up the 'Hull Mint' or 'tree' coinage in Massachusetts. The coins produced were used until 1685 when it was removed from circulation by a British decree.

- In 1675 a private land bank was set up in South Carolina, issuing paper bank notes as convertible securities (collateralised by secured estates). It was however ultimately unsuccessful, because although South Carolina could create money, it failed to get it accepted for general payments.[11] A private land bank was also set up in Boston in 1686, and failed for similar reasons.

- In 1690 the state of Massachusetts began issuing 'Bills of Credit'. This "paper money of Massachusetts was backed only by the 'full faith and credit' of the government", (Goodwin, 2003, p. 36), rather than land or some other commodity. Although initially not intended to be legal tender (a special tax was planned to be levied the next year that could be paid in real goods, specie or tax bills), it became more and more accepted for payments, with subsequent positive impacts on trade and production. As such, the Massachusetts assembly declared it legal tender for all payments in 1692 (Hutchinson, 1936).

- In 1709 and 1710, Hartford, New Hampshire and Rhode Island followed Massachusetts' lead and issued their own Bills of Credit. These circulated

---

11.   As Hyman Minsky noted, "anyone can create money, the problem is in getting it accepted." (Minsky, 1986)

across borders and at par with one another, and in 1712 became legal tender for public and private debts (McCallum, 1992). However, with many of the states at war against the French, too many bills were produced (for military expenditure) and the value of the currency declined substantially. Yet despite the eventual problems with the currency, the infrastructure it helped to build and the memory of the positive effect it initially had on the economy remained (Zarlenga, 2002).

Colonial monies could (and did) fail for a variety of reasons. Some were unsuccessful due to external events (such as the British shutting them down), while others failed because they could not get accepted. Several were unsuccessful (in the long run) because of the temptation to those issuing the currency to create too much. Yet not all colonial monies were beset by problems – New York, for example, had a highly regarded currency, as did Pennsylvania. But what made these currencies work when others failed?

In the lead up to the 1720s Pennsylvania found its economy suffering. Reflecting on this situation some years later, Francis Rawle, a successful Philadelphia merchant, wrote that "a running Stock of Money now wanting is the Cause of this Decay: The common Necessaries for Families brought to the Market are not bought, because Change (as Silver and Copper is commonly called) is not to be had; all our Domestic Trade is become nothing but Discount, a miserable Make-shift good for Nought, but to enrich Knaves and beggar Fools". (As quoted in Lester R., 1938, cited in Zarlenga, 2002.)

The problems arising from the lack of a medium of exchange were exacerbated by the South Sea Bubble bursting in 1720, which caused a financial crisis and a wave of bankruptcies (as those who had borrowed to invest lost more than their initial investment). With Britain (and some parts of America) in recession and prices deflating, people began hoarding their money. This had three effects on Pennsylvania. Firstly, the lower demand for goods negatively affected Pennsylvania's exports to Britain. Secondly, imports from Great Britain to Pennsylvania (which included a variety of commodities that had not been manufactured in the colonies because of the underdevelopment of its infrastructure and division of labour) began to fall. Thirdly, the hoarding of currency led to further scarcity in an already scarce medium of exchange. The combination of these three factors led to a sharp fall in the availability of a currency to make transactions: "When British purchases fell off and the colonies shipped less than would pay for their imports, sterling bills became scarce

and expensive, and people sought hard money to make payments abroad."
(Ferguson, 1953)

With exports to Britain depressed, and no currency to trade between themselves, the economy and people of Pennsylvania were in trouble. So, in 1723
the governor of Pennsylvania told the legislature: "I daily perceive more and
more that the People languish for want of some Currency to revive Trade and
Business, which is wholly at a Stand; therefore I am of Opinion, that all the
Dispatch imaginable ought to be given to the Paper Bill." (Lester R., 1938)
Crucially, he also added that in order to maintain the value of the currency
"the Quantity must be moderate". So, on March 2, 1723, the Pennsylvanian
assembly passed an act for the provision of a 15,000 issue of paper money.
Eleven thousand was to be loaned into the economy (to businesses and individuals at 5 percent interest), while 4,000 was to be spent into the economy
on public works - i.e. it did not enter with a corresponding debt. (Province
and Commonwealth of Pennsylvania, 1723) Additionally, the loans had to be
secured on land and were to be paid back in eight annual instalments (with
the money to be relent upon repayment). No more than 100 could be loaned
to any one person, since this paper money chiefly was intended to benefit the
poor and industrious.

Within a short period of time business and trade was revived with the governor of Pennsylvania stating that "a prodigious good effect immediately ensued
on all the affairs of that province", (Keith 1740, p. 213, cited in Zarlenga, 2002,
p. 370). Throughout the first year average prices changed little. With demand
for new loans high and the currency a success, the assembly decided to issue
another 30,000 in December of the same year. This time 26,500 was loaned
into existence and the remaining 3,500 was spent into circulation.[12]

In 1726, the assembly stated in a "Representation" to the authorities in
England that with "the whole Quantity that was struck thus in a very short
Time emitted, and diffused into the Peoples Hands, the Face of our Affairs
appeared entirely changed." (Lester, 1938) With business and trade revived,
prices began to recover and stabilise. Property values also recovered with the
issues of paper money. These developments relieved debtors, merchants, and
producers by helping to restore profit margins. With money issued by the

---

12.   Until 1729 several additional amounts of paper money were issued in Pennsylvania, but overall no more than 85,000 came into circulation at any time during
the first half of the eighteenth century (see Middleton 2002).

state rather than private banks, "the interest received by the government from money out on loan supported the costs of provincial administration, without the necessity of direct taxes. This relative freedom from taxation probably contributed to Pennsylvania's remarkable growth". (Ferguson, 1953, p. 169)

Yet a currency, high growth rates, freedom from taxation and a source of funding to allow government to undertake socially beneficial investments were not the only advantages of state issued money. Lester found that prices from 1721 until 1775 were more stable than in any subsequent period of equal length. Furthermore, loans of paper money at 5 percent interest tended, for a time, to lower the general rate of interest in Pennsylvania, which had been at 8 percent. (Lester, 1938, cited in Zarlenga, 2002)

In conclusion, historians agree that Pennsylvania's system of issuing currency was 'to the manifest benefit of the province' (Ferguson, 1953). Indeed, Ferguson notes that "Pennsylvania's currency was esteemed by all classes and regarded as having contributed to the growth and prosperity of the colony" (p. 159), and that "Favourable testimony can be found in nearly all commentators, modern or contemporary". (p. 163) Adam Smith, writing in the Wealth of Nations, commented that the success of the system was dependent on three circumstances:

> "First, upon the demand for some other instrument of commerce, besides gold and silver money, or upon the demand for such a quantity of consumable stock as could not be had without sending abroad the greater part of their gold and silver money, in order to purchase it; secondly, upon the good credit of the government which made use of this expedient; and, thirdly, upon the moderation with which it was used, the whole value of the paper bills of credit never exceeding that of the gold and silver money which would have been necessary for carrying on their circulation, had there been no paper bills of credit." (Smith, 1776)

It is clear that the reason for the success of the Pennsylvanian system was the adherence in particular to the third circumstance, the moderation in issuing the currency. Indeed, Smith goes on to say, "The same expedient was, upon different occasions, adopted by several other American colonies; but, from want of this moderation, it produced, in the greater part of them, much more disorder than conveniency."

Conclusions from historical examples

These case studies provide some insight into when money creation is and is not inflationary. In short, money creation that is undertaken solely to boost government revenue, with little or no regard for the consequences for the economy as a whole, will be inflationary (as was the case in Zimbabwe). Conversely, printing money to spend into the economy, when performed responsibly and with a view to providing a means of exchange, can deliver a low inflation environment (as was the case in Pennsylvania). While the Pennsylvanian experiment shows that a low inflation environment is achievable, it relied on the responsible behaviour of those administering it.

Many governments are not known for spending responsibly, particularly when elections are approaching. In order to prevent this conflict of interest, the proposals in this book splits the decision over how much money to create from the decision over how that money will be spent, to ensure that money is only created, if necessary, during periods when inflation is low and stable.

APPENDIX II

REDUCING THE NATIONAL DEBT

As discussed in Chapter 7, one potential use of newly created money could be to pay down the existing national (government) debt. In this appendix we explain the basic concepts necessary to understand the national debt. We then discuss the reasons why in the context of these reforms, paying down the national debt should not be the top priority.

What is the national debt?

The government has three main sources of revenue:

1. Taxes & fees - such as Income Tax, National Insurance, Value Added Tax (VAT), taxes on alcohol, fuel, flights and so on.

2. Borrowing - this is mainly achieved through the issuing of bonds.

3. Creation of money - the revenue from this source is negligible under the current monetary system.

If government spends more than it collects in taxes the difference is called the 'deficit'. If it collects more in taxes than it spends, this difference is called a 'surplus'. Surpluses have been relatively rare in the UK in recent decades, with the government typically running deficits, spending more than they collect in taxes and borrowing to make up the difference. These deficits have increased the outstanding nominal value of the national debt (whereas surpluses would have reduced it).

Who does the government borrow from?

Rather than borrowing from banks, the government typically borrows from the 'market' - primarily pension funds and insurance companies. These companies lend money to the government by buying the bonds that the government issues for this purpose. Many companies favour investing money in government bonds due to the lack of risk involved: the UK government has never defaulted on its debt obligations and is unlikely to in the future, primarily because it is able to collect money from the public via taxation. The market in government debt also tends to be stable and liquid, and offers an interest rate in excess of that which is available on other riskless investments (i.e. physical cash).

Does government borrowing create new money?

In most cases the process of government borrowing does not create any new money. While most individuals and businesses accept bank deposits in payment, the UK government does not; they require that the purchasers of new bonds 'settle' the transaction by transferring central bank reserves into a government-owned account at the Bank of England. This means that new money is not created in the process of borrowing.

For example, let's say a pension fund holds an account at MegaBank, and wishes to buy £1 million in government bonds. The fund asks MegaBank, which is one of the Gilt-Edged Market Makers (a bank authorized to deal directly with the government in the purchase of new bonds), to buy £1 million of new government bonds. MegaBank decreases the pension fund's account by £1 million and then purchases the bonds on behalf of the pension fund. To settle its transaction with the government, it transfers £1 million of reserves to the government's account at the Bank of England. The balance of MegaBank's account at the Bank of England will drop by £1 million. The government now has £1 million of central bank reserves in its account at the Bank of England, which can be used to make payments. It has borrowed the money without any additional deposits being created.

To spend the money it could now transfer the reserves to Regal Bank where an NHS hospital holds an account. Regal bank would then receive £1 million of central bank reserves, and could increase the account balance of the hospital by £1 million.

So through a rather convoluted process, £1 million of bank-created bank deposits have been taken from pension fund contributors and passed to an NHS hospital. No additional money has been created; only pre-existing deposits have been moved from one place to another. Because the majority of government borrowing is done in this way it does not constitute a monetary stimulus to the economy.

Is it possible to reduce the national debt?

The debt is currently higher (in nominal terms) than it's ever been before. While the government talks about reducing the deficit, the reality is that the total national debt will keep growing. Even if it stops the debt growing, taxpayers will continue paying around £120 million a day in interest on the national debt.

It is very unlikely that the government will be able to reduce debt in the current system. To understand why, consider what would need to happen for the debt to be paid down. First, the government would need to start paying the annual interest on the national debt each year out of tax revenue, rather than simply borrowing the money to pay it. Interest payments totalled £43bn for 2012, so if the government wanted to reduce the debt it would have to find an additional £43bn in taxes, which would require, for example, raising VAT (sales tax) to roughly 30% (from its current level of 20%).

In addition, in the five years before the banking crisis the government spent an average of 10.6% more than it received in taxes every year. So even after the £43bn interest on the national debt is paid, to run a 'balanced budget' right now, it would need to raise an extra £22bn in taxes (to cover the 10.6% shortfall), or cut public services by £22bn - equivalent to shutting down a fifth of the UK's National Health Service.

So far in this example, the government has raised VAT by 30% and cut £22bn of public services and has still only managed to stop the debt growing. In order to actually reduce the debt, it needs to raise taxes even further, or reduce public spending even more. If the government decided that it wanted to pay off £30bn of national debt every single year, then it would need to raise another extra £30bn in taxes: equivalent to doubling council tax. Even at this level it would take 30 years to pay down the national debt, assuming tax revenue is unaffected by these changes.

Of course, increasing taxes by such large amounts is likely to lead to a recession and even a depression: businesses will pass on the costs of higher taxes to their consumers, with the increase in prices likely to lower demand for goods and services. Likewise, faced with higher taxes, individuals will have lower levels of disposable income, and, independent of the increase in prices this will negatively affect demand. Both factors will feed through to lower sales and therefore lower sales taxes, forcing the government to further increase taxes to hit its debt reduction target. Lower demand for goods and services will also lead to businesses cutting employment, lowering the government's income from employment taxes. Higher levels of unemployment will also increase the government's spending on unemployment benefits, which will have to be funded through further borrowing, again preventing the government from hitting its targets.

Alternatively the government could cut its spending. However, this is likely to have similar effects to increasing taxes. During recessions people tend to cut their spending - if the government cuts its spending at the same time the result can be a catastrophic drop in demand. This of course lowers output and therefore the tax take. Indeed, in a paper looking at eight episodes of fiscal consolidations (i.e. cuts in government spending), Chick and Pettifor (2010) find that:

> "The empirical evidence runs exactly counter to conventional thinking. Fiscal consolidations have not improved the public finances. This is true of all episodes examined, except at the end of the consolidation after World War II, where action was taken to bolster private demand in parallel to public retrenchment."

As they point out this runs contrary to mainstream thinking, where recessions are thought to be, at least in the long-term, self-correcting. The presumption is that eventually the fall in demand will lead to lower prices, at which point demand increases (as the fall in prices increases relative wealth), which increases demand (the Pigou-Pantinkin effect). However, as was discussed in Chapter 9, when money is created with a corresponding debt, a fall in prices leads to an increase in the real value of debt, thus the negative effect on the real value of debt offsets the positive effects on real wealth. Thus lowering spending/increasing taxes is likely to lead to a fall in tax revenues, requiring even further tax increases/spending cuts and so on. In fact, in this situation a debt deflation scenario is far more likely if the population is highly indebted to begin with.

Is it desirable to reduce the national debt?

On the surface, paying off government debt may be beneficial because lower government debt frees up government revenue for core services. It is argued that high levels of government debt may also be problematic in the long run because:

1. Government bonds compete with private sector investments for funds, so government borrowing diverts money away from private sector

investments and increases the rate of interest the private sector pays to attract investment.

2. Individuals may start saving more (and so spending less) in expectation of an increase in future taxes (to pay off the debt). (This is known as Ricardian Equivalence).[1]

3. Because of the potential for adverse effects to long term interest rates and the exchange rate.

There is also the danger that excessive government debt can lead to a sovereign debt crisis, as seen in Greece and other Eurozone countries. However, for countries that retain control of their currencies (i.e. those that have central banks that are able to print currency, such as the UK, the US, Japan, but crucially not the Eurozone countries) defaulting on debt is only one of two options, as the country could simply print currency to pay off its debts. Of course, if this printing of currency caused significant inflation it would reduce the real value of the debt and represent a form of hidden default, in that the holders of the debt would not be repaid as much, in real terms, as they initially invested.

However it is important to also recognise the positive effects that come from having a national debt. First, as mentioned previously, the debt gives the private sector a safe asset in which it can invest. This strengthens private sector balance sheets, increasing their robustness in the face of downturns and negative shocks. Second, it allows a degree of certainty for institutional investors looking for long term returns. Third, it allows the private sector (excluding the government), in aggregate to hold a positive balance of wealth (see for example Godley and Lavoie (2012)). Fourth, it is misleading to think of the national debt in the same way as we think about private debts. The major holders of the national debt are UK investors: mainly pension funds and insurance companies. Thus, it is in many senses a debt we owe to ourselves (albeit it one owed by current taxpayers to current holders of the debt, which can create an inter-generational transfer of wealth). That said, approximately 40% of the national debt is owned to foreign investors (also pension funds and insurance companies).

---

1. While these are theoretical possibilities, there are also theoretical reasons why crowding out and Ricardian Equivalence may not occur (for Ricardian Equivalence see for example Feldstein (1976). In addition the empirical evidence for these effects is mixed at best.

fig. II.1 National debt as % of GDP

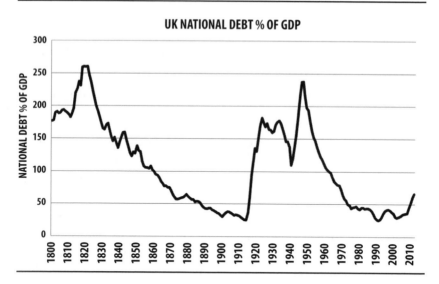

UK NATIONAL DEBT % OF GDP

Source: Krugman, 2011

In addition, it is important to remember that the nominal value of the debt is not actually important; it is the level of debt (and its maturity) relative to the earning capacity of the economy that is the important figure. For example, an individual with no income and no assets may consider a debt of £10,000 impossible to repay, yet an individual that earns £1 million a year would consider the same debt an inconsequential sum. Broadly speaking, the 'income' of the nation can be represented by GDP (Gross Domestic Product). Figure II.1 shows the national debt as a percentage of the country's GDP.

This brings into context the comments made earlier about the government never really paying off its debt. Instead of paying off the debt by actually reducing its nominal value, the debt tends to be reduced over time in terms of its burden. Rather than decrease the nominal amount of the debt, the earning ability of the economy (GDP) is increased.

Unsurprisingly the national debt to GDP ratio tends to shoot up during wars – such as World War I (from £650m in 1914 to £7.4bn in 1919) and World War II (from £7.1bn in 1939 to £24.7bn in 1949). It also shot up significantly in 2008 onwards, as the tax take plummeted due to the recession and spending (for example on unemployment benefits) increased. (The borrowing to bailout banks is not included in the main national debt figures.) It is pertinent to note here that despite the financial crisis, public debt is actually at a relatively low level. In addition, we must be clear that the largest part of the recent increase in public debt came about not due to too much spending, but rather as a result of the government's reaction to the financial crisis.

This brings us to the crux of the argument. The first half of this book was largely concerned with the effect of the banking sector on the economy and society as a whole. The excessive creation of private debt was shown to be a major cause of boom bust cycles, financial crises, recessions, etc. As can be seen from figure 4.1, the level of private debt far exceeds the level of public debt, and as such this should be the focus of debt reduction efforts.

As well as looking at absolute values, the cost of debt (i.e. the interest rate on the debt) should also be considered. In this context the overall interest rate on the national debt between 2000 and 2012 worked out at around 5.6% per annum (Webb & Bardens, 2012). In contrast, the interest rate for household debt ranges between 6% and above for mortgages, right up to 17% on credit cards and up to 29% on store cards. Overall, the average interest rate is undoubtedly higher for households than it is for the government. For these reasons, the government should focus on enabling the public to reduce its debts.

Paying down the national debt in a reformed monetary system

As outlined in Chapter 7, one use for newly created money in a reformed banking system is to pay down a part of the national debt. Given the arguments above, it would be misguided to concentrate on attempting to do this immediately following the reforms. A far better use of the money would be to encourage people to pay down their own, larger, more expensive debts (via tax cuts, public spending or direct payments to citizens). However, in the longer term it may be considered desirable to reduce the debt to GDP ratio, and even perhaps pay down some of the debt in nominal terms if conditions allow for it.

However, reducing the absolute level of the debt may also be undesirable for other reasons. Paying off part of the national debt involves reducing the quantity of government bonds in circulation, which, if it is done too quickly, will force pension funds to shift their investments from bonds to other investments, such as corporate bonds (riskier) and the stock market (much riskier). Furthermore, if this was done too quickly the effect of over £1 trillion (the current national debt, approximately) shifting from the bond market to the stock market and corporate bond market would be like tipping a bath of water into a small pond – creating huge waves in the market and possibly creating bubbles.

In addition, any money that is used to repay government debt will be transferred to those institutions that were holding government bonds. Because most of these bonds were initially a form of savings, it is likely that this money will be put back into the financial markets (i.e. people won't suddenly start spending money they had allocated as savings). Therefore using newly-created money to pay down the national debt will pump this money into the financial markets, where it may stay circulating, fuelling financial market bubbles and doing little or nothing to help the real economy.

To avoid this, if it was thought desirable to reduce the nominal value of the debt, bonds should be removed from circulation over a period of time. Fund managers would be well aware that a portion of government bonds were being 'phased out', but would have around ten to fifteen years in which they could gradually shift their investments away from the bond market and into corporate bonds and the stock market. This would avoid causing any bubbles in the market, avoid a flood of 'cheap' money into the corporate bond market, and safeguard the value of pensions.

Is this 'monetising' the national debt?

The proposals outlined in this book do not permit the elected government to have any say over how much money is created, or to create money simply to pay off the national debt. This decision is given to an independent committee, the Money Creation Committee. Money would only be created as long as inflation is low, steady, and within the target range. If money used to pay off the national debt started to feed into inflation, the MCC would then be unable to continue creating new money and the government would be restricted to paying down the national debt using money from tax revenue.

A similar argument applies to the charge that this would allow the government to inflate away the debt by printing money. In this situation savers suffer as the purchasing power of their savings falls as a result of the inflation. Conversely debtors benefit, as their debts, which do not increase with inflation, are smaller in real terms. It is however not possible for the government to simply turn on the printing press, for the same reason as before – the MCC is an independent body that will only create money, if necessary, during periods when inflation is low and stable.

APPENDIX III

ACCOUNTING FOR THE MONEY CREATION PROCESS

The reforms outlined in this book modernise the process by which money creation is accounted for at the Bank of England and the Treasury.

Instead of treating money as a liability of the issuer (as is the current setup for bank notes), we treat money as a token, issued by the state. This money is accepted and used by people and businesses because they are confident they can exchange these tokens with other people for goods or services of equivalent value. In general, if too many of these tokens are issued, their value will fall, in terms of the amount of goods or services they can buy. This is inflation. Conversely, if insufficient tokens are issued, their value will rise – this is deflation.

The current 'backing' for banknotes

The concept of 'backing' the currency is a hangover from the days when pound sterling bank notes were in effect receipts for gold held at the Bank of England. Banknotes have not been backed by or redeemable for gold since 1931, and despite the phrase "I promise to pay the bearer on demand the sum of £10" on a ten pound sterling bank note, if you return this note to the Bank of England, you will be given not gold, but an identical note of equal value. The Bank of England's own website is quite clear about this:

> "The words 'I promise to pay the bearer on demand the sum of five [ten/ twenty/fifty] pounds' date from long ago when our notes represented deposits of gold. At that time, a member of the public could exchange one of our banknotes for gold to the same value. For example, a £5 note could be exchanged for five gold coins, called sovereigns. But the value of the pound has not been linked to gold for many years, so the meaning of the

---

Box III.A - Bank of England's Balance Sheet

Ever since the 1844 Bank Charter Act, the Bank of England has been required by law to maintain two separate balance sheets. One of the balance sheets, the Issue Department, covers the business of issuing bank notes (coins are dealt with by the Treasury), while the other – the Banking Department – covers all the rest of the bank's activities. The Issue Department does not correspond to any actual department or office in the Bank of England; it is simply a set of accounts that measures a certain part of the Bank of England's assets and liabilities.

---

promise to pay has changed. Exchange into gold is no longer possible and Bank of England notes can only be exchanged for other Bank of England notes of the same face value." (Bank of England website – FAQs)

However, the Bank of England still retains the accounting structure it used when bank notes were redeemable for gold. Bank notes are recorded as liabilities (promises to pay) on the balance sheet of the Bank of England's Issue Department. These liabilities are backed by assets, in the form of government bonds and other financial assets. The Issue Department's balance sheet, as of February 2012, was as follows:

Assets	2012 £million
British government bonds	5,749
Deposit with the Banking Department of the Bank of England (i.e. central bank reserves)	47,172
Reverse Repurchase Agreements (repos)	1,610
Total assets	**54,921**

Liabilities	
Notes issued in circulation	54,921
Total Liabilities	**54,921**

The implication of this balance sheet is that the note issue is backed by government bonds i.e. the debt of the government. (The £47bn 'Deposit with the Banking Department of the Bank of England' is a liability of the Bank of England's 'Banking Department' balance sheet, which is effectively itself backed by another holding of government bonds.)

There is one logical reason why the note issue is 'backed' by bonds. When notes are first printed, they are sold to commercial banks at face value. Commercial banks can pay for these notes by handing over an equivalent value of British government bonds, or with a transfer from the bank's reserve account at the Bank of England. So the bonds and the deposit at the Banking Department which appear on the assets side of the Issue Department's balance sheet actually represent the financial assets that banks have used to 'pay' for the notes issued to them.

But in reality, notes should have ceased to be liabilities of the Bank of England, or of any part of the state, when they ceased to be redeemable for gold in 1931. A liability is a promise to pay some value in the future, but the Bank of England is not required to give anything of value to holders of bank notes, other than identical banknotes. So although the notes appear to be 'backed' by the government bonds, this is nonsensical; if notes are backed by government bonds, then what backs government bonds? The answer is that government bonds are backed by the ability of government to collect money from the public, forcibly, through taxation. So claiming that notes are 'backed' by government bonds is entirely circular: the argument would be that notes are backed by bonds, which are backed by the ability of the government to get notes from the public through taxation. In other words, the notes would be backed indirectly by themselves.

The reality is that notes get their value, not from what assets are on the balance sheet of the Bank of England, but from what they can be exchanged for in the economy. So there is no need for the Bank of England to hold backing assets to 'back' the currency it issues. This applies to notes, and will equally apply to electronic money issued by the state, post-reform. Surprisingly however, it already applies to coins issued in the United States, as described below.

The process for issuing coins in the USA

The accounting regime used by the United States government for the issuances of coins is much more appropriate, and with some small adaptations, provides the basis for the issuance of electronic money in a reformed system.

Within the existing system in the US, coins are manufactured by the US Mint, which sells the coins at face value to the Federal Reserve Banks, who in turn sells them at face value to commercial banks. The profit on the creation of coins,[1] which is the difference between the cost of manufacture and the face value, is known as seigniorage, as described in the US Mint's annual report:

> "Seigniorage equals the face value of newly minted coins less the cost of production (which includes the cost of metal, manufacturing, and transportation). Seigniorage adds to the government's cash balance, but unlike the payment of taxes or other receipts, it does not involve a transfer of financial assets from the public. Instead, it arises from the exercise of the government's sovereign power to create money and the public's desire to hold financial assets in the form of coins." (US Mint, 2011)

The key differences between US coins and UK notes

As described above, notes are still considered to be liabilities of the Bank of England, even though the 'promise to pay' element of the note is meaningless, as it can only be exchanged for another identical note. In the UK, coins are also treated as a liability of the government and recorded as part of the national debt, even though there is no logical basis for this.

In contrast, coins in the US are treated as a token, created by the US Mint, but then held as an asset of the Federal Reserve. Once in circulation, coins are an asset of the holder, but they are not a liability of any part of the government or the US Mint.

We believe that the process of issuing notes should be adapted to be consistent with the process for issuing coins used in the US, and that the issuance of electronic money post-reform should also be consistent with the process for coins. This would mean that coins, notes and electronic pounds would all be assets of the holder, but would not be a liability to anybody. This same approach is endorsed in a working paper from IMF economists considering the original Chicago plan for monetary reform:

> "[It] is critical to realize that the stock of reserves, or money, newly issued by the government is not a debt [i.e. liability] of the government. The reason is that fiat money is not redeemable, in that holders of money cannot claim repayment in something other than money. Money is therefore properly treated as government equity rather than government debt,

---

1.   In practice the cost of certain metals can mean that smaller coins, such as 1p and 2p coins in the UK, or 5 cent coins in the US, can at times cost more to produce than the actual face value, and so have negative seigniorage. However, this is always offset by the positive seigniorage on larger value coins.

which is exactly how treasury coin is currently treated under U.S. accounting conventions." (Benes & Kumhof, 2012)

The post-reform process for issuing electronic money

Electronic, state-issued currency will simply be a number in an account at the Bank of England. These accounts will be held off the Bank of England's balance sheet, so these numbers are not liabilities of the Bank of England. Instead, they should be seen as electronic tokens, held in custody for the owners of the tokens (money). The owners may be banks (for the Investment Pools and Operational Accounts), the government (for the Central Government Account) or members of the public (for the aggregated Customer Funds Accounts).

When the Money Creation Committee makes a decision to create money, they will do so simply by increasing the balance of the Central Government Account by that amount.

Ensuring that electronic money cannot be forged

There are two approaches to ensuring that electronic money cannot be forged or created by anyone other than the state. The first, most complex approach is to make every electronic pound a unique token, with serial numbers and some form of encryption and validation process to check that each token is valid. But no matter how secure the encryption, this process would be a magnet for computer hackers, since successfully 'breaking the code' would mean that the hacker had quite literally acquired the power to create money.

A far simpler way, and the approach we have taken, is to hold all state-issued electronic currency in accounts at the central bank (the Bank of England). With this approach, there is no need to encrypt the money – it can simply be numbers in a database. The Bank of England's current payment system, the 'RTGS processor', would be more than sufficient for this purpose. Banks would connect to this system (as they currently do to the Bank of England's RTGS system). However, the system would only accept one type of message, in the format:

"Move £… from Account Y to Account Z".

This ensures that the total balance of all accounts – and therefore the total electronic money supply – cannot be increased in any way by banks. Banks would only be able to transfer money from one account to another.

Reclaiming seigniorage on notes & electronic money

Post-reform, the state will earn the seigniorage on the creation of electronic money. The cost of production of electronic money is practically zero, meaning that the seigniorage is effectively 100% of the face value. Strictly speaking the only costs of the production of electronic money would be paying an official at the Bank of England to increase the balance of the Central Government Account, plus a couple of other officials (probably including the Governor) to validate the process and enter necessary passwords.

This reform therefore reclaims the seigniorage on the creation of money from commercial banks. However, unlike in the current system where commercial banks only earn the interest on the money they create, in the reformed system the state spends the money into circulation, thus benefiting from the full face value of the electronic money. As a result the cost to banks of losing their money-issuing power is lower than the benefit to the state (and taxpayers) of reclaiming it.

Modernising the note issuance

There is one final modernisation to make to the issuance of bank notes and coins. As described above, bank notes are sold to banks at face value, in exchange for government bonds. The government continues to pay interest on these bonds to the Bank of England, and the Bank of England records this as a profit of its Issue Department's balance sheet and returns 100% of this profit back to the government. So within the current system, the seigniorage on bank notes is not the difference between cost of production and the face value, but the interest that is earned on the bonds that are 'bought' with the notes. In effect, this convoluted process simply means that some of the interest that the government must pay on national debt is returned directly to the government, making this part of the national debt effectively interest free.

However, post-reform, coins and notes will not be sold to the banks in exchange for bonds and other assets. Instead, they will be printed in response to demand from banks and then swapped, one-for-one, with electronic state-issued currency owned by the banks. So if a bank wishes to increase the amount of physical cash it is holding, the Bank of England will provide the cash and deduct an equivalent amount of electronic money from the bank's Operational Account at the Bank of England. The electronic money deducted will be transferred into an account called the 'Cash in Circulation Dummy

Account', which will effectively keep the electronic money out of circulation, so that the issuance of extra physical cash into the economy (for example, in the run up to the Christmas shopping period) does not alter the overall stock of money.

Seigniorage will be earned at the point when electronic money is created. Coins and notes become, in effect, physical portable versions of the electronic money, and so no seigniorage will be earned at the point where electronic currency is swapped for physical cash.

AN ALTERNATIVE ACCOUNTING TREATMENT

The accounting treatment outlined in this book is not the only way in which the accounting for a reformed system can be presented. Whichever system of accounting is used is mainly a matter of taste and is largely immaterial. Accountancy is after all not the reality, rather it is the recording of the reality. The American Institute of Certified Public Accountants (AICPA) defines accountancy as:

> "the art of recording, classifying, and summarizing in a significant manner and in terms of money, transactions and events which are, in part at least, of financial character, and interpreting the results thereof." (AICPA Committee on Terminology, 1953).

In their book 'Creating New Money' (2000), Joseph Huber and James Robertson present a monetary reform which served as the inspiration for the proposals outlined in this book. However, unlike the treatment presented in Chapter 8, Huber and Robertson's proposal maintains customer accounts on the liabilities side of the central bank's balance sheet.

In order to understand how money, and the assets 'backing' money are classified on a balance sheet in a reformed system, we must first briefly examine the current arrangements. This is addressed in Box III.B.

The diagrams at the end of this section show how the balance sheet of the central bank appears under the alternative accounting system proposed here, on the day after the reform and also 30 years after the reform. The other balance sheets (of the commercial banking sector and the household sector) are identical to those that appear in chapter 8.

Box III.B - Classifying money on a balance sheet

Within the current system accounting rules and associated legislation require that the currency issued by banks – reserves and customer accounts – be classed as liabilities of those banks. (Coins are treated as contingent liabilities of the central government in the UK.) However, a liability implies that value is expected to be paid over to a creditor. This is inappropriate treatment for fiat money since fiat money is its own means of settlement. In addition, the assets that back or balance these liabilities are in general government bonds or loans (repos) collateralised with government bonds. Yet bonds are merely promises to pay money at a future date – as a result, the current regime implies that money held in hand today is supposedly backed by the promise of money in the future.

The current system is therefore logically incoherent – money neither has anything backing it nor conforms to the proper definition of a liability. However, this leaves us with the question of how should money then be accounted for on a balance sheet? One option, which was outlined in chapter 8, was to remove money from the balance sheet entirely and treat it as an electronic token. While this method is perfectly legitimate, it is also possible to account for money creation under a reformed system using the conventional approach.

To see how this can work, consider the idea that within countries, those that use a currency constitute an economic community that co-operate in the production of goods and services: those that accept money trust that there will be things available to spend the money on in the future, entailing production by other members of the community. Holding currency therefore entitles the holder to a share of the productive capacity of the economy in line with their money holding. What backs money is therefore not bonds or loans, but the belief that there will be something available to swap that money for in the future. As Niall Ferguson puts it in the Ascent of Money: "Money is not metal. It is trust inscribed. And it does not seem to matter much where it is inscribed: on silver, on clay, on paper, on a liquid crystal display" (Ferguson, 2008). Money is in fact backed by the productive capacity and output of the economy – this can be seen quite clearly with reference to certain historical episodes of inflation. For example, as outlined in Appendix I , in the case of Zimbabwe it was the sudden drop in the productive capacity of the economy that lead to the initial surge in inflation – the change in economic output lead to a change in the value of the Zimbabwean dollar.

What backs money is therefore the 'productive capacity of the economy', and the asset side of the central bank's balance sheet should reflect this fact. This leaves us with the question of just how to classify the actual monetary unit itself.

As mentioned previously, a liability implies that value is expected to be paid over to a creditor, which is an inappropriate treatment for fiat money since fiat money is its own means of settlement. Since accounts at the central bank (under the current or the reformed system) cannot reasonably be classified as liabilities of the issuing authority, whereas they are undoubtedly assets of the holder, they can only be classed as capital (equity). Indeed, this is the accounting method used by the US Treasury to account for coins.

Should money be classified as capital? Again consider that within countries, those that use a currency constitute an economic community that co-operate in the production of goods and services. Within this community individuals that give their own resources are partners in the enterprise, receiving money in exchange for their efforts. By accepting money these individuals are trusting that there will be things available to spend the money on in the future, which entails production by other members of the community. Holding money therefore entitles individuals to a share of the output (i.e. the productive capacity) of the enterprise, and as such those that hold currency can be thought of as shareholders in the enterprise (i.e. the country).

In conclusion, if using the conventional accounting approach, the 'asset' backing money is in fact the productive capacity of the economy, while money itself should be classified as equity in the commonwealth rather than government debt.

On the day after the reform, the Bank of England's assets are exactly the same as under the accounting treatment used in chapter 8. There is however a difference in the composition of the liabilities side – equity has been split into four parts, three of which are the monetary accounts held by a) banks, b) individuals, and c) the government, and one of which is the Bank of England's 'shareholder equity' (with the UK government being the only shareholder). Otherwise, everything else is exactly the same, as it should be – after all the accounting outlined here is simply a different accounting method of representing the same reality.

The transition then proceeds exactly as outlined in Chapter 8. To repay loans individuals pay money from their Transaction Accounts to the bank from whom they borrowed. Money moves from their Transaction Account to the bank's Investment Pool and is then transferred to the Operational Account (all of these accounts would be recorded on the liabilities side of the Bank of England's balance sheet). The money is then paid to the Bank of England, who would in normal circumstances automatically grant this money to the government to be spent back into the economy. The same process also applies to the repayment of loans that were initially made from the central bank to the commercial banks.

The creation by the central bank of new money to be granted to the government will first increase the government's account at the central bank, then, as the money is spent, the Transaction Accounts of individuals. This will increase the liabilities side of the Bank of England's balance sheet, which, if it is not matched by an increase in its assets, will make the central bank technically insolvent. In this case the central bank will increase the 'productive potential of the economy' asset, which will account for the benefits accruing to the economy from the newly issued money. So, if the Money Creation Committee wishes to create new money it will simultaneously increase the balance of the Central Government Account and the 'productive potential of the economy' asset on the central bank's balance sheet. Any loans from the central bank to private banks will be accounted for in the normal way.

It is important to note that the 'productive capacity of the economy' asset is merely a nominal balancing asset –the newly issued money will necessarily increase the productive capacity of the economy (although the increase in demand caused by the new money may lead to increases in production). Rather it is intended to reflect the fact that in reality money is backed by the productive capacity of the economy. This can be seen quite clearly with reference to certain historical episodes of hyperinflations. For example, in Zimbabwe it was a sudden drop in production that lead to the initial inflation – changes in output lead to a change in the value of the Zimbabwean dollar.

Because the MCC will only be charged with creating money when inflation is below its target rate, this ensures that inflation will not result from newly created money increasing spending at a faster rate than the productive capacity of the economy. However, if inflation is occurring (as a result of too much money chasing too few goods), the MCC may choose to slow or stop the creation of new money. It may even wish to reduce the stock of money in circulation. This could be achieved by the Bank of England removing some tax revenue from the government's account (working in collaboration with the Treasury) while simultaneously reducing the 'productive capacity of the economy' asset. Alternatively, the central bank may choose to reduce the money supply through one of the other methods outlined in section 7.7.

Balance sheets: alternative treatment (with money as a liability of the Bank of England)

System the day after transition

Bank of England

Assets	Liabilities
Loans to Commercial Banks	Other Liabilities
Gilts	Transaction Accounts*
Other Assets	Operational Accounts and Investment Pools*
Commercial Liability (Commercial Bank Liability to Bank of England)	Central Government Account*
	Equity

*in equity

System 20 years after transition

Bank of England

Assets	Liabilities
Other Assets	Other Liabilities
	New Money Transaction Accounts*
Productive Potential of the Nation	Transaction Accounts*
	Operational Accounts and Investment Pools*
	Central Government Account*
	Equity

*in equity

BIBLIOGRAPHY

Ackermann, J. (2010). IIF Calls on Group of 20 to Promote Multilateral Coordination in Addressing Key Economic and Financial Regulatory Reform Challenges. Retrieved from: http://www.iif.com/press/press+releases+2010/press+163.php on the 4.1.2013.

Adrian, T., & Shin, H. S. (2008). *Liquidity and Leverage*. Paper Presented at the Financial Cycles, Liquidity, and Securitization Conference, Hosted by the International Monetary Fund.

AICPA Committee on Terminology. (1953). *Accounting Terminology Bulletin No. 1. Review and Résumé*. American Institute of Accountants.

Akerlof, G. A., & Romer, P. (1993). *Looting: The Economic Underworld of Bankruptcy for Profit. Brookings Papers on Economic Activity, 2*, (pp. 1-73).

Alessandri, P., & Haldane, A. (2009). *Banking on the State*. Bank of England.

Arestis, P., & Sawyer, M. (2003). Can Monetary Policy Affect the Real Economy. *The Levy Institute Public Policy Brief, 71*.

Baffes, J., & Haniotis, T. (2010). *Placing the 2006/08 Commodity Price Boom into Perspective*. The World Bank Development Prospects Group.

Baker, G. (2007, January). Welcome to 'The Great Moderation'. *The Times*. Retrieved from: http://www.timesonline.co.uk/tol/comment/columnists/article1294376.ece on 27.7.2011.

Bank of England. (1999). *The Transmission Mechanism of Monetary Policy*. Bank of England.

Bank of England. (2009). *Payment Systems Oversight Report 2008*. Bank of England.

Bank of England. (2012). The Bank of England's Real-Time Gross Settlement Infrastructure. *Bank of England Quarterly Bulletin,* 2012 Q3. Bank of England.

Bank of England. (2012). *The Red Book: The Framework for the Bank of England's Operations in the Sterling Money Markets.* Bank of England.

Bannock, G. B. (1978). *Dictionary of Economics.* Harmondswort: Penguin Books.

Baxter, W. (1945). *The House of Hancock: Business in Boston, 1724-1775.* Cambridge, MA: Harvard University Press.

Benes, J., & Kumhof, M. (2012). *The Chicago Plan Revisited.* International Monetary Fund.

Bernanke, B., & Gertler, M. (1989). Agency Costs, Net Worth, and Business Fluctuations. *American Economic Review, 79* (1), (pp. 14-31).

BERR (Department for Business, Enterprise and Regulatory Reform). (2007). *Tackling Over-Indebtedness, Annual Report 2007.*

Berry, S., Harrison, R., Thomas, R., & de Weymarn, I. (2007). Interpreting Movements in Broad Money. *Bank of England Quarterly Bulletin,* 47 Q3, p. 377.

Binswanger, M. (2009). Is There a Growth Imperative in Capitalist Economies? A Circular Flow Perspective. *Journal of Post Keynesian Economics.*

Bisschop, W.R. (2001 [1896]). *The Rise of the London Money Market 1640-1826.* Kitchenor: Batoche Books.

Black, O. (2011). *Wealth in Great Britain. Main Results from the Wealth and Assets Survey: 2008/10.* The Office for National Statistics.

Blanchard, O. (2006). *Macroeconomics, 4th Edition.* Pearson Prentice Hall.

Cagen, P. (1956). *The Monetary Dynamics of Hyperinflation.* In: M. Friedman. (1956). *Studies in the Quantity Theory of Money.* Chicago: University of Chicago Press.

Chang, H. J. (2007). *Bad Samaritans; The Guilty Secrets of Rich Nations and the Threat to Global Prosperity.* Random House.

Cecchetti, S. & Kharroubi, E. (2012). *"Reassessing the impact of finance on growth".* BIS Working Papers No 381. Bank for International Settlements.

Chick, V. (1992). The Evolution of the Banking System and the Theory of Saving, Investment and Interest, in P. Arestis and S. Dow (eds), Chapter 12 in *On Money, Method and Keynes: Selected Essays*. New York: St. Martins Press.

Chick, V., & Pettifor, A. (2010). *The Economic Consequences of Mr. Osborne*.

Chick, V. (2013). *The current banking crisis in the UK: an evolutionary view*. In G Harcourt and J Pixley (eds), *Financial crises and the nature of capitalist money: Mutual developments from the work of Geoffrey Ingham*. London: Palgrave Macmillan

Cohen, E. O. (1997). *Athenian Economy & Society: A Banking Perspective, 3rd Edition*. Princeton University Press.

Coltart, D. (2008, March 24th). A Decade of Suffering in Zimbabwe. Economic Collapse and Political Repression under Robert Mugabe. *Economic Development Bulletin*.

Constâncio, V. (2011). *Challenges to monetary policy in 2012*. Speech at the 26th International Conference on Interest Rates. Frankfurt am Main.

Daffin, C. (2009). *Wealth in Great Britain. Main Results from the Wealth and Assets Survey 2006/08*. Office for National Statistics.

Davidson, P. (2008). The Financial Crisis, the US Economy, and International Security in the New Administration. *Looking for Solutions to the Crisis*. International Initiative for Rethinking the Economy.

Daly, H. (1991). *Steady-State Economics, 2nd edition*. Island Press, Washington, DC.

Davies, R., Richardson, P., Katinaite, V., & Manning, M. (2010). Evolution of the UK Banking System. *Bank of England Quarterly Bulletin, 50 (4)*, (pp. 321-332).

Davis, A. (1900). *Currency and Banking in the Province of Massachusetts Bay*. New York: Macmillan.

De Soto, J. H. (2009). *Money, Bank Credit and Economic Cycles*. Ludwig von Mises Institute.

Demirguc-Kunt, A., & Detragiache, E. (2002). Does Deposit Insurance Increase Banking System Stability? An Empirical Investigation. *Journal of Monetary Economics, 49 (7)*, (pp. 1373-1406).

D'Hulster, K. (2009). *Crisis Response Note Number 11: The Leverage Ratio.* The World Bank Group.

Diamond, D., & Dybvig, P. (1983). Bank Runs, Deposit Insurance, and Liquidity. *Journal of Political Economy, 91 (3),* (pp. 401–419).

Disyatat, P. (2010). *The bank lending channel revisited.* BIS Working Papers No. 297.

Driver, R. (2007). The Bank of England Credit Conditions Survey. *Bank of England Quarterly Bulletin,* Q3, (pp. 389-401).

Dyson, B., Greenham, T., Ryan-Collins, J., & Werner, R. (2011). *Towards A Twenty-First Century Banking And Monetary System.* Centre for Banking, Finance and Sustainable Development at the University of Southampton, New Economics Foundation, Positive Money.

Erturk, I., Froud, J., Johal, S., Leaver, A., Moran, M., & Williams, K. (2011). City State against National Settlement. *UK Economic Policy and Politics after the Financial Crisis.* Working Paper No.10, CRESC.

Evans, A. (2010). *Public Attitudes to Banking.* The Cobden Centre.

Feldstein, M. (1976). Perceived Wealth in Bonds and Social Security: A Comment. *Journal of Political Economy.* University of Chicago Press, vol. 84(2), pages 331-36, April.

Ferguson, J. (1953, April). Currency Finance: An Interpretation of Colonial Monetary Practices. *The William and Mary Quarterly,* 10 (2), (pp. 153-180).

Ferguson, N. (2008). *The Ascent of Money: A Financial History of the World.* Allen Lane.

Financial Services Authority. (2009). *The Turner Review; A Regulatory Response to the Global Banking Crisis.* Financial Services Authority.

Financial Services Compensation Scheme. (2009). *Annual Report and Accounts: 2008/09 Financial Services Compensation Scheme.*

Fisher, I. (1933). The Debt-Deflation Theory of Great Depressions. *Econometrica, 1* (4), (pp. 337-357).

Fisher, I. (1935). *100% Money: Designed to keep checking banks 100% liquid; to prevent inflation and deflation; largely to cure or prevent depressions; and to wipe out much of the National Debt.* New York: The Adelphi Company.

Fisher, I. (1936). *100% Money and the Public Debt*. Economic Forum, Spring Number, April-June 1936, 406-420.

Friedman, M. (1960). *A Program for Monetary Stability*. Fordham University Press.

Friedman, M. (1970, September 16th). Wincott Memorial Lecture. London.

Galbraith, J. K. (1997). Time to Ditch the NAIRU. *The Journal of Economic Perspectives, 11* (1), (pp. 93-108).

Gary, S. (2008). *Handbook - No. 27 Liquidity Forecasting*. Bank of England Centre for Central Banking Studies.

Godley, W. & Lavoie, M. (2012). *Monetary Economics: An Integrated Approach to Credit, Money, Income, Production and Wealth*. London: Palgrave Macmillan.

Goodhart, C. (1984). *Monetary Policy in Theory and Practice*. London: Macmillan.

Goodhart, C. (1994). What Should Central Banks Do? What Should Be Their Macroeconomic Objectives and Operations? *The Economic Journal, 104* (p. 427).

Goodhart, C.A.E. (2001), *The Endogeneity of Money*. In P. Arestis, M. Desai, and S. Dow (eds.), *Money, Macroeconomics and Keynes, Essays in Honour of Victoria Chick*, vol. 1. London: Routledge, (pp. 14–24).

Goodhart, C., & Hofmann, B. (2007). *House Prices and the Macroeconomy: Implications for Banking and Price Stability*. Oxford: Oxford University Press.

Goodwin, J. (2003). *Greenback*. New York: Henry Holt & Co.

Graeber, D. (2011). *Debt: The First 5000 Years*. New York: Melville House.

Greenspan, A. (2007). *The Age of Turbulence - Adventures in a New World*. New York: Penguin.

Guttentag, J., & Herring, R. (1984). Credit Rationing and Financial Disorder. *The Journal of Finance, 39* (5), (pp. 1359-1382).

Haldane, A. (2012). *The $100 Billion Question*. Bank of England.

Hanke, S. & Krus, N. (2012). *World Hyperinflations*. Cato Institute.

Hanke, S., & Kwok, A. (2009). On the Measurement of Zimbabwe's Hyperinflation. *Cato Journal, 29* (2), (pp. 353-364).

Hart, M., & Levie, J. (2011). *Global Entrepreneurship Monitor United Kingdom 2010 Monitoring Report.* London: Global Entrepreneurship Research Association.

Hart, O., & Zingales, L. (2011, May). *Inefficient Provision of Inside Money.*

He, P., Huang, L., & Wright, R. (2005). Money and Banking in Search Equilibrium. *International Economic Review*

Herring, R., & Wachter, S. (2002). *Bubbles in Real Estate Markets.* Working Paper 402. Zell/Lurie Real Estate Center.

Hill, G. (2003). *The Battle for Zimbabwe.* Cape Town: Zebra.

HMRC. (2011). *Personal Wealth Statistics 2001-03 and 2005-07.*

HMRC. (2011). *Pay-As-You-Earn and Corporate Tax Receipts from the Banking Sector.*

HMRC. *Public Finance Databank.*

Hodgson, G. (Forthcoming). *Redistribution of Wealth through Interest.* Positive Money

Holmes, A. (1969). *Operational Constraints on the Stabilization of Money Supply Growth. Controlling Monetary Aggregates.* Federal Reserve Bank of Boston.

House of Commons Treasury Committee. (2011). *Competition and Choice in Retail Banking.*

Howells, P. (2005). *The Endogeneity of Money: Empirical Evidence.* University of the West of England.

Huber, J., & Robertson, J. (2000). *Creating New Money; A Monetary Reform for the Information Age.* New Economics Foundation.

Hudson, M. (2004). *The Development of Money-of-Account in Sumer's Temples,* in Hudson, M. and Wunsch, C. (eds.), *Creating Economic Order.* Bethesda: CDL.

Hutchinson, T. (1936). *History of the Colony and Province of Massachusetts Bay, 1764–1828.* Cambridge, MA: Harvard University Press.

IMF. (2010). *Zimbabwe: Challenges and Policy Options After Hyperinflation.* Washington D.C: International Monetary Fund.

Independent Commission on Banking. (2011). *Interim Report.* Her Majesty's Stationery Office.

Institute for Fiscal Studies. (2011). *Dimensions of Tax Design.* Institute for Fiscal Studies.

Jordá, O. Schularick, M. & Taylor, A. (2011). Financial Crises, Credit Booms and External Imbalances: 140 Years of Lessons. *IMF Economic Review* 59 (pp. 340–378).

Kalecki, M. (1943). Political Aspects of Full Employment. *Political Quarterly.*

Kauffman Foundation. (2009). *The Anatomy of an Entrepreneur.* Ewing Marion Kauffman Foundation.

Kay, J. (2009). *Narrow Banking.*

Keen, S. (2011). *House Prices and the Credit Impulse.* Retrieved from: www. debtdeflation.com

Keen, S. (2012). *The Debtwatch Manifesto.* Retrieved from: www.debtdeflation. com

Keen, S. (2012a). "Ignoring the role of private debt in an economy is like driving without accounting for your blind-spot". *LSE blog.* Retrieved from: http:// blogs.lse.ac.uk/politicsandpolicy/2012/03/14/ignoring-the-role-of-private-debt-in-an-economy-is-like-driving-without-accounting-for-your-blind-spot/ on 4.1.2013

Keen, S. (2012b). The Crisis in 1000 words or less. *Debtwatch.*

Keynes, J. M. (1930). *A Treatise on Money Volume 1 (The Pure Theory of Money).*

Keynes, J. M. (1936). *The General Theory of Employment, Interest and Money.* Palgrave Macmillan.

Kindleberger, C. (2007). *A Financial History of Western Europe.* London: Routledge.

King, M. (1994). The Transmission Mechanism of Monetary Policy. *Bank of England Quarterly Bulletin,* (Q3), (pp. 261-267).

King, M. (2010a, October 25). *Banking: From Bagehot to Basel and Back Again.* Speech presented at the Second Bagehot Lecture, Buttonwood Gathering, New York City.

King, M. (2010b). Speech presented at The Black Country Chamber of Commerce, West Midlands, Tuesday 19th October.

King, M. (2012). Speech presented at the South Wales Chamber of Commerce at the Millenium Centre, Cardiff, 23rd October.

King, M. (2012b). *Twenty years of inflation targeting*. Speech presented at the Stamp Memorial Lecture, London School of Economics , 9th October.

Kotlikoff, L. (2010). *Jimmy Stuart Is Dead*. John Wiles & Sons.

Krugman, P (2011, December). A Thought on Debt History. The Conscience of a Liberal. *The Opinion Pages, The New York Times*. Retrieved from http://krugman.blogs.nytimes.com/2011/12/31/a-thought-on-debt-history/ on 4.1. 2013

Krugman, P. (2012, March 27). Minksy and methodology wonkish. The Conscience of a Liberal. *The Opinion Pages, The New York Times*. Retrieved 2012, 4th September from: http://krugman.blogs.nytimes.com/2012/03/27/minksy-and-methodology-wonkish/

Kydland, F., & Prescott, E. (1990). *Business cycles: Real facts and a monetary myth*. Federal Reserve Bank of Minneapolis.

Laeven, L., & Valencia, F. (2012). *Systemic Banking Crises Database: An Update*. IMF Working Paper. International Monetary Fund.

Lester, R. (1938). Currency Issues to Overcome Depressions in Pennsylvania, 1723 and 1729. *Journal of Political Economy, 46* (3), (pp. 324-375).

Lewis, M. (2011, March). When Irish Eyes Are Crying. *Vanity Fair*. Retrieved 2012, 4th September from: http://www.vanityfair.com/business/features/2011/03/michael-lewis-ireland-201103

Macleod, H. D. (1889). *Theory of Credit*.

McCallum, B. (1992). Money and Prices in Colonial America, a New Test of Competing Theories. *Journal of Political Economy*, (pp. 143-161).

McIndoe, T. (2009, July 31st). *Hyperinflation in Zimbabwe: Money Demand, Seigniorage and Aid Shocks*. IIIS discussion paper No. 293. Institute for International Integration Studies.

Michener, M. (2010). *Money in the American Colonies*. Economic History Association. Retrieved from http://eh.net/encyclopedia/article/michener.american.colonies.money

Middleton, R. (2002). *Colonial America, a History: 1565-1776.* Malden, MA: Blackwell Publishing Company.

Mill, J. S. (1909). *Principles of Political Economy with some of their Applications to Social Philosophy, 7th Edition.* (A. William, Ed.) London: Longmans, Green and Co.

Minsky, H. (1966). *Financial Instability Revisited: The Economics of Disaster. Fundamental Reappraisal of the Discount Mechanism.*

Minsky, H. (1986). *Stabilizing an Unstable Economy.* New York: McGraw-Hill.

Moore, B. (1988). *Horizontalists and Verticalists.* Cambridge: Cambridge U.P.

Nationwide. (2012). *House Price Index.* Nationwide.

Noko, J. (2011). Dollarization: The Case of Zimbabwe. *The Cato Journal,* 31 (2), (p. 339).

Norman, B., Shaw, R., & Speight, G. (2011). *The History of Interbank Settlement Arrangements: Exploring Central Banks' Role in the Payment System.* Working Paper, Bank of England.

Noss, J., & Sowerbutts, R. (2012). *The Implicit Subsidy of Banks.* Bank of England.

ONS (Office for National Statistics) (2010), Annual Employment Statistics (BRES) 2010, Table 1b - UK level employment (thousands) by Broad Industry Group, and Table 2b - Total employment (thousands) by 2 and 3 digit SIC.

Padgett, J. F. (2009). *The Emergence of Large, Unitary Merchant Banks in Dugento, Tuscany.* Working Paper No 8. Chicago: University of Chicago.

Poliakov, L. (1977). *Jewish Bankers and the Holy See.* London: Routledge & Kegan.

Province and Commonwealth of Pennsylvania. (1723). An Act For The Emitting and Making Current Fifteen Thousand Pounds in Bills of Credit. *The Statutes at Large of Pennsylvania.*

Radford, R. *(1945) The Economic Organisation of a P.O.W. Camp.* Economica, 12(48): 189-201.

Ratnovski, L. & Huang, R. (2010). *The Dark Side of Bank Wholesale Funding.* IMF Working Papers. International Moetary Fund.

Reinhart, C. M., & Rogoff K. S. (2008). *"This Time is Different: A Panoramic View of Eight Centuries of Financial Crises"*. NBER Working Paper 13882. National Bureau of Economic Research.

Reinhart, C. M., & Rogoff K. S. (2009). *"This Time is Different: Eight Centuries of Financial Folly"*. Princeton, N.J.: Princeton University Press.

Richardson, C. (2005, November 14th). How the Loss of Property Rights Caused Zimbabwe's Collapse. *Economic Development Bulletin.*

Rousseau, P., & Stroup, C. (2011). Monetization and Growth in Colonial New England, 1703-1749. *Explorations in Economic History, 48* (4), (pp. 600-613).

Ryan-Collins, J., Greenham, T., Jackson, A., & Werner, R. (2011). *Where Does Money Come From? A Guide to the UK Monetary and Banking System*. New Economics Foundation.

Salmon, C. (2011, July). *The Case for more CHAPS Settlement Banks.* Speech presented at the Yorkshire and Humberside Network of the ifs School of Finance, Leeds.

Salmon, F. (2012, September 3rd). *Why you won't find hyperinflation in democracies.* Reuters. Retrieved from http://blogs.reuters.com/felix-salmon/2012/09/03/why-you-wont-find-hyperinflation-in-democracies/ on 4.1.2013.

Sanchez, M. (2005). *"The Link Between Interest Rates and Exchange Rates: Do Contractionary Depreciations Make a Difference?"* European Central Bank Working Paper Series No. 548. European Central Bank.

Schularick, M., & Taylor, A. (2009). *"Credit Booms Gone Bust: Monetary Policy, Leverage Cycles, and Financial Crises, 1870-2008"*. NBER Working Paper 15512. National Bureau of Economic Research.

Schumpeter, J. A. (1934). *The Theory of Economic Development: An Inquiry into Profits, Capital, Credit, Interest and the Business Cycle.* Cambridge, MA: Harvard University Press.

Schutter, O. D. (2010). *Food Commodities Speculation and Food Price Crises.* United Nations.

Shiller, R. J. (1999). *Human Behavior and the Efficiency of the Financial System,* in J. B. Taylor, & M. Woodford. (1999). *Handbook of Macroeconomics.* Elsevier. (pp. 1305-1340).

Smith, A. (2005 [1776]). *An Inquiry into the Nature and Causes of the Wealth of Nations*. Electronic Classics Series, Pennsylvania State University.

Smithin, J. (2003). *Inflation*. In J. E. King. (2003). *The Elgar Companion to Post Keynesian Economics*. Bodmin, Cornwall: Edward Elgar. (pp. 186-190).

Spufford, P. (2002). *Power and Profit: The Merchant in Medieval Europe*. London: Thames and Hudson.

Stiglitz, J., & Weiss, A. (1981). Credit Rationing in Markets with Imperfect Information. *American Economic Review,* (pp. 393-410).

Stiglitz, J., & Weiss, A. (1988). *Banks as Social Accountants and Screening Devices for the Allocation of Credit*. National Bureau of Economic Research.

Sugunan, V. (1997). *Fisheries Management of Small Water Bodies in Seven Countries in Africa, Asia and Latin America*. Rome: Food and Agriculture Organization, United Nations.

Taylor, A. (2012). *The Great Leveraging*. NBER Working Papers 18290.

The Economist. (1993, June 19th). *A Japanese Puzzle*. The Economist.

The Economist. (2008, July 17th). *A Worthless Currency*. Retrieved December 7th, 2011.

The Occupational Pensions Schemes (Investment) Regulations 2005. The Stationary Office Limited.

Tibaijuka, A. K. (2005). *Report of the Fact-Finding Mission to Zimbabwe to Assess the Scope and Impact of Operation Murambatsvina by the UN Special Envoy on Human Settlements Issues in Zimbabwe*. United Nations.

Tobin, J. (1984), *On the efficiency of the financial system*. Lloyds Bank Review 153, (pp. 1–15).

Tobin, J. (1987). *The Case for Preserving Regulatory Distinctions, in Restructuring the Financial System*. Federal Reserve Bank of Kansas City, 1987.

Tucker, P. (2012). *Shadow Banking: Thoughts for a Possible Policy Agenda*. European Commission High Level Conference, Brussels. Bank of England.

Turner, A. (2010). *What Do Banks Do? Why Do Credit Booms and Busts Occur and What Can Public Policy Do About It?* In *The Future of Finance: The LSE Report*. London: London School of Economics and Political Science. (pp. 3-63).

Turner, A. (2011, September). *Credit Creation and Social Optimality.* Speech presented at Southampton University. Financial Services Authority.

Turner, A. (2012, November). *Monetary and Financial Stability: Lessons from the Crisis and from Classic Economics Texts.* Speech presented at South African Reserve Bank, Pretoria.

Tymoigne, É. (2009). *Central Banking, Asset Prices and Financial Fragility.* Taylor and Francis e-Library: Routledge.

US Mint. (2011). *Annual Report 2010-2011.*

Webb, D., & Bardens, J. (2012). *Government Borrowing, Debt and Debt Interest Payments: Historical Statistics and Forecasts.* Economic Policy and Statistics Section, House of Commons Library.

Werner, R. (1992). *Towards a quantity theory of disaggregated credit and international capital flows.* Paper presented at the Royal Economic Society Annual Conference, York, April 1993 and at the 5th Annual PACAP Conference on Pacific-Asian Capital Markets in Kuala Lumpur, June 1993.

Werner, R. (1997). Towards a New Monetary Paradigm: A Quantity Theorem of Disaggregated Credit, with Evidence from Japan. *Kredit und Kapital,* vol. 30, no. 2. Berlin: Duncker & Humblot, pp. 276-309.

Werner, R. (2003). *Princes of the Yen, Japan's Central Bankers and the Transformation of the Economy.* New York: M. E. Sharpe

Werner, R. (2005). *New Paradigm in Macroeconomics: Solving the Riddle of Japanese Macroeconomic Performance.* New York: Palgrave Macmillan.

Werner, R. (2010). *Towards Stable and Competitive Banking in the UK.* University of Southampton, Centre for Banking, Finance and Sustainable Development.

Werner, R. (2011). Economics as if Banks Mattered – A Contribution Based on the Inductive Methodology. *The Manchester School,* 79, September, 25–35.

Wolf, M. (2010, November 9th) *The Fed is right to turn on the tap.* Retrieved on 1.4.2013

Wolf, M. (2012, June 28th). *The Case for Truly Bold Monetary Policy.* Retrieved from on the 4.1.2013

Zarlenga, S. (2002). *The Lost Science of Money.* New York: American Monetary Institute.

Index

C

capital 57
  buffer 57
  requirements / ratios 95–97
capital ratios
  confusion with reserve ratios 58
capital requirements
  distortions caused by 153–154
  simpification post-reform 271–272
cash
  accepting deposits from customers
    67
  how cash gets into the economy 87
  providing to customers 66
  supplying to the economy, post-
    reform 316
  withdrawals by customers 66
  withdrawals to customers 66
cashflow
  management of, post-reform 272
central bank. *See* Bank of England
central bank reserves 49, 70
  acquiring 71
  as a restriction on lending 78
  creation of, 70
cheques 41
Citizens' Dividends 212
coins
  issuance of, USA 313
  minting of, 32
  vs UK notes 313
commercial bank money 49. *See
    also* deposits
commercial banks. *See* banks
Competition and Credit Control
    (1971) 44
competition in banking
  effects on money creation 94
Consolidated Fund 224
control of money supply 95–107

Conversion Liability 228–230
  as a means of reducing money supply
    218
  repayment of 233
costs of banking
  upon society 171
counterfeiting 279
credit
  credit risk 61
  demand for 82–85
    identifying shortages, post-reform
      214
  demand for, vs demand for money 87
  for businesses, post-reform 215
  provision of, post-reform 231
  sources of funds for lending, post-
    reform 231
  vs. money 61
credit rationing 110
current accounts
  post-reform 177, 178
Customer Funds Accounts 185
  and transaction accounts 186

D

debt
  need for, 271
  private
    effect on employment 142
    effect on financial crises 135,
      140–144
debt deflation 133–135
debt repayment
  effects of 68, 88
debt repayments
  effects of 158
deficit 303
  reduction of, 305
deleveraging
  post-reform 233
demand deposits 54

ABOUT THE AUTHORS

Andrew Jackson holds a BSc in Economics and a MSc in Development Economics from the University of Sussex, and is currently studying for a PhD at the University of Surrey. He is also a co-author of the book *"Where Does Money Come From? A guide to the UK monetary and banking system"* with Josh Ryan-Collins and Tony Greenham from the New Economics Foundation, and Professor Richard Werner from the University of Southampton.

Andrew can be contacted at andrew.jackson@positivemoney.org

Ben Dyson has spent the last 5 years researching the current monetary system and understanding the impacts it has on the economy and society as a whole. He is the founder and director of Positive Money, a not-for-profit dedicated to raising awareness of problems with our monetary system amongst the general public, policy makers, think tanks, charities, academics and unions. He has spoken at events around the UK and internationally.

Ben can be contacted at ben.dyson@positivemoney.org

You can keep in touch with Positive Money by signing up to its regular email updates at **www.positivemoney.org**